HOT CARS OF THE
70s

THE BEST CARS OF THE DECADE

HOT CARS OF THE
70s

THE BEST CARS OF THE DECADE

GENERAL EDITOR: CRAIG CHEETHAM

Grange
BOOKS

First published in 2004 for Grange Books
An imprint of Grange Books plc
The Grange
Kingsnorth Industrial Estate
Hoo, Nr Rochester
Kent ME3 9ND
www.grangebooks.co.uk

Reprinted in 2005

A catalogue record for this book is available from the British Library.

ISBN 1-84013-638-3

Produced by
Amber Books Ltd
Bradley's Close
74–77 White Lion Street
London N1 9PF
www.amberbooks.co.uk

Printed in Singapore

All photographs © 2004 International Masters Publishers BV,
except pages 6, 7 & 9 © TRH Pictures

Contents

Introduction

Hot Cars of the '70s celebrates the achievements of some of the greatest engineers in automotive history. Often working in a torrid environment of industrial unrest, political dispute, and economic decay, the men and women of the motor industry overcame the odds of a difficult era to bring some of the finest cars ever made to our roads—and they are all gathered here, in this historic collection that puts you, the reader, behind the wheel of some great machines.

By 1970, most families in America had an automobile, and those in Europe were not far behind, with an average of one car for every 1.7 homes. The motor industry had become the most money-spinning business in world industry as more and more people craved transport of their own. The companies that had grown powerful started to take over the world. Ford had sprouted into a global empire of its own, selling cars in more than 70 different countries, while America's other "big two" were on a worldwide campaign of their own.

General Motors had already claimed the Chevrolet, Buick, and Pontiac names as its own in the indigenous North American market, but its expansion further afield meant it rapidly bought a share in other markets. By the start of the decade, it had brought Germany's Opel, Britain's Vauxhall, and Australia's Holden into its portfolio and had a strong foothold into the world's most profitable markets. Determined not to be outdone, Chrysler had swept up the ailing Rootes Group in Britain, bringing the names of Hillman, Humber, Sunbeam, and Singer under its wing, while in Europe Chrysler was making its mark, stealing Simca from under the nose of Ford.

After years of enjoying immense success exporting cars across the Atlantic, the once-formidable British car industry was left reeling at

The BMW 2002 Turbo was Europe's first turbo-charged production-line car. It could achieve a top speed of 130 mph and inspired many imitators.

One of Pontiac's most successful muscle cars, the second-generation Firebird remained in production for 11 years. This 1976 model includes additional front- and rear-end styling to satisfy safety requirements.

the enormous power of its American rivals. In 1968, British Leyland was formed, incorporating most of Britain's top manufacturers. Morris, Austin, Jaguar, Triumph, Standard, Rover, Wolseley, Riley, and MG were all brought together under one big umbrella—and BL's aim was world domination. Its policy was one of "badge-engineering," where identical cars would be sold with different badges and trim levels in order to satisfy the demands of traditional customers. But the policy did not work. By the mid-1970s, once-famous names such as Riley and Wolseley were gone for good, and the likes of Triumph and Morris would only survive into the early 1980s before they, too, disappeared forever.

AN AILING ECONOMY
Part of the blame could be put on the economy. The Western world suffered badly as a result of the Arabian oil embargo in 1973. Angry with the West over its stance on the Arab-Israeli war, where the NATO countries supported Israel, Arab countries refused to export their oil and fuel became strictly rationed. Industry suffered, and it was the British car makers that felt the pinch most. Britain itself was plunging into its first major post-war recession, jobs were lost, and militant unions made life difficult for factory bosses. British Leyland was brought to its knees. Its one great

hope—the all-new Austin Allegro—had consumed most of its remaining development money, but BL was optimistic that the Allegro would become "a car for Europe," winning sales in markets where British makers had never had a presence, thanks to its advanced technology and distinctive style.

Critics did not see it that way. Part of the Allegro's failure was its gimmick-led design. A square steering wheel, rounded profile, and complex, gas-filled suspension did it no favors in markets where simplicity was preferred, while in other areas the car failed because of underdevelopment. Costing issues meant BL had to use old and established engines, which were too big for the original design and forced the car to become taller and wider. With projected sales targets of at least two million over a seven year production life, BL bosses must have felt bitterly disappointed that just 650,000 Allegros were sold over a decade of production, most of them in the home market.

The British car industry still produced some gems, though, and the likes of the Jaguar XJ-C, Jaguar XJ6, MGB GT V8, Range Rover, Triumph

Stag, and Triumph Dolomite Sprint are given the recognition they deserve in *Hot Cars of the '70s*. Each brought something original to the global car market, thanks to the work of genius designers and planners.

But over all, the British car industry had fallen from grace and its once-brilliant products became a international laughing stock. in the 21st century, Britain has only one car manufacturer left. Struggling MG Rover is based at BL's original plant in Longbridge, Birmingham, and is a shadow of its former glory.

Over in America, the fuel crises had a different effect. US makers were strong enough to withstand the effects of cost-cutting, but some rapid rethinking had to be done to bring in a raft of new, compact, and economical cars. The results were not as good as their rivals from Europe and the Far East, and America found itself swamped by imported models such as the VW Bug and Volvo 240. The gas-guzzling excesses of the past and the glory of the Muscle Car era were dead, making way for new designs such as the AMC AMX, Ford Mustang Mach 1, and Chevy Chevelle.

NEW COMPETITION, NEW TECHNOLOGIES

While Britain and America were hit hard, manufacturers in other countries were ready to capitalize on the decline of the traditional car-manufacturing centers. Japan—once perceived as a bit-player in the car industry that catered solely for its own market—suddenly found itself exporting more than ever. Datsuns and Toyotas provided welcome relief for British drivers, tired of their indigenous products' poor reliability, while Americans laughed when Datsun said it was about to introduce a sports car. But in 1970 it did just that—and it wasn't a laughing matter for other car makers. The Datsun 240Z took just a year to become the fastest selling sports car in history, as US buyers shunned thirsty home-market products and antiquated imported MGs in favor of the sporty Japanese newcomer. The Japanese car industry was established, and it was set to become very, very powerful…

However, it was not just Japan whose car industry grew. Across Europe, open markets made it much easier for companies to sell their cars where they never had before, while new technologies such as anti-lock brakes, airbags, central door locking, and air conditioning meant cars were much safer than ever before. In France, Citroën continued to lead the field in technology with the radical GS, the most aerodynamic

Sister car to the Lotus Eclat, the British-produced Lotus Esprit offered race car-like handling and performance at an affordable price.

production sedan of its generation. The beautiful SM combined Citroën's forward thinking with Maserati's glorious engines to create a car that stunned thousands of drivers. They are all here, along with other fine French offerings from Peugeot and Renault.

Germany, too, was entering something of a golden era. BMW, which retained its independence throughout the industry's period of globalization, gave us the remarkable 2002 Ti and Turbo, as well as the stunning M1 supercar. Porsche continued to develop the 911, adding a turbo to give it even more power, while NSU introduced the world's first mainstream production rotary engine in the technologically brilliant, yet ultimately ill-fated Ro80. Those, along with other illustrious European marques such as Fiat, Ferrari, Maserati, Lamborghini, Saab, TVR, and Volvo are all celebrated with our fantastic studio photography and first-hand driving impressions, bringing you as close to the metal as possible without actually putting you in the driving seat.

The 1960s and 70s Triumph Dolomite was a revival of an old 1930s Triumph name. It appeared in many versions, ranging from a front-wheel drive 1300 cc model, to the rear-wheel drive 1850 cc Sprint model.

Hot Cars of the '70s aims to immerse you in the four-wheeled action of the decade in which Elvis Presley died, the video recorder was invented, and President Nixon fell after the Watergate scandal. Flared trousers, big perms, and multicolored interior decor were in—and these cars reflect this culture as much as they do the technological innovations of the era.

The criteria for selecting the vehicles that feature in this book is simple: they are either cars that were on the roads in the 1970s, or were produced in that stylish decade. Each and every one of them is a classic and is described here in glorious detail. Fasten your seatbelt and enjoy the ride—and if this has whetted your appetite be sure to check out the other two books in this series—*Hot Cars of the '50s* and *Hot Cars of the '60s*.

AC **3000ME**

Based on the Diablo show car designed by Peter Bohanna, the 3000ME marked a return to true sports machines for Britain's oldest car maker. It suffered from development problems, however, and only a small number were built.

"...superbly responsive."

"Compact is that word that best describes the 3000ME on first sight. Its cockpit is a fairly tight squeeze, but the interior is neatly laid out and well equipped. Acceleration is good, but not outstanding, with 0-60 mph taking 9.0 seconds. Thanks to its mid-engined layout and all-independent suspension, it corners nicely. The rack-and-pinion steering is superbly responsive, and disc brakes at all corners enable rapid stops to be made."

For a mid-engined sports car, the 3000ME has a well-appointed and well-trimmed cabin.

Milestones

1972 Peter Bohanna

pens a stylish two-seater mid-engined roadster—the Diablo—which is intended to be powered by an Austin Maxi 1,750-cc engine. On a trip to AC Cars, the Diablo catches Derek Hurlock's eye and the company decides to build a version of it using the Ford 3.0-liter V6 engine.

Fitting a Ford V8 engine into the Ace sports car resulted in the fearsome Cobra.

1979 After a

lengthy development period, the production car—the 3000ME—finally goes on sale.

AC's latest creation using Ford power is the Ace luxury GT.

1984 With only 70

cars having been built, AC Cars Scotland takes over 3000ME production. Although press reviews are favorable, sales are sluggish and production ends in 1985 after some 30 cars have left the Scottish factory.

UNDER THE SKIN

A mixed bag

Unlike previous ACs, the 3000ME has a pressed-steel perimeter frame chassis onto which the fiberglass body is mounted. Positioning the engine centrally required a specially designed Hewland geared transmission to take drive to the rear wheels. For optimum handling, a double wishbone suspension is employed front and rear, although poor rear suspension geometry results in tricky handling at the limit.

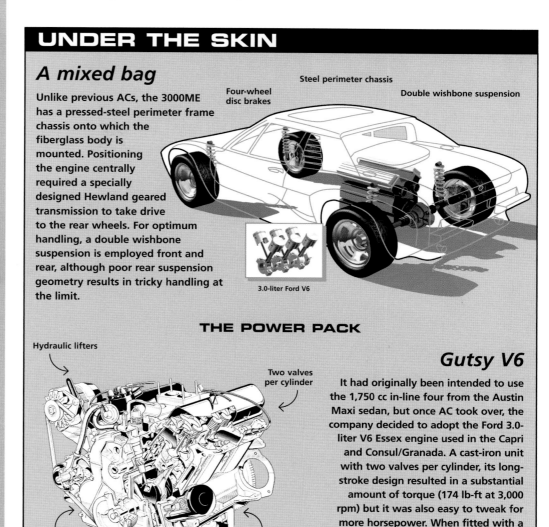

Four-wheel disc brakes

Steel perimeter chassis

Double wishbone suspension

3.0-liter Ford V6

THE POWER PACK

Hydraulic lifters

Two valves per cylinder

Cast-iron block and cylinder heads

Five main-bearing crankshaft

Gutsy V6

It had originally been intended to use the 1,750 cc in-line four from the Austin Maxi sedan, but once AC took over, the company decided to adopt the Ford 3.0-liter V6 Essex engine used in the Capri and Consul/Granada. A cast-iron unit with two valves per cylinder, its long-stroke design resulted in a substantial amount of torque (174 lb-ft at 3,000 rpm) but it was also easy to tweak for more horsepower. When fitted with a turbocharger, the power output jumped from 138 bhp to a healthy 200 bhp.

Turbocharged

Although the standard 3000ME was a decent performer in its day, Rooster Turbos later converted a small number of cars to turbocharged power. With 200 bhp and improved suspension, they are more invigorating to drive than stock 3000MEs.

A small number of 3000MEs were reworked with turbocharged power.

AC 3000ME

It seemed like the 3000ME, with its fiberglass body, racing-style suspension and reliable Ford V6 power, would be the answer to AC's problems. Alas, it took so long for the car to enter production that interest waned and only 70 were built.

Luggage space
With the engine mid-mounted, the luggage is carried up front. However, the small lid hinders access.

Fiberglass body
Unlike previous ACs, which had aluminum or steel bodies, the 3000ME has a fiberglass shell. This was cheap to manufacture and allowed considerable weight savings to be made.

Steel-perimeter chassis
A huge perimeter steel chassis was a first for AC. This makes the 3000ME very strong, but a side effect was too much weight and thus performance is adequate rather than sporty.

Hewland transmission
Because the V6 sat virtually on top of the transmission, AC had to design a new sump/transmission casing to house the Hewland gears. Unusually, drive is taken through a triple-row chain.

Protruding air cleaner
Because the V6 is shoehorned in, it protrudes from the rear bodywork. AC therefore fabricated a special external air cleaner to cover the carburetor.

Front radiator

The radiator is mounted at the front in the usual way, and the air forced through its large grill above the nose.

Stunning looks

The original Diablo created quite a stir, due mainly to its sleek shape. Not surprisingly, AC decided to leave the lines virtually unchanged for the production 3000ME.

Specifications
1979 AC 3000ME

ENGINE
Type: V6

Construction: Cast-iron block and heads

Valve gear: Two valves per cylinder operated by a single camshaft with pushrods and rockers

Bore and stroke: 3.7 in. x 2.85 in.

Displacement: 2,994 cc

Compression ratio: 8.9:1

Induction system: Weber carburetor

Maximum power: 138 bhp at 5,000 rpm

Maximum torque: 174 lb-ft at 3,000 rpm

Top speed: 120 mph

0-60 mph: 9.0 sec.

TRANSMISSION
Five-speed manual

BODY/CHASSIS
Steel perimeter chassis with fiberglass two-door body

SPECIAL FEATURES

A special protruding air cleaner covers the carburetor.

These vents are functional air extractor units.

RUNNING GEAR
Steering: Rack-and-pinion

Front suspension: Double wishbones with coil springs and telescopic shock absorbers

Rear suspension: Double wishbones with coil springs and telescopic shock absorbers

Brakes: Discs (front and rear)

Wheels: Forged magnesium, 7 x 14 in.

Tires: 195/60HR16

DIMENSIONS
Length: 157.0 in.   **Width:** 65.0 in.

Height: 45.0 in.   **Wheelbase:** 90.5 in.

Track: 55.0 in. (front) 56.8 in. (rear)

Weight: 2,483 lbs.

Aston MARTIN DBS

After many years of top-class DB models, Aston Martin produced the radically new DBS. It was larger and screamed for a V8 engine—which it eventually received in 1969. This was one of the fastest grand tourers of the late 1960s.

"...highly muscular performer."

"You've heard of British bulldogs—well, the DBS V8 is the automotive equivalent. It is a highly muscular performer, especially in the upper reaches, though acceleration at any given speed is very impressive. The manual transmission certainly helps, though you do have to struggle with one of the heaviest clutches in history. At least there's power steering on the V8 model, providing fairly crisp turn-in and a good degree of feel."

Traditional British elegance and solid build quality are hallmarks of the cabin.

Milestones

1967 While the DB6 continues in production, the all-new DBS, equipped with a 3,995-cc straight-six engine, becomes the Aston Martin flagship. It handles nicely, but it is a heavy car and most critics believe it needs more power.

Produced alongside the DBS, the DB6 uses the same engine.

1969 The DBS V8 arrives with its all-new quad-cam V8 engine and power steering as standard.

V8 versions of the DBS give the car the power it deserves.

1972 The DBS V8 is renamed simply 'V8.'

1973 The six-cylinder DBS is dropped and the V8 continues with Weber carburetors in place of fuel injection. This model goes out of production after the 1990 model year.

UNDER THE SKIN

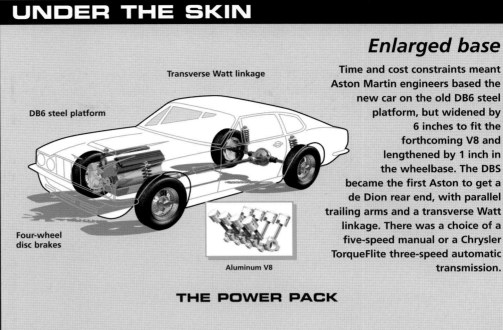

Transverse Watt linkage

DB6 steel platform

Four-wheel disc brakes

Aluminum V8

Enlarged base

Time and cost constraints meant Aston Martin engineers based the new car on the old DB6 steel platform, but widened by 6 inches to fit the forthcoming V8 and lengthened by 1 inch in the wheelbase. The DBS became the first Aston to get a de Dion rear end, with parallel trailing arms and a transverse Watt linkage. There was a choice of a five-speed manual or a Chrysler TorqueFlite three-speed automatic transmission.

THE POWER PACK

Aristocratic engines

At launch, the DBS came with the latest version of the long-running straight-six Aston engine, as fitted to the DB6. In standard tune it develops 282 bhp, and in Vantage tune a full 325 bhp. In 1969, a brand-new Tadek Marek-designed V8 engine was introduced. With twin overhead camshafts for each bank of cylinders, all-aluminum construction and Bosch mechanical fuel injection, it is a mighty powerplant. Aston Martin never quoted a power output, but estimates put it between 310 and 375 bhp.

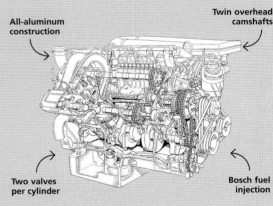

All-aluminum construction

Twin overhead camshafts

Two valves per cylinder

Bosch fuel injection

V8 classic

The six-cylinder DBS is a stunning machine even though it is underpowered for an Aston Martin. This is why most collectors are attracted to the more powerful V8 models. These classic GT cars represent the 'entry-level' Aston in the classic-car marketplace.

Now—as then—the V8 models are most in demand.

ASTON **MARTIN DBS**

Just right for the era, the DBS is a heavy and muscular beast. It is also a beautifully hand-crafted machine with a very high degree of luxury and a quality of finish that can easily be compared with Rolls-Royce.

Luxurious interior

The cabin is a picture of traditional Aston crafts-manship. The sumptuous leather seats are superb, and there are lots of nice touches, such as a wood-rimmed steering wheel, seven round gauges housed in an oval instrument panel, standard air conditioning, power windows and a radio.

Quad-cam V8

Despite the first versions of the DBS that used a six-cylinder engine, the car was designed for V8 power. The 5.3-liter V8—raced in a Lola T70—was designed by Tadek Marek.

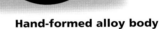

Hand-formed alloy body

Like all Aston Martins, each body was lovingly hand-formed in aluminum by highly skilled craftsmen. Some parts were formed in steel.

Block-like aerodynamics

The styling may have been muscular and brawny but the shape is nowhere near as slippery through the air as the previous DB6. Early tests indicated a drag coefficient figure between 0.42 and 0.47 for the DBS, compared with 0.36 for the DB6.

Disc brakes
The DBS was launched with solid disc brakes on all four wheels. For the V8 model, these had to be uprated and vented.

William Towns styling
The DBS was the first Aston designed by young British designer William Towns, who had worked with General Motors and Rootes. He was open in admitting influence from contemporary GM styling.

Specifications
1971 Aston Martin DBS V8

ENGINE
Type: V8
Construction: Aluminum block and heads
Valve gear: Two valves per cylinder operated by twin overhead camshafts per bank
Bore and stroke: 3.94 in. x 3.35 in.
Displacement: 5,340 cc
Compression ratio: 9.0:1
Induction system: Bosch fuel injection
Maximum power: 320 bhp at 5,000 rpm
Maximum torque: 360 lb-ft at 4,000 rpm
Top speed: 160 mph
0-60 mph: 5.9 sec.

TRANSMISSION
Five-speed manual

BODY/CHASSIS
Unitary monocoque construction with aluminum and steel two-door coupe body

SPECIAL FEATURES

Aston's hallmark side air intake first emerged in the late 1950s.

The DBS features dual exhaust pipes—one pipe on each side exits through the rear valance panel.

RUNNING GEAR
Steering: Rack-and-pinion
Front suspension: Wishbones with coil springs, shock absorbers and anti-roll bar
Rear suspension: De Dion axle with parallel radius arms, Watt linkage, coil springs and shock absorbers
Brakes: Vented discs (front and rear)
Wheels: Alloy, 15-in. dia.
Tires: GR70 VR15

DIMENSIONS
Length: 180.5 in. **Width:** 72.0 in.
Height: 52.3 in. **Wheelbase:** 102.8 in.
Track: 59.0 in. (front and rear)
Weight: 3,800 lbs.

Audi **100 S COUPE**

With the 100 S Coupe, Audi transformed its image and took the first step toward producing a high-class, sports coupe that gave enough performance and handling to match its arch rival, BMW.

"...a fine-handling car."

"Forget the front-heavy design; the 100 S is free of the ponderous feel and monumental understeer that its layout suggests. Instead, it's a fine-handling car, which is at its best on fast, open roads, where it can cruise untroubled at high speeds. Levels of grip are high although under really hard cornering it tends to understeer. The inline transmission helps give one of the best gear shifts on a front-wheel drive car, and the brakes are excellent."

Wood-trimmed panels and well-shaped seats ensure occupants travel in comfort.

Milestones

1969 Audi unveils its new 100 S Coupe at the Frankfurt Motor Show. It has an enlarged, bored-out version of an existing 1.7-liter engine. It is based on the 100 sedan range but has a shorter wheelbase and fastback 2+2 body.

Audi's late 1960s 100 sedan was ahead of its time in many ways.

1974 A minor restyle sees the front grill made narrower and the interior trim upgraded. The brakes are also improved.

The second generation Coupe was more popular than the first.

1975 More changes include the introduction of negative-offset front suspension settings and brake revisions.

1976 Production ends after just under 31,000 have been made. Audi's next Coupe will have sharper, harder-edged lines and will be one of its all-time hottest sellers.

UNDER THE SKIN

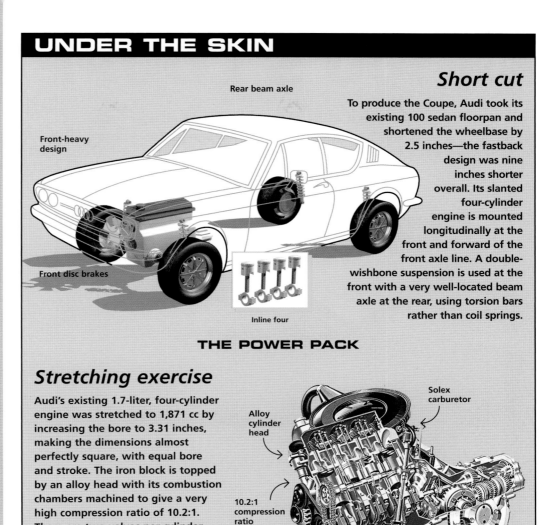

Rear beam axle

Front-heavy design

Front disc brakes

Inline four

Short cut

To produce the Coupe, Audi took its existing 100 sedan floorpan and shortened the wheelbase by 2.5 inches—the fastback design was nine inches shorter overall. Its slanted four-cylinder engine is mounted longitudinally at the front and forward of the front axle line. A double-wishbone suspension is used at the front with a very well-located beam axle at the rear, using torsion bars rather than coil springs.

THE POWER PACK

Stretching exercise

Audi's existing 1.7-liter, four-cylinder engine was stretched to 1,871 cc by increasing the bore to 3.31 inches, making the dimensions almost perfectly square, with equal bore and stroke. The iron block is topped by an alloy head with its combustion chambers machined to give a very high compression ratio of 10.2:1. There are two valves per cylinder operated by a single centrally mounted camshaft and fuel is fed in by a single Solex carburetor.

Solex carburetor

Alloy cylinder head

10.2:1 compression ratio

The final cut

The Coupe was at its best by the end of production. By then Audi had modified it for more advanced negative-offset front suspension settings and greatly improved the brakes, as well as making the wheels and the interior trim more attractive.

The later versions of the Coupe are the best—visually and mechanically.

Audi 100 S COUPE

Luckily for Audi, the appeal of its 100 S, four-cylinder Coupe was enhanced because, by chance, its styling had a very close resemblance to the more exotic and expensive Aston Martin DBS supercar.

Slant four-cylinder

To enable the engine to fit easily under the low hood, Audi tilted the engine at a 45-degree angle with the carburetor and its large air intake near the center of the hood.

Rear-mounted battery

To help minimize the Coupe's excessive front-heavy weight distribution, Audi mounted the battery below the rear seat rather than in the engine bay.

Rear drum brakes

Another effect of having such a front-heavy design is that the Coupe can easily get away with rear-mounted drum brakes at the back. At a mere 7.9 inches in diameter, they are quite small.

Inboard front brakes

Audi mounted the front disc brakes inboard right next to the transmission. On later cars they were moved to the more traditional outboard location.

Torsion bar

Audi paid a lot of attention to the Coupe's rear suspension. The beam axle has a Panhard rod for sideways location, as well as trailing arms working as transverse torsion bars.

Front-heavy

Because Audi mounted the iron-block engine longitudinally at the front, slightly ahead of the front axle line, the car has a 62/38 percent front-to-rear weight ratio.

Specifications
1971 Audi 100 S Coupe

ENGINE
Type: Inline four-cylinder
Construction: Cast-iron block and alloy head
Valve gear: Two valves per cylinder operated by a single block-mounted camshaft via pushrods and rockers
Bore and stroke: 3.31 in. x 3.32 in.
Displacement: 1,871 cc
Compression ratio: 10.2:1
Induction system: Single Solex carburetor
Maximum power: 112 bhp at 5,600 rpm
Maximum torque: 118 lb-ft at 3,500 rpm
Top speed: 112 mph
0-60 mph: 10.9 sec.

TRANSMISSION
Three-speed automatic

BODY/CHASSIS
Unitary monocoque construction with steel two-door 2+2 coupe body

SPECIAL FEATURES

The grills behind the rear side windows keep the cabin well ventilated.

The Coupe's three-speed automatic transmission was advanced for its time.

RUNNING GEAR
Steering: Rack-and-pinion
Front suspension: Double wishbones with coil springs, telescopic shock absorbers and anti-roll bar
Rear suspension: Beam axle with trailing arms, Panhard rod, torsion bars, telescopic shock absorbers and anti-roll bar
Brakes: Vented discs,11.0-in. dia. (front), drums, 7.9-in. dia. (rear)
Wheels: Pressed steel disc, 5 x 14 in.
Tires: 185/70 HR14

DIMENSIONS
Length: 175.8 in.   **Width:** 68.8 in.
Height: 52.5 in.   **Wheelbase:** 101.0 in.
Track: 56.5 in. (front), 56.8 in. (rear)
Weight: 2,410 lbs.

Bentley CORNICHE

The name Corniche evokes images of the mountains rising up behind the coast of Nice and Monaco. This is precisely the location that this exclusive two-door Bentley was aimed at, to be driven by rich playboys on their way to the casino.

"...experience to savor."

"If you have never driven a Bentley before, the experience is one to savor. Turn the ignition key and you'll wonder if something is wrong, because you can't hear the engine start up. Put the column shifter into 'drive' and the car sedately and serenely moves ahead. The ride is magic-carpet soft—too soft for the suspension to cope with fast cornering as the body rolls excessively. But that really isn't the point. This car is for rapid, comfortable cruising."

The cabin is very luxurious with Connolly leather, wood veneer and Wilton carpets.

Milestones

1967 A two-door coupe
version of the Bentley T Series sedan is announced with a drophead coming to market one year later.

1971 The Mulliner Park Ward
two door is adopted as an official Bentley with the name Corniche. It is offered in fixed-head and drophead versions.

There was also a Rolls-Royce badged version of the Corniche.

1972 Vented disc brakes
are now standard.

1976 A split-level
air conditioning system is adopted.

The Azure has taken the place of the convertible Corniche.

1977 A facelift adds a front
spoiler and rubber-faced bumpers.

1984 The Corniche name
is abandoned in favor of the name Continental.

UNDER THE SKIN

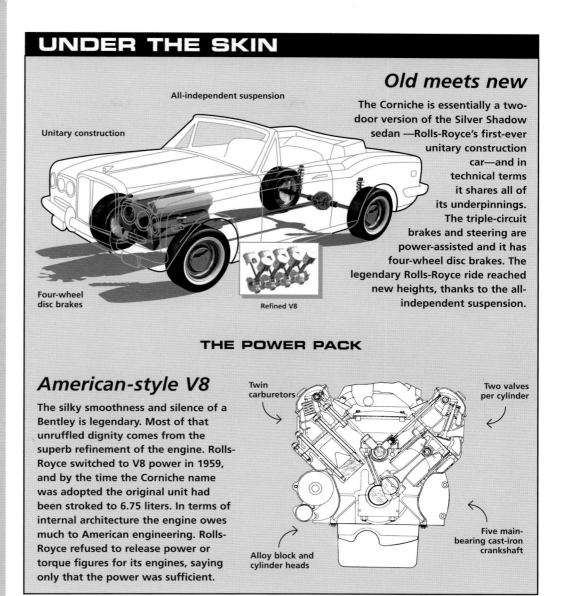

All-independent suspension

Unitary construction

Four-wheel disc brakes

Refined V8

Old meets new

The Corniche is essentially a two-door version of the Silver Shadow sedan —Rolls-Royce's first-ever unitary construction car—and in technical terms it shares all of its underpinnings. The triple-circuit brakes and steering are power-assisted and it has four-wheel disc brakes. The legendary Rolls-Royce ride reached new heights, thanks to the all-independent suspension.

THE POWER PACK

American-style V8

The silky smoothness and silence of a Bentley is legendary. Most of that unruffled dignity comes from the superb refinement of the engine. Rolls-Royce switched to V8 power in 1959, and by the time the Corniche name was adopted the original unit had been stroked to 6.75 liters. In terms of internal architecture the engine owes much to American engineering. Rolls-Royce refused to release power or torque figures for its engines, saying only that the power was sufficient.

Twin carburetors

Two valves per cylinder

Five main-bearing cast-iron crankshaft

Alloy block and cylinder heads

Drop-top

Of the two Corniche models produced by Bentley—the coupe and convertible—the latter is the more sought after. While the coupe is merely a more exclusive two-door version of the Bentley T-Series sedan, the convertible is an icon in its own right.

The Bentley convertible commands higher prices than the coupe.

Bentley CORNICHE

Except for the badges and shape of the grill, the Bentley Corniche is identical to the Rolls-Royce car of the same name. But the Bentley is more exclusive, with its sporty heritage and great rarity.

V8 engine
To produce a respectable power output and torque at unruffled engine speed, an American GM V8 engine was heavily adapted by Rolls-Royce engineers. Power output was never quoted since it was tuned for refinement and effective pulling power rather than outright performance.

Subframe construction
The Corniche uses chassis-less unitary construction. Subframes are used front and rear to carry the main mechanical components such as suspension, powertrain and steering.

Self-levelling suspension
Citroën invented the idea of an oil-based damping system using pressurized air and Bentley used this setup to minimize the rear end stiffness of the Corniche. It provides a self-levelling function: no matter what the load, the rear suspension maintains a constant height.

Fixed or drophead roof
The Corniche was available in two body styles. The first was a fixed-head two-door which, according to British custom, was described as a two-door saloon (sedan). The more expensive was the drop-head model, with its power-operated convertible roof.

Bentley grill

The only major difference between the Rolls-Royce Corniche and its Bentley sibling is the grill. Although it is equally imposing, it features more rounded edges, a slightly lower profile and better aerodynamic characteristics.

Hand-crafted bodywork

The exquisite bodywork was hand-built by the Mulliner Park Ward company that styled this body shape. The company later became a subsidiary of Rolls-Royce.

Specifications
1973 Bentley Corniche

ENGINE
Type: V8
Construction: Aluminum block and heads
Valve gear: Two valves per cylinder operated by a single camshaft via pushrods and rockers
Bore and stroke: 4.10 in. x 3.90 in.
Displacement: 6,750 cc
Compression ratio: 9.0:1
Induction system: Two carburetors
Maximum power: Not quoted
Maximum torque: Not quoted
Top speed: 122 mph
0-60 mph: 9.6 sec.

TRANSMISSION
Three-speed automatic

BODY/CHASSIS
Steel unitary construction with two-door coupe or convertible body

SPECIAL FEATURES

Every panel and all trim is finished in the highest quality leather upholstery.

The only exterior differences between the Rolls-Royce and Bentley is the badging and front radiator grill.

RUNNING GEAR
Steering: Power-assisted recirculating ball
Front suspension: Wishbones with coil springs and shock absorbers
Rear suspension: Semi-trailing arms with coil springs and self-levelling shock absorbers
Brakes: Discs (front and rear)
Wheels: Steel, 15-in. dia
Tires: 235/70 HR15

DIMENSIONS
Length: 203.5 in. **Width:** 71.0 in.
Height: 59.75 in. **Wheelbase:** 119.5 in.
Track: 57.5 in (front and rear)
Weight: 4,815 lbs.

BMW **2002 TURBO**

When BMW won the European Touring Car Championship in 1969 with a turbocharged 2002, it inspired the factory to produce Europe's first turbo production car, the 170-bhp 2002 Turbo. Other manufacturers soon jumped on the turbo bandwagon.

"...real boosted performance."

"Put your foot down and... nothing happens until the revs have climbed past 3,800 rpm, then you quickly realize that this BMW has real boosted performance. You need antici-pation to really use all the Turbo's power. Stiffened, lowered suspension stops the tendency to lift a rear wheel in hard cornering, and even if it did, the limited slip differential would keep the power on. The direct steering gives you a better chance of catching the car if your over-exuberant right foot causes the semi-trailing arm rear to lose grip and swing the back end out."

The engine bay layout meant that only left-hand drive cars were available.

Milestones

1968 BMW drops its largest 2-liter engine into the 1,600 two-door coupe body to produce the 2002. The original car has a single carburetor and just 100 bhp. Later the twin-carb 2002 ti is launched with 120 bhp.

1969 Dieter Quester and the 290-bhp turbocharged 2002 win four rounds and the title in the European Touring Car Championship.

Kugelfischer fuel injection gave 2002 tii 130 bhp.

1971 Fitting Kugelfischer fuel injection to the road cars and raising the compression ratio produces the 130-bhp 2002 tii. The Cabriolet appears, with a built-in steel rollbar. The range also includes the hatchback touring model.

1973 The 2002 Turbo is launched.

The energy crisis spelled the end for the thirsty 2002 Turbo.

1974 The 2002 Turbo's career is cut short as sales plummet due to the energy crisis.

UNDER THE SKIN

Lower, stiffer

The Turbo took the 130-bhp 2002 tii and improved on its strut front and semi-trailing arm rear suspension by lowering it, fitting stiffer springs and firmer shocks, bulging the wheel arches to take the wider alloy wheels and bigger tires. A limited slip differential is standard and you could choose between a four- and five-speed transmission.

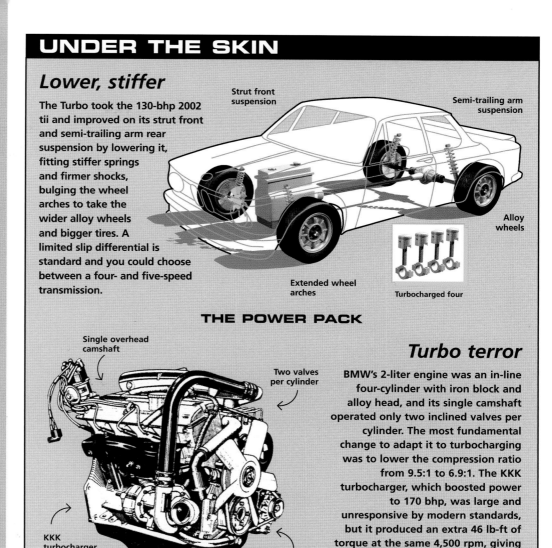

Strut front suspension

Semi-trailing arm suspension

Alloy wheels

Extended wheel arches

Turbocharged four

THE POWER PACK

Single overhead camshaft

Two valves per cylinder

KKK turbocharger

Cast-iron block

Turbo terror

BMW's 2-liter engine was an in-line four-cylinder with iron block and alloy head, and its single camshaft operated only two inclined valves per cylinder. The most fundamental change to adapt it to turbocharging was to lower the compression ratio from 9.5:1 to 6.9:1. The KKK turbocharger, which boosted power to 170 bhp, was large and unresponsive by modern standards, but it produced an extra 46 lb-ft of torque at the same 4,500 rpm, giving outrageous performance for its time.

Flaunting it

BMW was proud of its 2002 Turbo and deliberately styled it to stand out as much as possible with its big skirts and flared wheel arches. This was to make it obvious it was a much faster car than the previous top of the 2002 range, the tii. The bold reversed 'turbo' script for the benefit of driver's mirrors, was soon deleted due to adverse publicity.

Deep chin spoiler, wheel arches and bold stripes tell you it's a Turbo.

BMW 2002 TURBO

In the mid-1970s no one cared that the 2002 Turbo had a problem with turbo lag. They were just delighted that BMW could produce a 2-liter car with 170 bhp and acceleration in Porsche's league.

Four-cylinder engine

The four-cylinder engine in the 2002 could trace its ancestry back to the 1500. The same iron block was also used in the BMW turbo F1 engine, which at one stage produced more than 1000 bhp.

Vented front brakes

To cope with its performance, the Turbo has vented disc brakes in the front, but it retains the 2002 tii's drums at the rear.

Square rear lights

The first 2002s had raised round tail lights, but when the Turbo was launched, BMW changed the design to these newer square lights.

KKK turbocharger

The KKK turbocharger that BMW used was large, by modern standards, and capable of producing tremendous power. But the inertia in its large rotors meant it was slow to start spinning when the throttle was pressed. Consequently, there was too much lag before the turbo began to make boost.

High-geared steering

To make the Turbo feel more responsive, it was given a higher ratio steering gear than the fuel-injected 2002 tii.

Front spoiler

The front spoiler reduces the amount of turbulent air flowing under the car which can hamper its performance.

Wider wheels

For the Turbo, BMW went up from the 5-inch wide steel wheels of the 2002 tii to 6-inch wide alloy rims, carrying wider 185/70 HR13 tires.

Lowered suspension

The 2002 was lowered to improve handling. With stiffer springs and shocks there was no danger of the wheels hitting the bodywork.

Specifications
1973 BMW 2002 Turbo

ENGINE
Type: In-line four cylinder
Construction: Cast-iron block and alloy cylinder head
Valve gear: Two inclined valves per cylinder operated by single chain-driven overhead cam
Bore and stroke: 3.50 in. x 3.14 in.
Displacement: 1,990 cc
Compression ratio: 6.9:1
Induction system: Kugelfischer fuel injection
Maximum power: 170 bhp at 5,800 rpm
Maximum torque: 177 lb-ft at 4,500 rpm
Top speed: 130 mph
0-60 mph: 7.6 sec

TRANSMISSION
Four- or five-speed manual

BODY/CHASSIS
Steel monocoque two-door sedan

SPECIAL FEATURES

When the driver you were following looked in his mirrors, the reversed badges on the front spoiler told him he was being caught by the Turbo.

Radical wheel arches are needed to cover the Turbo's wide tires.

RUNNING GEAR
Steering: ZF worm-and-roller
Front suspension: MacPherson struts and anti-roll bar
Rear suspension: Semi-trailing arms, coil springs, telescopic shocks and anti-roll bar
Brakes: Vented discs 10 in. dia. (front), drums 9 in. dia. (rear)
Wheels: Alloy, 6 in. x 13 in.
Tires: 185/70 HR13

DIMENSIONS
Length: 166.1 in.   **Width:** 63.8 in.
Height: 55 in.   **Wheelbase:** 98.4 in.
Track: 62.2 in. (front and rear)
Weight: 2,381 lbs.

BMW **M1**

Built in small numbers and too late for the racing formula it was designed for, the M1 was turned into BMW's first mid-engined, street-legal supercar with a 277-bhp, twin-cam six.

"...designed as a race car."

"At high speeds, you can feel that the M1 was designed as a racing car. It's as solid as a rock with great reserves of power everywhere. Unfortunately, it is simply too heavy to be a competitive racing car. It takes a lot of effort to drive the M1, with both the clutch and brake needing a firm push...though that's a small penalty. Its steering feel and response is pure BMW, rewarding you with endless confidence and unflappable poise."

The M1's disappointingly unattractive cabin hasn't stood the test of time in the way that the ageless Giugiaro exterior shape has.

Milestones

1972 Paul Bracq, head of BMW styling,

creates the Turbo Coupe concept car. The head of BMW Motorsport feels the design could be modified to create a racing car to contest Group 4 endurance events. Giugiaro is asked to style the car.

Giorgetto Giugiaro styled the M1 for BMW.

1978 After many delays, the M1 appears at the Paris Show.

The M635CSi and M1 share same basic 24-valve, six-cylinder engine, but the coupe has more power.

1979 Too late and too heavy to be a

competitive racer, BMW and FOCA arrange for the M1 to star in the one-marque 'Procar' series to support Grands Prix.

1981 Production ends after 450 cars have been

produced—397 road cars and 53 racers.

UNDER THE SKIN

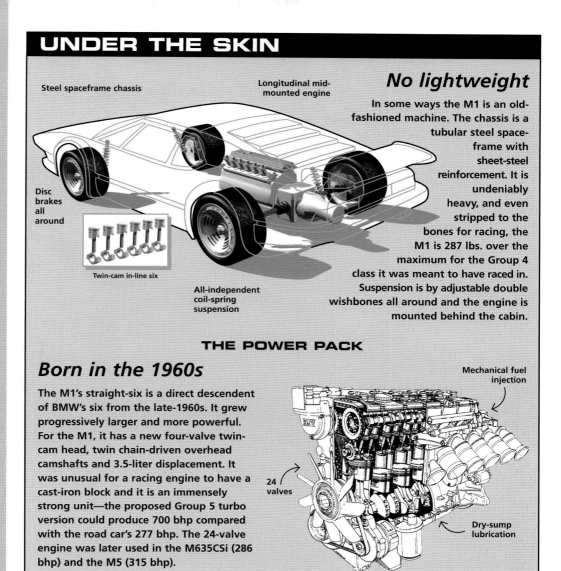

Steel spaceframe chassis

Longitudinal mid-mounted engine

Disc brakes all around

Twin-cam in-line six

All-independent coil-spring suspension

No lightweight

In some ways the M1 is an old-fashioned machine. The chassis is a tubular steel space-frame with sheet-steel reinforcement. It is undeniably heavy, and even stripped to the bones for racing, the M1 is 287 lbs. over the maximum for the Group 4 class it was meant to have raced in. Suspension is by adjustable double wishbones all around and the engine is mounted behind the cabin.

THE POWER PACK

Born in the 1960s

The M1's straight-six is a direct descendent of BMW's six from the late-1960s. It grew progressively larger and more powerful. For the M1, it has a new four-valve twin-cam head, twin chain-driven overhead camshafts and 3.5-liter displacement. It was unusual for a racing engine to have a cast-iron block and it is an immensely strong unit—the proposed Group 5 turbo version could produce 700 bhp compared with the road car's 277 bhp. The 24-valve engine was later used in the M635CSi (286 bhp) and the M5 (315 bhp).

Mechanical fuel injection

24 valves

Dry-sump lubrication

Effective racer

Racing M1s were tuned to almost 200-bhp more than the road car, and their engines could rev to 9,000 rpm. Although it was an overweight racer, it could still be effective. Hans-Joachim Stuck's M1 led more potent cars at Le Mans one year.

The M1 provided plenty of excitement, running in Procar and Group 4 circuits.

BMW **M1**

It might not look as spectacular as its exotic Ferrari and Lamborghini rivals, but don't let that fool you. The M1 has one major advantage—it was designed as a real racing car.

Fiberglass bodywork

All the M1 body panels are fiberglass and they are both riveted and bonded to the tubular steel frame. The body was produced by Italian company TIR (Transformazione Italiana Resina) to a very high standard.

Tubular steel chassis

Originally, it made sense to farm out the chassis construction to Lamborghini because they had far more experience than BMW in building tubular steel chassis. Eventually Marchesi of Modena made the chassis.

Twin-cam straight-six

In street-legal form the BMW's six-cylinder, twin-cam engine produces 277 bhp from 3.5 liters.

Pirelli P7 tires

The low-profile Pirelli P7 tire was a huge advance in its day and the car's suspension was set up to suit the tire's characteristics.

Slatted engine cover

Hot air from the engine compartment escapes between these large slats. Rearward vision is very good for a mid-engined supercar, and a glass window behind the driver's head insulates the cockpit from the engine bay.

Air intakes

Slots just behind the nearside, rear window feed air to the engine's induction system. The matching slots on the other side are for engine bay ventilation.

Classic grill

The distinctive BMW grill was kept for the M1 and it is functional because both the radiator and the engine oil cooler are at the front. After the air passes over them, it exits through the vents on top of the hood.

Servo brakes

Street-legal M1s have servo-assisted brakes but these were left off the racers, although the driver could adjust the brake balance between front and rear wheels.

Double-wishbone suspension

Most BMWs have some form of semi-trailing arm suspension at the rear but the M1 is different, with racing-type double wishbones in the front and rear.

Specifications
1980 BMW M1

ENGINE
Type: Straight-six twin cam
Construction: Cast-iron block and alloy head
Valve gear: Four valves per cylinder operated by two chain-driven overhead camshafts
Bore and stroke: 3.68 in. x 3.31 in.
Displacement: 3,453 cc
Compression ratio: 9.0:1
Induction system: Bosch-Kugelfischer mechanical fuel injection
Maximum power: 277 bhp at 6,500 rpm
Maximum torque: 239 lb-ft at 5,000 rpm
Top speed: 162 mph
Engine type: straight-six

TRANSMISSION
ZF five-speed manual

BODY/CHASSIS
Fiberglass two-door, two-seat coupe body with tubular steel chassis

SPECIAL FEATURES

Rear screen louvers afforded reasonable rearward vision and helped to keep engine temperatures down.

Dated wheel with Pirelli P7s that are narrow by today's standards.

RUNNING GEAR
Steering: Rack-and-pinion
Front suspension: Double wishbones, coil springs, telescopic shocks and anti-roll bar
Rear suspension: Double wishbones, coil springs, telescopic shocks and anti-roll bar
Brakes: Vented discs front and rear
Wheels: Alloy, 7 in. x 16 in. (front), 8 in. x 16 in. (rear)
Tires: Pirelli P7, 205/55 VR16 (front), 225/50 VR16 (rear)

DIMENSIONS
Length: 171.7 in.   **Width:** 71.7 in.
Height: 44.9 in.   **Wheelbase:** 100.8 in.
Track: 61 in. (front), 60.9 in. (rear)
Weight: 3,122 lbs.

Buick RIVIERA GRAN SPORT

Bigger and heavier for 1971, Buick's personal luxury coupe also got dramatic new styling—especially at the rear, which gave rise to its 'boat-tail' nickname. Some saw it as the ultimate land yacht, but the GS™ model's 330 bhp made for fast, executive-style driving.

"...easy and effortless ."

"When viewed from the outside, the Riviera looks positively huge, but take your place behind the wheel and it feels much smaller. Easy and effortless to drive, this big Buick is at its best on long, straight roads, but with the GS package it will corner hard, ultimately only let down by its tires and sheer girth. The V8 is another matter; with the GS option it packs 330 bhp and 455 lb-ft of torque. This car will reach 60 mph quicker than many other personal luxury cars of its era."

A radiused gauge cluster and close-mounted console garnish the Riviera's lavish interior.

Milestones

1971 Replacing the 1966 vintage

Riviera is a new, larger model, with a wheelbase three inches longer and swoopy styling. Weighing about 100 lbs. more, sales drop to 33,810 due in part to its controversial rear end.

The Riviera was reborn as a personal luxury coupe in 1963.

1972 Chrome side spears

and a new grill mark the 1972 model. The Gran Sport package is still around, though power is down because of its low-lead, 8.5:1 compression ratio. The big 455-c.i. V8 makes 225 bhp—250 in GS tune.

1974 saw the heaviest Riviera yet, weighing in at 4,572 lbs.

1973 A bigger front bumper

and toned down rear deck styling give the Buick's personal luxury car a less distinctive look. Sales creep up slightly to 34,080.

UNDER THE SKIN

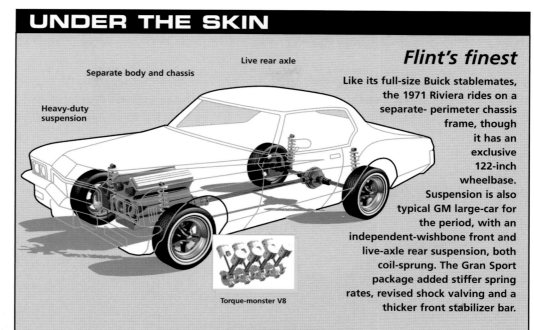

Separate body and chassis

Heavy-duty suspension

Live rear axle

Torque-monster V8

Flint's finest

Like its full-size Buick stablemates, the 1971 Riviera rides on a separate- perimeter chassis frame, though it has an exclusive 122-inch wheelbase. Suspension is also typical GM large-car for the period, with an independent-wishbone front and live-axle rear suspension, both coil-sprung. The Gran Sport package added stiffer spring rates, revised shock valving and a thicker front stabilizer bar.

THE POWER PACK

Mammoth motor

With fuel selling for around 30 cents per gallon in 1971, the Riviera naturally came with Buick's largest V8. Displacing 455-cubic inches, it was an outgrowth of the 1967 430. A very long (3.90-inch) stroke makes it a torque monster; it thumps out a whopping 455 lb-ft at just 2,800 rpm. Driving such a car as the Riviera Gran Sport, it is possible to entice drivers of smaller and lighter muscle cars to a traffic light duel. Though it has a lot of torque, the engine is still well behaved and will provide relaxed high-speed cruising.

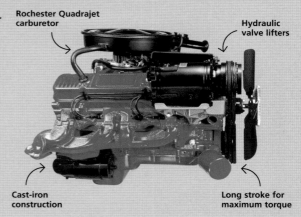

Rochester Quadrajet carburetor

Hydraulic valve lifters

Cast-iron construction

Long stroke for maximum torque

Speed boat

Although large and unique, the boat-tail Riviera does have a following. The 1971-1972 models have the unusually styled rear end, which was toned down for 1973. The 1971 GS is also the most sporty version and luckily can still be bought at reasonable prices.

1971 is the pinnacle year for boat-tails in terms of styling and performance.

Buick **RIVIERA GRAN SPORT**

Penned by Jerry Hirschberg, the 1971 Riviera was a unique design because it broke away from the conservative luxury so often associated with Buick cars. This is what elevated this short-lived car to cult status in later years.

Giant V8

Powering one of the largest and heaviest Rivieras is Buick's largest passenger car engine. Displacing a monster 455-cubic inches, this giant packs 330 bhp in Gran Sport trim and 455 lb-ft of torque. The Riviera GS was the perfect street sleeper for those who were looking for something different.

Heavy-duty suspension

Ordering the Gran Sport package in 1971 brought with it stiffer coil springs and shock absorbers, plus a thicker stabilizer bar. It made for one of the most sporty luxury coupes then on sale.

Body-on-the-frame construction

Rivieras in 1971 had their own E-body chassis but shared their separated chassis structure with the other GM B- and C-body full-size cars.

Boat-tail deck styling

Riviera stylist Hirschberg gave the new Riviera a very dramatic rear deck style which extended right to the bumper. This necessitated an offset rear license plate bracket.

Cornering lights

Costing just $36 in 1971, cornering lights are mounted in the front fenders. These come on with the turn signals. At night, the front and side signals flash alternately instead of in time.

Dual exhaust

Initially, Rivieras had dual exhaust, each with individual mufflers. This system prevailed until 1975, when the adoption of a catalytic convertor necessitated the need for a single setup.

Counterbalanced hood

Like most U.S. cars of the period, the 1971 Riviera has a counterbalancing hood. When opened, heavy-duty hinges support it, eliminating the need for a prop rod. The hood latch is located in the front-grill assembly.

1971 Buick Riviera Gran Sport

ENGINE
Type: V8
Construction: Cast-iron block and heads
Valve gear: Two valves per cylinder operated by pushrods and rockers
Bore and stroke: 4.31 in. x 3.90 in.
Displacement: 455 c.i.
Compression ratio: 8.5:1
Induction system: Rochester Quadrajet four-barrel carburetor
Maximum power: 330 bhp at 4,600 rpm
Maximum torque: 455 lb-ft at 2,800 rpm
Top speed: 120 mph
0-60 mph: 8.1 sec.

TRANSMISSION
GM TurboHydramatic 400 three-speed automatic

BODY/CHASSIS
Steel-perimeter chassis with separate two-door coupe body

SPECIAL FEATURES

Pillarless styling is a feature of Rivieras built up to 1974.

1971-72 models are the only true boat-tail-styled Rivieras.

RUNNING GEAR
Steering: Recirculating ball
Front suspension: Unequal-length A-arms with coil springs, telescopic shock absorbers and stabilizer bar
Rear suspension: Live axle with coil springs and telescopic shock absorbers
Brakes: Discs (front), drums (rear)
Wheels: Steel 7 x 15
Tires: G70-15 in.

DIMENSIONS
Length: 217.4 in.   **Width:** 79.9 in.
Height: 56.4 in.   **Wheelbase:** 122.0 in.
Track: 60.4 in.
Weight: 4,325 lbs.

Chevrolet CHEVELLE SS 454

In 1970, Chevrolet introduced the ultimate powerhouse for its midsize muscle car. It was also the year GM lifted its displacement ban on all of its midsize cars. For the Chevelle, it meant 450 bhp from a stout LS-6 454 V8 for the Super Sport model. Today, it is regarded as one of the most fearsome muscle cars of all time.

"...all-out performance."

"This is not a toy—it's an LS-6 Chevelle SS. It's one of those cars GM built just to show up Ford and Mopar. For years, the SS used semi-powerful 396 V8s, but when Chevy® released the LS-6 454, the competition shuddered. The all-out performance engine has a factory rating of 450 bhp—no other muscle car production engine had a higher rating. The LS-6 Chevelle's only limitation was its tires. But even with the stock tread, the SS could be power shifted to 13.7 seconds in the ¼ mile."

While most Chevelle Super Sports were ordered with custom buckets, this one has a bench seat.

Milestones

1969 SS is an option package. Top-of-the-line engine continues to be the L78 396 with 375 bhp. However, Vince Piggins, GM's performance products manager, had 323 COPO (Central Office Production Order) Chevelles built with L72 427 V8s. They produce 425 bhp, and run the ¼ mile in 13.3 seconds at 108 mph.

Earlier Chevelles had much boxier styling.

1970 General Motors unleashes its wildest muscle cars yet, with revised styling. The LS-5 (360 bhp) and LS-6 (454 bhp) 454 V8s join the 396 in the Chevelle SS line up as a regular production order.

In 1970, the smaller-engined SS 396 was still available.

1971 The SS 454 returns, though the LS-6 option is dropped. The less powerful LS-5 actually gains 5 bhp, to 365. Only 9,402 SS 454s are built. A new Chevelle arrives for 1973.

UNDER THE SKIN

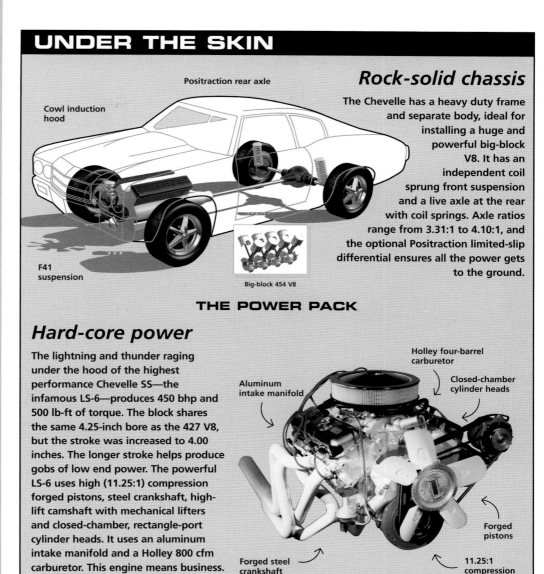

Positraction rear axle

Cowl induction hood

F41 suspension

Big-block 454 V8

Rock-solid chassis

The Chevelle has a heavy duty frame and separate body, ideal for installing a huge and powerful big-block V8. It has an independent coil sprung front suspension and a live axle at the rear with coil springs. Axle ratios range from 3.31:1 to 4.10:1, and the optional Positraction limited-slip differential ensures all the power gets to the ground.

THE POWER PACK

Hard-core power

The lightning and thunder raging under the hood of the highest performance Chevelle SS—the infamous LS-6—produces 450 bhp and 500 lb-ft of torque. The block shares the same 4.25-inch bore as the 427 V8, but the stroke was increased to 4.00 inches. The longer stroke helps produce gobs of low end power. The powerful LS-6 uses high (11.25:1) compression forged pistons, steel crankshaft, high-lift camshaft with mechanical lifters and closed-chamber, rectangle-port cylinder heads. It uses an aluminum intake manifold and a Holley 800 cfm carburetor. This engine means business.

Aluminum intake manifold

Holley four-barrel carburetor

Closed-chamber cylinder heads

Forged pistons

11.25:1 compression

Forged steel crankshaft

Collector's cars

The 1970 Chevelle Super Sport was restyled from the 1969 model and again in 1971. A 1970 SS with the LS-6 is as rare as it is powerful. Only 4,475 of these venomous vehicles were produced, making them popular and valuable among auto collectors.

Not many muscle cars come close to the tire-shredding power of the LS-6 SS.

Chevrolet CHEVELLE SS 454

The LS-6 Chevelle was one of the most powerful muscle cars ever produced. It combined Chevrolet's largest engine with its sporty midsize car to give outrageous results.

Body stripes

By 1970 style was every bit as important as performance, and SS Chevelles were available with twin stripes running over the hood and rear decklid.

LS-6 454-cubic inch V8

The biggest performance option in 1970 was the LS-6 engine. It produces 450 bhp at 5,600 rpm and 500 lb-ft of torque at 3,600 rpm. It has high compression pistons, rectangle port cylinder heads, and solid valve lifters. Few other muscle machines could rival the power of the LS-6.

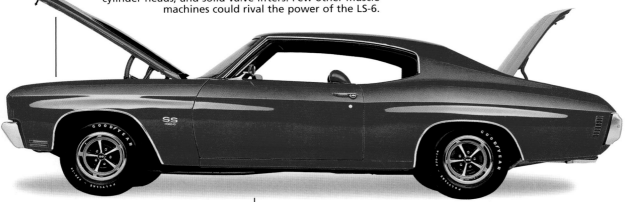

M-22 'Rock crusher' transmission

With 500 lb-ft of torque, only two transmissions were strong enough to cope with the LS-6 engine. This one has a Muncie M22 'Rock crusher' four-speed. This stout unit has a 2.20:1 straight-cut first gear.

Magnum 500 wheels

Magnum 500 steel wheels were used on all 1970 Chevelle Super Sports. The Polyglas F70x14 could barely handle the engine's torque.

Hardtop body

While all LS-6 engines were supposed to be installed in hardtops only, it's rumored that a few found their way into convertibles.

Upgraded suspension

The SS package included the F41 suspension which has stiffer front springs to compensate for the weight of the big-block engine.

Cowl induction hood

A vacuum-controlled flap at the top of the hood draws air in from the high-pressure area at the base of the windshield to help the engine exploit its power. This is known as cowl induction.

Dual exhaust

A full-length 2.5-inch dual exhaust system enables the LS-6 to optimize the engine's performance.

Specifications
1970 Chevrolet Chevelle SS 454

ENGINE
Type: V8
Construction: Cast-iron block and heads
Valve gear: Two valves per cylinder operated by pushrods and rockers
Bore and stroke: 4.25 in. x 4.00 in.
Displacement: 454 c.i.
Compression ratio: 11.25:1
Induction system: Holley four-barrel carburetor and aluminum intake manifold
Maximum power: 450 bhp at 5,600 rpm
Maximum torque: 500 lb-ft at 3,600 rpm
Top speed: 125 mph
0-60 mph: 6.1 sec

TRANSMISSION
Manual four-speed, close-ratio M-22

BODY/CHASSIS
Steel body on separate steel chassis

SPECIAL FEATURES

All Chevelle Super Sports came with Magnum 500 steel wheels and Polyglas F70x14 tires in 1970.

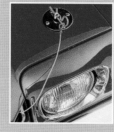

These NASCAR-style tie down hood pins were a popular item and helped keep the hood from lifting at high speed.

RUNNING GEAR
Steering: Recirculating ball
Front suspension: Independent with wishbones, anti-roll bar, coil springs and telescopic shock absorbers
Rear suspension: Live axle with coil springs and telescopic shock absorbers
Brakes: Disc, 11-in. dia. (front), drum 9-in. dia. (rear)
Wheels: Magnum 500, 14-in. dia.
Tires: Polyglas F70x14

DIMENSIONS
Length: 189 in.   **Width:** 70.2 in.
Height: 52.7 in.   **Wheelbase:** 112 in.
Track: 56.8 in. (front), 56.9 in. (rear)
Weight: 4,000 lbs.

Chevrolet **CAMARO SS 396**

Unveiled in February 1970, the all-new second-generation Camaro was an instant design classic. Benefitting from a smoother ride and better handling, it could still be optioned with a pile-driving 375 bhp 396. Because of the immediate popularity of the then-new 350 bhp, 350 LT-1™, few buyers specified the big engine.

"...no ordinary Camaro."

"If you want a good handler, try the Z28® but if it's outright power that makes your mouth water, slide in and start 'er up. Inside the SS396, you're quickly greeted with a rough-idling engine and a loudly roaring exhaust. That's just one sign that lets you know this is no ordinary Camaro. Coax the shifter into first, bring up the rpm and drop the clutch—the tires spin with ease from the SS396's massive 415 lb-ft of torque. Then, powershift into second and hang on it'll reach 60 mph in 6.2 seconds."

Supportive front bucket seats and a well laid-out instrument panel are Camaro traits.

Milestones

1970 An all-new, second-generation

Camaro makes its debut in February. Offered only as a coupe, it comes in base, SS™ and Z28 versions. A United Auto Workers strike causes production to dip to 124,889 units. The SS gets a new 402 big block during the year but is still badged as a 396.

The Camaro was introduced in September 1966 in both coupe and convertible bodystyles.

1971 Few changes occur this year, although emissions begin to bite. The 402-cubic inch V8 has a lower 8.5:1 compression ratio and power drops from 350 to 300 bhp.

Second-generation Camaros got their final facelift for 1978.

1972 Power ratings are switched to SAE net ratings, with all engine ancillaries attached. The SS is still offered with 350-cubic inch, four-barrel and 402-cubic inch engines, but power is down to 200 and 240 bhp, respectively. The SS is replaced by the LT for 1973.

UNDER THE SKIN

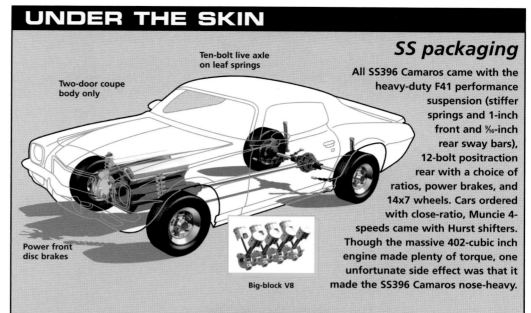

Ten-bolt live axle on leaf springs

Two-door coupe body only

Power front disc brakes

Big-block V8

SS packaging

All SS396 Camaros came with the heavy-duty F41 performance suspension (stiffer springs and 1-inch front and ⁹⁄₁₆-inch rear sway bars), 12-bolt positraction rear with a choice of ratios, power brakes, and 14x7 wheels. Cars ordered with close-ratio, Muncie 4-speeds came with Hurst shifters. Though the massive 402-cubic inch engine made plenty of torque, one unfortunate side effect was that it made the SS396 Camaros nose-heavy.

THE POWER PACK

Is it a 396 or a 402?

Though the popular combination for the Camaro in 1970 was the Z-28 with 360-bhp, LT-1 power, customers were still offered the 396 big block. Although its bore was increased to 4.125 inches making its actual displacement 402-cubic inches, GM still badged the engine as a 396. If ordered in Camaro SS trim, the massive motor was available in two states of tune—350 (L-34) or 375 bhp (L-78). 350 bhp versions had 10.25:1 compression, a cast-iron intake manifold and a Rochester Quadrajet carburetor. 375-bhp versions came with higher compression, an aluminum intake manifold and a Holley four-barrel carburetor.

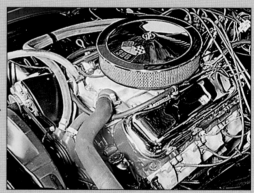

Rare find

Although the SS was in its prime in 1969, one year later it was eclipsed by the LT-1-powered Z28. The rarest of the 1970 SS396 Camaros have the elusive 375-bhp, L78 engines. Only 600 were built. Today, these powerful Camaros are hard to find and have kept their value well.

The original SS leaves the lineup in 1972 due to a changing market.

Chevrolet CAMARO SS 396

Overshadowed by the better balanced Z28, the 1970 SS396 was the weapon of choice for drag racers. As the muscle car dynasty of the 1960s began to unfold during the early 1970s, Chevrolet still offered a truly brutal performer.

Standard front

The standard front-end treatment consists of a full-length chrome bumper with turn signals mounted below it. RS-equipped Camaros have an Endura nose and twin bumperettes.

Big-block V8

With more than 400-cubic inches and 415 lb-ft of torque, the SS396 could run with the best cars the competition had to offer. Improved suspension also gave the factory SS ¼-mile times in the low 14-second range.

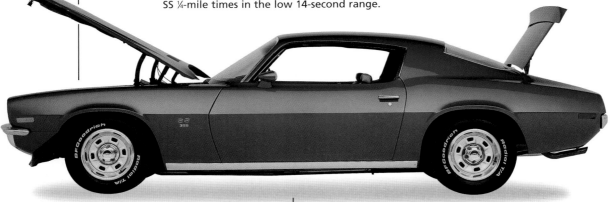

Unitary chassis

Camaros retained a unitary body/chassis for 1970, but greater attention was paid to refinement, including greater use of sound-deadening in the body.

Hardtop styling

Two bodystyles were initially planned, although with a growing buyer preference for closed bodystyles, it was decided to drop the convertible early in the development stage.

Small rear window

GM stylists originally intended to give the 1970 Camaro a wraparound rear window, but problems with the installation delayed this until 1975. Thus, all early cars got small back windows, which led to criticism of rearward visibility.

SS equipment group

The SS package included a stiffer suspension and a refreshing appearance package with twin sport mirrors, blacked-out grill and a sporty interior.

External spoilers

Front and rear spoilers were optional on any Camaro. The rear spoilers increased in size later in the 1970 model year.

Specifications
1970 Chevrolet Camaro SS396

ENGINE
Type: V8
Construction: Cast-iron block and heads
Valve gear: Two valves per cylinder operated by pushrods and rocker arms
Bore and stroke: 4.125 in. x 3.76 in.
Displacement: 402 c.i. (396 c.i.)
Compression ratio: 10.25:1
Induction system: Rochester Quadrajet carburetor
Maximum power: 375 bhp at 5,600 rpm
Maximum torque: 415 lb-ft at 3,200 rpm
Top speed: 128 mph
0-60 mph: 6.2 sec.

TRANSMISSION
Muncie M21 four-speed manual

BODY/CHASSIS
Steel unitary chassis with two-door body

SPECIAL FEATURES

Quad taillights mimic its big brother, the Corvette.

The SS396's transmission, the Muncie M21 four-speed, was named after the town they were made in—Muncie, Indiana.

RUNNING GEAR
Steering: Recirculating ball
Front suspension: Unequal-length A-arms with coil springs, telescopic shock absorbers and anti-roll bar
Rear suspension: Live axle with semi-elliptic leaf springs and telescopic shock absorbers
Brakes: Discs (front), drums (rear)
Wheels: Super Sport, 7 x 14 in.
Tires: Firestone Wide Oval, F70-14

DIMENSIONS
Length: 188.0 in.   **Width:** 74.4 in.
Height: 50.1 in.   **Wheelbase:** 108.0 in.
Track: 61.3 in. (front), 60.0 in. (rear)
Weight: 3,550 lbs.

Citroën SM

Combining the eccentricity of Citroën with the quad-cam engine technology of Maserati produced the perfect blend of luxury and performance for those brave enough to try it.

"...best when driven smoothly."

"The SM isn't a car you take by the the neck to wring out performance. It needs the most delicate of inputs in every department. The power steering and brakes are ultrasensitive and over-enthusiastic cornering produces massive amounts of roll. Grip, however, remains outstanding. It's at its best when driven smoothly through long sweeping bends. The SM's ride is fantastic and it has a smooth gearshift. The SM is fast, too and pulls surprisingly strongly."

Citroën's design for the SM's interior was typically quirky and very 1970s in style.

Milestones

1969 Citroën takes over Maserati, the company which will build the engines for the SM.

1970 The SM goes into production. Four cars take part in the Morocco Rally of 1971, finishing 1st, 3rd and 4th.

SM used many parts from the DS parts bins.

1972 Bosch fuel injection is fitted and a short-wheelbase version called the SM Rallye is built with lightweight body panels. One comes 3rd in the TAP Rally in Portugal.

1974 With sales falling, SM production is transferred to the racing car builders Ligier. As Citroën merges with Peugeot, putting Maserati into receivership, the SM is doomed.

Maserati's mid-engined Merak shared the SM's V6.

1975 Production ends at the Ligier factory at Abrese in France.

UNDER THE SKIN

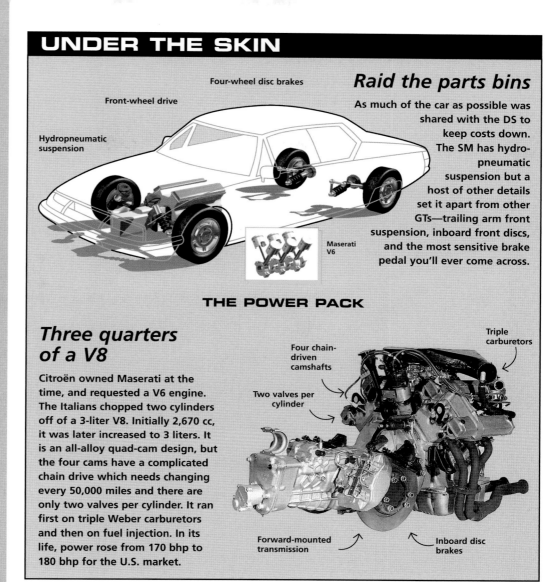

Four-wheel disc brakes

Front-wheel drive

Hydropneumatic suspension

Maserati V6

Raid the parts bins

As much of the car as possible was shared with the DS to keep costs down. The SM has hydropneumatic suspension but a host of other details set it apart from other GTs—trailing arm front suspension, inboard front discs, and the most sensitive brake pedal you'll ever come across.

THE POWER PACK

Three quarters of a V8

Citroën owned Maserati at the time, and requested a V6 engine. The Italians chopped two cylinders off of a 3-liter V8. Initially 2,670 cc, it was later increased to 3 liters. It is an all-alloy quad-cam design, but the four cams have a complicated chain drive which needs changing every 50,000 miles and there are only two valves per cylinder. It ran first on triple Weber carburetors and then on fuel injection. In its life, power rose from 170 bhp to 180 bhp for the U.S. market.

Four chain-driven camshafts

Two valves per cylinder

Triple carburetors

Forward-mounted transmission

Inboard disc brakes

Chop-top

As though the standard SM wasn't extraordinary enough, there were four-door convertibles built specially for the French president, as well as an attractive two-door by Henri Chapron, who built many special Citroën bodies. Despite the unusual look of the two- and four-seat bodies, Citroëns were quite popular in Europe.

Coachbuilder Chapron converted SMs to open-top specifications.

Citroën SM

Designed to be a luxury grand tourer for the man who wanted to be different from everyone else, the SM's character was as complex as its unique engineering.

Transmission ahead of engine

To help weight distribution the five-speed transmission is mounted ahead of the engine so all the V6 is behind the front axle line.

Maserati V6 engine

The SM's V6 engine is derived from the Maserati V8 design—it is compact, light, and powerful.

Hatchback design

The fastback styling meant there was no room for a trunk—the SM became one of the world's most expensive hatchbacks.

Trailing arm front suspension

The SM's front suspension has two trailing arms that are sprung and dampened by the usual Citroën hydropneumatic system.

Power brakes

The SM's very high-pressure hydraulic system powers the four disc brakes. The brake feel is closer to a push button than a conventional brake pedal and needs only the slightest touch to produce very effective braking.

Variable ride height

Citroën hydropneumatic suspension can be set to different heights. Here it's at the maximum, which would never have been used on normal roads.

Inboard front discs

To help with unsprung weight, the front disc brakes are mounted inboard next to the transmission.

Power-assisted steering

At low speeds the assistance is great, dropping away as road speed rises. It's very direct with just two turns lock-to-lock and the self-centering action is extremely strong.

Central hydraulic pump

An engine-driven hydraulic pump is mounted in the center of the engine's V, pressurizing the hydropneumatic suspension, power steering, and brakes.

Specifications
1973 Citroën SM

ENGINE
Type: V6
Construction: Alloy block and cylinder heads; wet liners
Valve gear: Two valves per cylinder operated by four chain-driven overhead camshafts
Bore and stroke: 3.42 in. x 2.95 in.
Displacement: 2,670 cc
Compression ratio: 9.0:1
Induction system: Bosch D-Jetronic fuel injection
Maximum power: 178 bhp at 5,500 rpm
Maximum torque: 171 lb-ft at 4,000 rpm
Top speed: 142 mph
0-60 mph: 8.5 sec

TRANSMISSION
Five-speed manual

BODY/CHASSIS
Unitary construction with two-door, four-seat hatchback body

SPECIAL FEATURES

The SM has a typically quirky Citroën dashboard with oval instruments and trademark single-spoke steering wheel.

As the SM turns through corners one pair of the powerful front lights also turns to illuminate the whole corner. The lights also self-level.

RUNNING GEAR
Steering: Rack-and-pinion
Front suspension: Twin trailing arms with hydropneumatic springs and anti-roll bar
Rear suspension: Trailing arms with hydropneumatic springs. Self levelling front and rear
Brakes: Four-wheel discs
Wheels: Steel, 6 in. x 15 in.
Tires: Michelin XVX 205/70 VR15

DIMENSIONS
Length: 192.8 in. **Width:** 72.5 in.
Height: 52.1 in. **Wheelbase:** 116.1 in.
Track: 60.1 in. (front), 52.2 in. (rear)
Weight: 3,197 lbs.

Citroën **GS BIROTOR**

The Birotor was an intriguing mixture of rotary-engined smoothness and advanced front-drive sedan. However, it proved a blind alley, like so many of the cars that used rotary power: it was expensive to build and expensive to run.

"...smooth and supple."

"Driving the Birotor is very much like driving any other GS derivative except it is much faster, quieter and smoother. The engine is exceptionally smooth and revs very freely to its 6,500-rpm redline, with most of its power coming on from 4,000 rpm onward. The transmission is a clutchless semi-automatic. It shifts like a typical manual transmission, but without the clutch. Like all GS models, the ride is smooth and supple, and the brakes are astoundingly sharp."

An array of gauges and a futuristic steering wheel compliment the cabin.

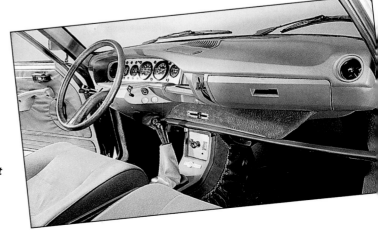

Milestones

1964 Citroën signs an agreement with NSU to build Wankel rotary engines under license.

Citroën first tried rotary power with the experimental M35.

1967 The CoMotor subsidiary is established to market and manufacture rotary engines.

1969 Work begins on the CoMotor factory at Sarre.

The standard, flat-four-powered GS was a big hit in 1972.

1971 Citroën builds 260 experimental single-rotor M35 cars to test the durability of the Wankel engine.

1973 The GS-based Birotor is becomes a reality.

1975 Production of the Birotor ends after just 847 cars have been built.

UNDER THE SKIN

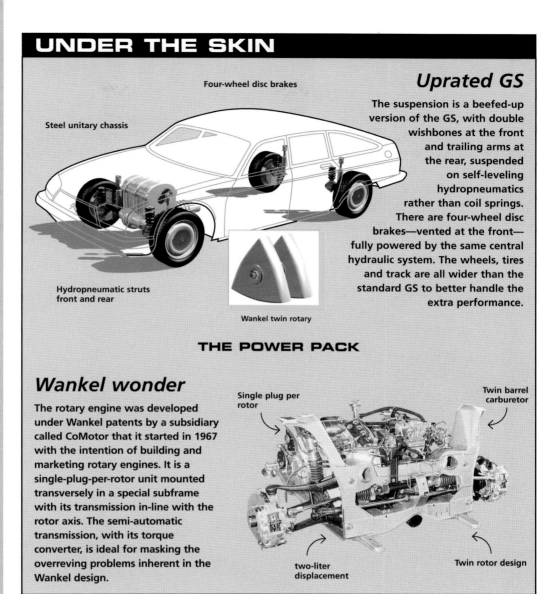

Four-wheel disc brakes

Steel unitary chassis

Hydropneumatic struts front and rear

Wankel twin rotary

Uprated GS

The suspension is a beefed-up version of the GS, with double wishbones at the front and trailing arms at the rear, suspended on self-leveling hydropneumatics rather than coil springs. There are four-wheel disc brakes—vented at the front—fully powered by the same central hydraulic system. The wheels, tires and track are all wider than the standard GS to better handle the extra performance.

THE POWER PACK

Wankel wonder

The rotary engine was developed under Wankel patents by a subsidiary called CoMotor that it started in 1967 with the intention of building and marketing rotary engines. It is a single-plug-per-rotor unit mounted transversely in a special subframe with its transmission in-line with the rotor axis. The semi-automatic transmission, with its torque converter, is ideal for masking the overreving problems inherent in the Wankel design.

Single plug per rotor

Twin barrel carburetor

two-liter displacement

Twin rotor design

Forgotten GS

Although the regular GS sold in large numbers, the Birotor was almost an unknown. Sealing problems with the rotary engine, difficulties with spares and incurable rust problems made them very difficult to own, but its performance is hard to find fault with.

Only 847 Birotors were built in the three-year production run.

Citroën GS BIROTOR

The GS Birotor was not only way ahead of its time, but perhaps too complex to succeed. When the gas crisis struck in 1973, sales of the Birotor fell sharply and Citroën tried to buy many back to avoid the extensive servicing they required.

Rotary engine
A super-smooth water-cooled rotary engine replaced Citroën's air-cooled flat four, the engine found in the conventional GS.

Special color scheme
The brown roof and beige body was a special Birotor color scheme, which was later adopted on the Pallas versions of the GS.

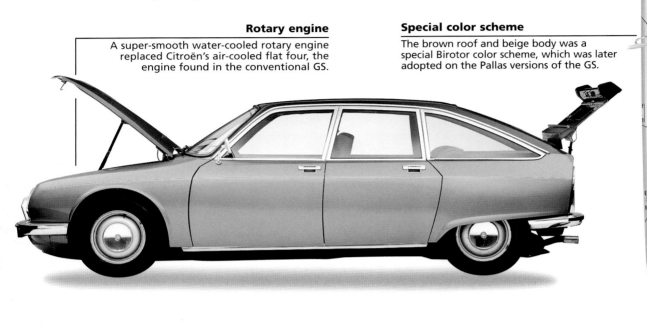

Flared arches
At a glance, the flared arches are the only way you can distinguish a Birotor from a conventional GS. They are needed to accom-modate the wider track.

Four-wheel disc brakes

Like the standard GS the Birotor has disc brakes, but the fronts are not in-board; they are mounted in the conventional position and are larger, to make stopping the car much easier.

High-backed seats

Another Birotor feature are the high-backed seats with integral head restraints.

Semi-automatic transmission

The semi-automatic transmission can be operated like a manual, but there is no clutch pedal. A touch-sensitive switch in the gear knob operates the clutch.

Specifications
1975 Citroën GS Birotor

ENGINE
Type: Wankel twin rotary
Construction: Alloy housings; nickel-silicon coated inside
Valve gear: N/A
Bore and stroke: N/A
Displacement: 1,990 cc
Compression ratio: N/A
Induction system: Solex twin-barrel carburetor
Maximum power: 107 bhp at 6,500 rpm
Maximum torque: 101 lb-ft at 3,000 rpm
Top speed: 109 mph
0-60 mph: 10.2 sec.

TRANSMISSION
Three-speed semi-automatic

BODY/CHASSIS
Unitary monocoque construction with steel four-door sedan body

SPECIAL FEATURES

The hydropneumatic suspension can be raised or lowered by a console lever.

To free up much needed luggage space in the trunk, the spare wheel is carried under the hood.

RUNNING GEAR
Steering: Rack-and-pinion
Front suspension: Double wishbones with interconnected hydropneumatic struts and anti-roll bar
Rear suspension: Trailing arms with interconnected hydropneumatic struts
Brakes: Discs, 10.6-in. dia. (front), vented discs, 6.9-in. dia. (rear)
Wheels: Steel, five-bolt fixing, 5.5-in. rim
Tires: Radial, 165 HR14

DIMENSIONS
Length: 150.2 in.   **Width:** 64.6 in.
Height: 53.9 in.   **Wheelbase:** 100.0 in.
Track: 56.3 in. (front), 53.2 in. (rear)
Weight: 2,514 lbs.

Cosworth VEGA

A limited production of Vegas received an engine transplant and turned it into a performance machine. It looks good, handles well and has an advanced twin-cam engine designed by British Formula One racing experts Cosworth.

"...exotic twin-cam engine."

"For its time the standard Vega was an advanced car, offering more power than its rivals, and the Cosworth version was even better. Unfortunately, because the U.S. was new at building emission-controlled performance cars, the exotic 2.0-liter, twin-cam engine lacks sufficient torque. The four-speed Muncie transmission offers precise shifts and the steering is responsive. The handling is exceptional and the Cosworth Vega can corner with the best of its rivals."

The interior is very European in character—stark but very functional.

Milestones

1970 Chevrolet® introduces the Vega

as a 1971 model in sedan and coupe forms. Chevy's® import fighter was available with a 2.3 liter engine with up to 110 bhp, but the engine is criticized for its roughness

Although Cosworth was known for its race engines, the Vega was never raced seriously.

1973 Further improvements make

the Vega quicker, but the appearance of the Cosworth, with a twin-cam engine, sees the fastest Vega yet. Chevrolet plans to build 5,000 for the 1975 model year.

Cosworth later helped Ford with rally cars like the Sierra and Escort Cosworth.

1976 Sales never reach projected figures and

having sold just 1,447 units in the 1976 model year, the Cosworth Vega is discontinued.

UNDER THE SKIN

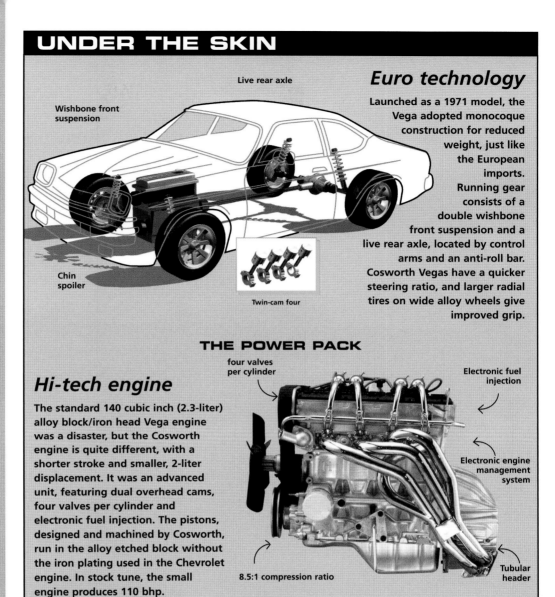

Live rear axle

Wishbone front suspension

Chin spoiler

Twin-cam four

Euro technology

Launched as a 1971 model, the Vega adopted monocoque construction for reduced weight, just like the European imports. Running gear consists of a double wishbone front suspension and a live rear axle, located by control arms and an anti-roll bar. Cosworth Vegas have a quicker steering ratio, and larger radial tires on wide alloy wheels give improved grip.

THE POWER PACK

four valves per cylinder

Electronic fuel injection

Electronic engine management system

8.5:1 compression ratio

Tubular header

Hi-tech engine

The standard 140 cubic inch (2.3-liter) alloy block/iron head Vega engine was a disaster, but the Cosworth engine is quite different, with a shorter stroke and smaller, 2-liter displacement. It was an advanced unit, featuring dual overhead cams, four valves per cylinder and electronic fuel injection. The pistons, designed and machined by Cosworth, run in the alloy etched block without the iron plating used in the Chevrolet engine. In stock tune, the small engine produces 110 bhp.

A hotter Vega

With just 3,508 built over a two-year production run, the Cosworth Vega is a real collector's item. It is also a historically important car, because it was built as an economical performance car when gasoline prices were driven up by the fuel crisis of the time.

The Cosworth is by far the most desirable Vega.

Cosworth VEGA

Using electronic fuel injection and four valves per cylinder in a 2-liter engine might have been normal in Europe during the 1970s, but not in the U.S. It's too bad this high-tech hot rod wasn't more successful.

Wide radials
Due to its better performance, the Cosworth deserves bigger tires so it uses with fatter BR70-13 radials as standard equipment.

High-tech horsepower
Small displacement, overhead cams and electronic fuel injection are common on U.S. cars today. But these features made the Cosworth an exotic high-tech hot rod with 110 bhp from its very small 122 cubic inch engine in 1975.

Twin-cam engine
Chevrolet followed the exotic import route and fitted the Vega with a Cosworth-designed twin-cam cylinder head, the first in a U.S. car for many years. When the engine first appeared the power output was an excellent 130 bhp and 115 lb-ft of torque, but in production the figures were much lower.

Four-speed transmission
In attempt to attract buyers of would-be imported small cars, the Cosworth Vega came with a Muncie four-speed transmission.

European styling
Vegas bore styling cues from the larger Camaro®, which was unmistakably European, although this was later marred by big bumpers.

Low rear axle ratio
All 1975 Cosworth Vegas used 3.73:1 rear axle ratios, while in 1976 they used 4.10:1s. The Cosworth's rear suspension is upgraded to handle the engine's power.

Alloy wheels
The standard Vega wheels have been replaced by wider 6-inch alloy wheels.

Specifications
1975 Chevrolet Cosworth Vega

ENGINE
Type: In-line four-cylinder twin-cam
Construction: Light alloy block and head
Valve gear: Four valves per cylinder operated by twin belt-driven overhead camshafts
Bore and stroke: 3.50 in. x 3.14 in.
Displacement: 122 c.i.
Compression ratio: 8.5:1
Induction system: Bendix electronic injection
Maximum power: 110 bhp at 5,600 rpm
Maximum torque: 107 lb-ft at 4,800 rpm
Top speed: 112 mph
0-60 mph: 12.3 sec

TRANSMISSION
Four-speed Muncie

BODY/CHASSIS
Unitary monocoque construction with two-door coupe body

SPECIAL FEATURES

Each Cosworth Vega has a dash-mounted plaque making it exclusive.

The twin-cam alloy engine is highly exotic for a 1970s American compact.

RUNNING GEAR
Steering: Recirculating ball, 16:1 ratio
Front suspension: Double wishbones with coil springs, telescopic shocks and anti-roll bar
Rear suspension: Live axle with upper and lower control arms, coil springs, telescopic shocks and anti-roll bar
Brakes: Discs, 9.9-in. dia. (front), drums, 9-in. dia. (rear)
Wheels: Alloy, 6 in. x 13 in.
Tires: Radial BR70-13 in. x 6 in.

DIMENSIONS
Length: 170.2 in.   **Width:** 65.4 in.
Height: 47.9 in.   **Wheelbase:** 97 in.
Track: 55.2 in. (front), 54.1 in. (rear)
Weight: 2,639 lbs.

Datsun 240Z

In one fell swoop Datsun slayed the American sports car market with the 240Z. It had everything: beautiful looks, a punchy six-cylinder engine, great handling, superb build quality and a bargain price.

"...the essence of sportiness."

"Compared to rival machinery from the early 1970s, the 240Z is quick. The six-cylinder engine pulls strongly through the well-chosen gear ratios and with the long-legged, five-speed transmission cruising is pleasant. Gas mileage is also surprisingly good. Fully-independent suspension results in excellent road manners and minimal understeer, with power oversteer readily available. The brakes are sharp and fade-free and the steering responsive."

Deeply-set gauges and a wood-rimmed wheel were fashionable for 1970s sports cars.

Milestones

1969 The 240Z makes its public debut at the Tokyo Motor Show.

1970 Automatic transmission is offered for the first time.

For 1975, the 240 was replaced by the larger-engined 260Z.

1971 Datsun scores a 1-2 in the East African Safari Rally, and the long-nose 240ZG is homologated. Standard cars receive altered differentials, and for the 1972 model year the engine is fitted with revised carburetors.

Despite a bigger engine, the 280ZX produces only 135 bhp.

1973 A 240Z again wins the East African Safari Rally. Road cars receive smog equipment and Federal bumpers.

1974 The 240Z is replaced by the new 260Z.

UNDER THE SKIN

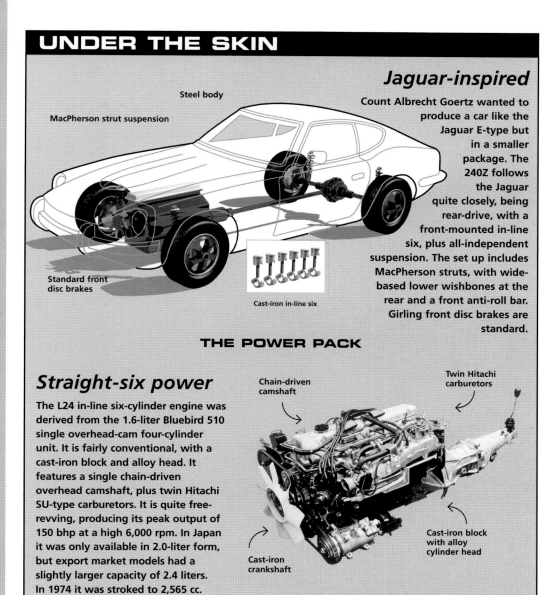

Steel body

MacPherson strut suspension

Standard front disc brakes

Cast-iron in-line six

Jaguar-inspired

Count Albrecht Goertz wanted to produce a car like the Jaguar E-type but in a smaller package. The 240Z follows the Jaguar quite closely, being rear-drive, with a front-mounted in-line six, plus all-independent suspension. The set up includes MacPherson struts, with wide-based lower wishbones at the rear and a front anti-roll bar. Girling front disc brakes are standard.

THE POWER PACK

Straight-six power

The L24 in-line six-cylinder engine was derived from the 1.6-liter Bluebird 510 single overhead-cam four-cylinder unit. It is fairly conventional, with a cast-iron block and alloy head. It features a single chain-driven overhead camshaft, plus twin Hitachi SU-type carburetors. It is quite free-revving, producing its peak output of 150 bhp at a high 6,000 rpm. In Japan it was only available in 2.0-liter form, but export market models had a slightly larger capacity of 2.4 liters. In 1974 it was stroked to 2,565 cc.

Chain-driven camshaft

Twin Hitachi carburetors

Cast-iron block with alloy cylinder head

Cast-iron crankshaft

Pure original

The original 240Z is undoubtedly the most sought after today. Later 260s and 280s are more luxurious, but are also heavier and less exciting to drive. Extremely desirable, but rare, are the lightweight Z432 (Japan only) and 240ZG specials.

Early Zs are characterized by their pure styling and better performance.

Datsun 240Z

Unashamedly created for and targeted at the U.S. market, the 240Z marked the beginning of the modern era of Japanese sports cars. It did almost everything right, and sales went straight through the roof.

High standard of finish

In addition to an attractive price, the Datsun Z's high level of build quality was very impressive. By comparison, European sports cars were not very well put together and could be unreliable in service. The Datsun was a more sensible proposition for everyday use.

Six-cylinder engine

Datsun's punchy in-line six gave impressive performance for a sports car, especially one which sold at such a low price. Unlike some of its rivals, the 240Z's engine was also incredibly strong and reliable.

Hatchback rear

In most sports cars practicality is overlooked, but the 240Z features an opening decklid, complete with spoiler, plus a useful storage area behind the seats. However, space is impeded by the intrusion of the suspension struts and the spare tire.

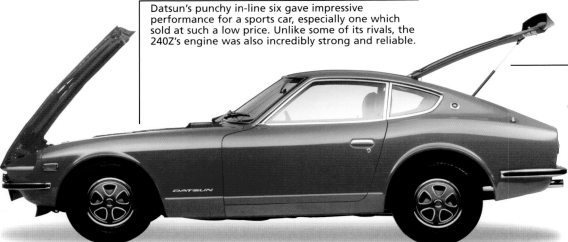

All-independent suspension

While rivals still used live rear axles and leaf springs, the 240Z was updated with an all-independent suspension front and rear giving the Z outstanding cornering ability.

Specifications
1971 Datsun 240Z

ENGINE
Type: In-line six-cylinder
Construction: Cast-iron block and alloy head
Valve gear: Two valves per cylinder operated by a chain-driven single overhead camshaft
Bore and stroke: 3.27 in. x 2.9 in.
Displacement: 2,393 cc
Compression ratio: 9.0:1
Induction system: Two Hitachi HJG 46W carburetors
Maximum power: 150 bhp at 6,000 rpm
Maximum torque: 148 lb-ft at 4,400 rpm
Top speed: 125 mph
0-60 mph: 8.7 sec

TRANSMISSION
Four- or five-speed manual or three-speed automatic

BODY/CHASSIS
Steel monocoque with two-door coupe body

SPECIAL FEATURES

The straight-six engine is reliable, and easily capable of lasting 150,000 miles.

Very few Datsun Zs retain their original wheels and trims. Most are now fitted with aftermarket alloy wheels.

RUNNING GEAR
Steering: Rack-and-pinion
Front suspension: MacPherson struts with coil springs, telescopic shock absorbers and anti-roll bar
Rear suspension: Chapman struts with coil springs, telescopic shock absorbers and anti-roll bar
Brakes: Discs (front), drums (rear)
Wheels: Steel, 14-in. dia.
Tires: 175 x 14 in.

DIMENSIONS
Length: 162.8 in.   **Width:** 64.1 in.
Height: 50.6 in.   **Wheelbase:** 90.7 in.
Track: 53.3 in. (front), 53.0 in. (rear)
Weight: 2,355 lbs.

Handsome styling
The smooth styling of the Z was probably its biggest selling point. Count Albrecht Goertz, who conceived the Z, had a solid track record in recognizing what the American public wanted. Goertz's other achievements include the BMW 507 and the Toyota 2000GT.

De Tomaso **MANGUSTA**

De Tomaso's first volume production sports car was a mid-engined, supercar designed to challenge Ferrari. It paved the way for the famous Pantera, although in some ways its design was more advanced and more like the racing car from which it was developed.

"...a perfect combination."

"A light front end, flexible chassis and less-than-perfect driving position ensure the Mangusta is a challenge. Against that, there's a perfect combination of power and torque, giving all the performance its shape promises; 100 mph comes up in an impressive 18.7 seconds. The steering is light and the straight line stability good, but don't throw this car into bends too hard; mid-engined cars, particularly this one, don't like it."

The fully-equipped dashboard gives the Mangusta a strong race car feel.

Milestones

1965 The Turin Motor Show
sees an open mid-engined racer, the 70P, appear. It has a central backbone much like De Tomaso's Vallelunga road car, but a 5.0-liter Ford engine rather than a 1.5-liter. It is styled by an ex-GM designer, Pete Brock, and built by coachbuilders Fantuzzi.

Conceived in the early 1960s, the Vallelunga was ahead of its time.

1966 The basic structure
of the 70P reappears at the next Turin Show, now covered by the stylish Giugiaro-designed body.

1967 Production of the Mangusta
begins with the one-of-a-kind fiberglass show body replaced by sheet metal and aluminum.

The Pantera was built in greater numbers than the Mangusta.

1971 Production ceases
after 400 Mangustas (including one convertible) have been made. About 300 were exported to the U.S.

UNDER THE SKIN

Racing heritage

Technically more advanced than the later and more famous Pantera, the Mangusta has a folded and welded sheet steel box-section central backbone. Onto the back of that is mounted the Ford V8 acting, as in a racing car, as a stressed chassis member. Right at the back is the ZF five-speed transmission with long shifter linkage. The Mangusta has a classic racing car suspension with double wishbones at the front and rear.

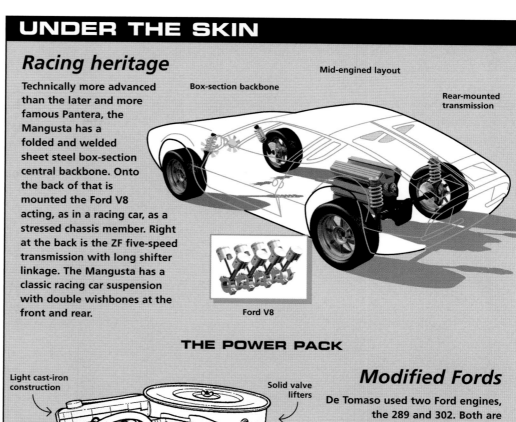

Box-section backbone

Mid-engined layout

Rear-mounted transmission

Ford V8

THE POWER PACK

Light cast-iron construction

Solid valve lifters

Pushrod, short-stroke design

Inlet and exhaust manifold modifications

Modified Fords

De Tomaso used two Ford engines, the 289 and 302. Both are essentially the same and share a surprisingly light cast-iron pushrod, short-stroke V8 design. The HiPo 289 with its stronger connecting rods, higher compression ratio and solid rather than hydraulic valve lifters is the unit used in the fast Mustangs, AC Cobras and the Shelby GT350. De Tomaso decided to have the same modifications as Shelby, using improved intake and exhaust manifolds to make the engine breathe better.

Euro models

Curiously for a car intended for the U.S., the European-spec Mangusta is the one to choose as it has the 289 V8 with 305 bhp compared with 230 bhp from a larger 302. Naturally, the Euro spec cars have quicker acceleration and a higher top speed, too.

European-spec versions are more powerful than those built for the U.S.

De Tomaso MANGUSTA

This is now one of the forgotten supercars, but it would have been a very different story if De Tomaso had given the powerful Mangusta the development its stunning Giugiaro design merited.

Glass engine covers
Giugiaro's solution to engine access was to design two transparent covers which opened up, pivoting from the center. They are an impressive sight when up, but access is awkward nevertheless.

V8 engine
Given De Tomaso's close links with Ford (the later Pantera was a joint Ford/De Tomaso enterprise), it was no surprise that De Tomaso chose to use the 289- and 302-cubic inch Ford V8s. They give plenty of power and are very reliable.

Front radiator
Although De Tomaso mounted the radiator at the front and ran pipes back to the engine to offset the car's weight distribution, the Mangusta was still very rear-heavy.

Rear-biased weight distribution
A combination of the all-iron V8, clutch, final drive and heavy ZF transmission at the back of the car gives the Mangusta a very heavy rear weight bias—as much as 68 percent of the weight at the back.

Giugiaro styling
After he moved on from Bertone, Giorgetto Giugiaro was, for a time, head of styling at Ghia (then owned by De Tomaso). During this time, he designed the body for the Mangusta. It still looks stunning today, more than thirty years after its debut.

Bigger rear tires

With the weight at the back of the car the front and rear tires are different sizes, with 185 HR15s at the front and 225 HR15s at the rear. Time has proven that the car needs even larger, more modern tires for its performance to be safely exploited.

Alloy hood

Strangely, given that the Mangusta's design ensures that it is light at the front, it has an alloy hood which makes the problem worse.

Specifications

1970 De Tomaso Mangusta

ENGINE
Type: V8

Construction: Cast-iron block and heads

Valve gear: Two valves per cylinder operated by single V-mounted camshafts via pushrods and rockers

Bore and stroke: 4.00 in. x 3.00 in.

Displacement: 4,950 cc

Compression ratio: 10.0:1

Induction system: Four-barrel carburetor

Maximum power: 230 bhp at 4,800 rpm

Maximum torque: 310 lb-ft at 2,800 rpm

Top speed: 130 mph

0-60 mph: 6.3 sec.

TRANSMISSION
Rear-mounted ZF five-speed manual

BODY/CHASSIS
Sheet steel backbone chassis with engine and transmission as stressed members and alloy and steel two-door coupe body

SPECIAL FEATURES

By way of a nod to Ferrari, the Mangusta has a gated shifter.

The triple line engine vents on the C-pillars are a neat styling touch.

RUNNING GEAR
Steering: Rack-and-pinion

Front suspension: Double wishbones with coil springs, telescopic shock absorbers and anti-roll bar

Rear suspension: Reversed lower wishbone with single transverse link and twin radius arms per side, coil springs, telescopic shock absorbers and anti-roll bar

Brakes: Girling discs, 11.5-in. dia. (front), 11.0-in. dia. (rear)

Wheels: Magnesium alloy, 7 x 15 in. (front), 7.5 x 15 in. (rear)

Tires: 185 HR15 (front), 225 HR15 (rear)

DIMENSIONS
Length: 168.3 in.   **Width:** 72.0 in.

Height: 43.3 in.   **Wheelbase:** 98.4 in.

Track: 54.9 in. (front), 57.1 in. (rear)

Weight: 2,915 lbs.

Dodge **CORONET R/T**

The Coronet R/T was the first mid-size Dodge muscle machine to feature all the performance and luxury features in a single package. With a powerful 440-cubic inch V8, it didn't disappoint.

"...it just keeps on going."

"Unlike previous mid-size Chrysler muscle cars, the Coronet R/T has a more sporty feel. With a distinctive start-up sound, the giant Magnum V8 roars into life. Smooth and refined, the big V8 has plenty of torque. Dropping the pedal launches the car forward and it just keeps on going, daring you to go faster. Watch out for the corners though; the nose-heavy R/T doesn't handle very well and its 480 lb-ft of torque will surely result in oversteer."

The Coronet R/T has standard bucket seats, a center console and full instrumentation.

Milestones

1967 Dodge introduces its
Coronet R/T (Road and Track). It is a complete high-performance package and is fitted with a standard 440-cubic inch V8, although the Hemi engine is also available. This year sales figures total 10,181.

The Coronet R/T debuted in both hardtop and convertible forms.

1968 The R/T returns
with handsome new sheet-metal on an unchanged wheelbase.

1969 After a major facelift
in 1968, changes this year are minor, with a new grill and rear tail panel. Engine choices remain the same.

The race-ready Super Bee was the Coronet's high performance stablemate.

1970 Greater competition
in a heavily crowded market takes its toll on the Coronet R/T and sales fall to just 2,615. Only 13 of these cars are fitted with the Hemi V8.

UNDER THE SKIN

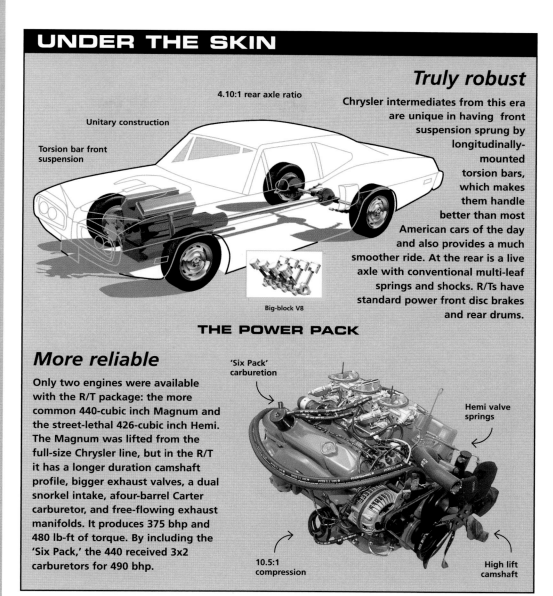

4.10:1 rear axle ratio

Unitary construction

Torsion bar front suspension

Big-block V8

Truly robust

Chrysler intermediates from this era are unique in having front suspension sprung by longitudinally-mounted torsion bars, which makes them handle better than most American cars of the day and also provides a much smoother ride. At the rear is a live axle with conventional multi-leaf springs and shocks. R/Ts have standard power front disc brakes and rear drums.

THE POWER PACK

More reliable

Only two engines were available with the R/T package: the more common 440-cubic inch Magnum and the street-lethal 426-cubic inch Hemi. The Magnum was lifted from the full-size Chrysler line, but in the R/T it has a longer duration camshaft profile, bigger exhaust valves, a dual snorkel intake, a four-barrel Carter carburetor, and free-flowing exhaust manifolds. It produces 375 bhp and 480 lb-ft of torque. By including the 'Six Pack,' the 440 received 3x2 carburetors for 490 bhp.

'Six Pack' carburetion

Hemi valve springs

10.5:1 compression

High lift camshaft

Short life

When the Coronet was launched in 1967, its styling was boxy and upright. A new, smoother body was introduced the following year, which was carried over to 1969 with few changes. 1970 models feature an aggressive twin 'horse collar'-type grill.

1970 was the last year for the convertible Coronet.

Dodge **CORONET R/T**

This peppermint green 1970 Coronet 440 is one of just 2,615 R/Ts built that year. With so much competition in the muscle car arena, sales plummeted in 1970, making this a desirable muscle car today.

Torsion bar suspension

Chrysler was unique in employing torsion bars for the front suspension. Mounted lengthways, they are extremely simple and robust.

Street racer's powerplant

Easier to maintain, more flexible and less temperamental than the Hemi, the 440 delivers plenty of torque and is perfect for drag racing. It is nicknamed the 'Wedge' because of the shape of its combustion chambers.

Bulletproof TorqueFlite

The V8 in this R/T is backed up by the optional 727 TorqueFlite three-speed automatic. This transmission is extremely reliable and has been used in countless Mopars over the years.

Bigger wheels

For 1970 handsome 15-inch Rallye wheels became available on the Coronet R/T. They feature chrome beauty rings and center caps.

Bumble bee stripe

A tail end stripe, usually in black, white or red, was available at no extra cost.

Aggressive front

Twin 'horse collar'-type grills are unique to 1970 Coronets and give the car an aggressive appearance. The hood scoops are an R/T-only feature and are non-functional.

Specifications
1970 Dodge Coronet R/T

ENGINE
Type: V8

Construction: Cast-iron block and heads

Valve gear: Two valves per cylinder operated by pushrods and rockers

Bore and stroke: 4.32 in. x 3.75 in.

Displacement: 440 c.i.

Compression ratio: 10.5:1

Induction system: Single Carter AFB downdraft four-barrel carburetor

Maximum power: 375 bhp at 4,600 rpm

Maximum torque: 480 lb-ft at 3,200 rpm

Top speed: 123 mph

0-60 mph: 6.6 sec

TRANSMISSION
TorqueFlite 727 three-speed automatic

BODY/CHASSIS
Steel monocoque with two-door body

SPECIAL FEATURES

Side-mounted scoops are only fitted to 1970 Coronet R/Ts and are purely decorative features.

Though the engine in this Coronet R/T makes 375 bhp, it is the base engine. Also available was a 390 bhp version with three two-barrel carbs, and a 426 Hemi that made 425 bhp.

RUNNING GEAR
Steering: Recirculating ball

Front suspension: Longitudinally-mounted torsion bars with wishbones and telescopic shocks

Rear suspension: Live rear axle with semi-elliptic leaf springs and telescopic shocks

Brakes: Discs (front), drums (rear)

Wheels: Steel disc, 15-in. dia.

Tires: Goodyear Polyglas GT F60 15

DIMENSIONS
Length: 207.7 in. **Width:** 80.6 in.

Height: 52.5 in. **Wheelbase:** 117 in.

Track: 58.9 in. (front and rear)

Weight: 3,546 lbs.

Dodge CHARGER R/T

For 1971, the Charger got all-new styling on an unchanged wheelbase. The R/T performance option was still available with standard 440 and optional 426 Hemi V8s. This was the last year for big-block R/Ts, but they went out with a bang.

"...straight-line screamer."

"In normal driving situations the R/T 440 is a docile animal, but on a straight, deserted two-laner the car really comes into its own. The pistol grip four-speed enables you to get the most out of the 440-cubic inch V8. Nail the throttle and the two outer carburetors open, pinning you back in the seat. As the speed increases, you can feel your hands fighting for control of the steering wheel to prevent the solid rear axle from cutting loose."

This Charger R/T is loaded to the max and has a pistol-grip, four-speed shift.

Milestones

1966 Radical fastback
styling and a futuristic interior allow the Charger to disguise its Coronet underpinnings. A 383-cubic inch V8 is standard on the performance-oriented R/T model, and the Hemi engine is an option.

The Charger debuted in 1966 based on the mid-size Coronet.

1967 The 375-bhp 440 Magnum
joins the list of Charger engines. Other changes are few this year.

1968 Perfect proportions
have made the second-generation Charger the best-looking of all time. In R/T trim the 440-cubic inch V8 is standard while the 426 Hemi remains an option.

Second-generation Chargers, like this 1969 model, are real classics.

1971 A Charger with curvier
styling arrives. A budget performance Super Bee joins the R/T. This is the last year for high compression big-block V8s.

UNDER THE SKIN

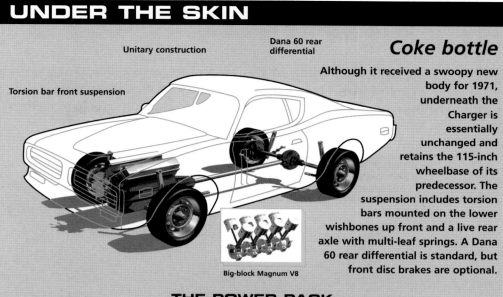

Unitary construction

Dana 60 rear differential

Torsion bar front suspension

Big-block Magnum V8

Coke bottle

Although it received a swoopy new body for 1971, underneath the Charger is essentially unchanged and retains the 115-inch wheelbase of its predecessor. The suspension includes torsion bars mounted on the lower wishbones up front and a live rear axle with multi-leaf springs. A Dana 60 rear differential is standard, but front disc brakes are optional.

THE POWER PACK

Six-barrel Magnum

The tractable Magnum 440 was a racer's dream engine, with its super strong forged-steel crankshaft and connecting rods. With the addition of a stiff cast-iron block, the combination of a 4.32-inch bore and 3.75-inch stroke, decent flowing cylinder heads and a highly effective intake manifold, it is easy to see why many NHRA championship drag races have been won with 440 power. In street car trim high-13-second, ¼-mile times are the norm. With six-barrel induction it is rated at 385 bhp.

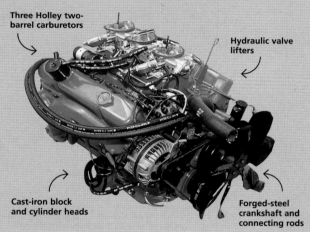

Three Holley two-barrel carburetors

Hydraulic valve lifters

Cast-iron block and cylinder heads

Forged-steel crankshaft and connecting rods

Overlooked

Many collectors prefer the first- and second-generation Chargers, and so even in mint condition 1971 R/Ts do not cost the earth. They still offer the performance and are rare: only 3,118 R/Ts were built in 1971 and only 63 were equipped with the Hemi.

1971 R/Ts are perhaps the best buy of the muscle era Chargers.

Dodge CHARGER R/T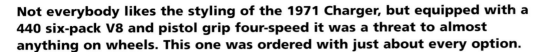

Not everybody likes the styling of the 1971 Charger, but equipped with a 440 six-pack V8 and pistol grip four-speed it was a threat to almost anything on wheels. This one was ordered with just about every option.

Big-block power

Although slightly detuned from previous years due to a lower compression ratio, the R/T's Magnum 440 engine remained just as powerful. The block's understressed cast-iron construction makes it very durable.

HD four-speed transmission

This car has an optional four-speed manual with a Hurst pistol-grip shifter.

Heavy-duty suspension

Like all Chrysler cars of the era, torsion bars are fitted up front. To give the new, bigger Charger a firmer ride and flatter handling, all R/Ts came with heavy-duty suspension components.

Elegant styling

The new exterior for 1971 was an evolutionary design and incorporated styling cues from the distinctively handsome 1968 Charger. With its dual racing body-colored mirrors, hood blackout treatment, louvered tail lights and body side stripes, the high-impact look has a very performance oriented appeal.

Racing wheels

G70 x 14-inch raised white lettered tires on silver steel Rallye wheels that sport chrome trim rings provided functional performance with a racy image.

Sporty interior

Twin bucket seats, a sporty steering wheel and a full complement of gauges give the R/T a high performance look.

Front-end styling

Wider than previously styled Chargers, the 1971-1974 body design incorporates a heavy, one-piece chrome bumper for increased crash protection. This car has the optional 'Ram-Charger' hood with a vacuum-operated scoop.

Specification
1971 Dodge Charger R/T

ENGINE
Type: V8

Construction: Cast-iron block and heads

Valve gear: Two valves per cylinder operated by pushrods and rockers

Bore and stroke: 4.32 in. x 3.75 in.

Displacement: 440 c.i.

Compression ratio: 9.5:1

Induction system: Three Holley two-barrel carburetors

Maximum power: 385 bhp at 4,800 rpm

Maximum torque: 490 lb-ft at 3,200 rpm

Top speed: 125 mph

0-60 mph: 6.0 sec.

TRANSMISSION
Pistol-grip four-speed with Hurst linkage

BODY/CHASSIS
Unitary steel body construction with front K-frame

SPECIAL FEATURES

A special vacuum-operated lift-up scoop feeds extra air into the carburetors.

Options on this R/T include hideaway headlights and even headlight wipers.

RUNNING GEAR
Steering: Recirculating ball

Front suspension: Adjustable torsion bars with upper and lower control arms and anti-roll bar

Rear suspension: Live solid axle with shock absorbers and leaf springs

Brakes: Drums (front and rear)

Wheels: 6 x 14 in.

Tires: G70 x 14

DIMENSIONS
Length: 206.0 in.   **Width:** 79.1 in.

Height: 52.2 in.   **Wheelbase:** 115.0 in.

Track: 59.5 in. (front and rear)

Weight: 3,785 lbs.

Ferrari DAYTONA

Until the arrival of the 550 Maranello, the Daytona was the last front-engined Ferrari supercar. Despite the old-fashioned layout, the Daytona is still one of the fastest supercars of all time.

"...meant to be driven hard."

"Ferrari made no compromises with the Daytona. It was meant to be driven fast and driven hard. At speed, the heavy unassisted steering—which makes parking a huge chore—lightens up. Drive the Daytona the way it was intended—hard—and it repays you. It seems to shrink around you and, despite its weight, it's agile and well behaved. You'll believe it was the fastest car of its time as it accelerates savagely long after other supercars have faded. The Daytona can easily go from 0-100 mph in just under 13 seconds."

The interior is classic Ferrari with a gated shifter and a steering wheel with a central Prancing Horse.

Milestones

1968 Ferrari unveils the 365 GTB/4 at the Paris Motor Show. The press calls it 'Daytona' in honor of Ferrari's success at the 1967 24-hour race. The name is unofficial, however, and never appears on the bodywork.

Daytona's predecessor was the 275 GTB, which also had a V12 engine.

1969 Production begins of both the coupe and convertible models. Ferrari also produces competition models. They have more power, with 400 bhp at 8,300 rpm and can reach more than 180 mph at tracks like Le Mans.

1971 Retractable headlights replace the original perspex-covered type.

1972 A competition Daytona wins its class at the 24 Hours of Le Mans, an achievement repeated in 1973 and 1974.

Daytonas took class victories at the 24 Hours of Le Mans in 1973 and 1974.

UNDER THE SKIN

Separate chassis

Rear-mounted transmission

Steel and alloy bodywork

Wishbone suspension all around

4.4-liter V12

Last of a kind

The Daytona is very traditional. Not only is it front-engined and rear-wheel driven, but the alloy and steel bodywork covers a multi-tube steel chassis, which is very sturdy and has no pretensions of saving weight. But with the transmission at the rear, weight distribution is perfect. Engine and transmission are connected by a hollow torque tube for the propshaft.

THE POWER PACK

V12 development

Nothing but a V12 would do for the Daytona and this is one of the best. Developed from the existing 275 GTB all-alloy, wet-liner engine, it has four instead of two camshafts. Driven by gears rather than chains it still has just two valves per cylinder. Six twin-choke carburetors were used to pour fuel directly and efficiently into each intake port. The car's official name, the 365 GTB/4, refers to capacity of each cylinder—365 cc.

Two valves per cylinder

Six twin-choke carburetors

Four chain-driven camshafts

Wet cylinder liners

Easy conversion

The rarest of the Daytonas is the Spyder. A little over 100 were built, although there are many fakes converted from the coupes. For factory and faker alike, the conversion was easy because the car has a strong separate chassis, so it does not rely on the roof for its strength.

Desirable and rare, the factory Spyder has often been copied.

Ferrari **DAYTONA**

The end of an era...but what a way to go! The combination of Pininfarina's perfectly proportioned body and a 4.4 liter Ferrari V12 makes it an instant classic, not to mention one of the world's fastest cars.

Quad-cam V12

The 365 GTB/4 model name helps explain the engine. The 365 stands for the size of each cylinder (which multiplied by the number of cylinders gives its 4.4 liter displacement).The 4 stands for the number of camshafts.

Rear-mounted transmission

The five-speed transmission shares the same alloy housing as the final drive. Because this is a two-seater with a short cabin, the length of gear linkage from the driver to the transmission is not excessive.

Engine air vents

After cool air has passed through the tiny front opening and through the V12's big radiator, it leaves the car via the two unobtrusive sunken vents in the hood.

Square-tube chassis

In the late-1960s, Ferrari was a very traditional manufacturer, so the Daytona's chassis is made up of many small-diameter square section tubes welded together. It is strong but heavy.

Front-to-rear torque tube

The engine and rear-mounted transmission are rigidly connected by a torque tube that houses the driveshaft.

Equal weight distribution

By setting the V12 back in the chassis and moving the transmission to the rear, Ferrari achieved a near-perfect 52/48 weight distribution without the complexity of a mid-engined car.

Wishbone suspension

Double wishbone suspension is fitted all around. To help the packaging, the rear spring/shock units are mounted above the top wishbone.

Alloy and steel body

The doors, hood and trunk lid are made of weight-saving alloy. The rest of the bodywork is steel.

Specifications

1970 Ferrari 365 GTB/4 Daytona

ENGINE

Type: V12

Construction: Alloy block and heads with wet liners

Valve gear: Two valves per cylinder operated by four gear-driven overhead camshafts

Bore and stroke: 3.19 in. x 2.8 in.

Displacement: 4,390 cc

Compression ratio: 9.3:1

Induction system: Six Weber 40DCN 20 downdraft carburetors

Maximum power: 352 bhp at 7,500 rpm

Maximum torque: 330 lb-ft at 5,500 rpm

Top speed: 174 mph

0-60 mph: 5.6 sec.

TRANSMISSION

Rear-mounted, five-speed manual

BODY/CHASSIS

Steel square tube separate chassis with alloy and steel two-door coupe or convertible body

SPECIAL FEATURES

Wrap-around front direction indicators were often mimicked after the Daytona's launch.

Four round tail lights and four exhausts tell you you've just been overtaken by a Daytona.

RUNNING GEAR

Steering: Recirculating ball

Front suspension: Double wishbones with coil springs, telescopic shocks and anti-roll bar

Rear suspension: Double wishbones with coil springs, telescopic shocks and anti-roll bar

Brakes: Vented discs, 11.3 in. dia. (front), 11.6 in. dia. (rear)

Wheels: Alloy, 7.5 in. x 15 in.

Tires: 215/7015

DIMENSIONS

Length: 174.2 in.   **Width:** 69.3 in.

Wheelbase: 94.5 in.   **Height:** 49 in.

Track: 56.7 in. (front), 56.1 in. (rear)

Weight: 3,530 lbs.

Ferrari DINO

One of Ferrari's best and most popular cars wasn't even officially called a Ferrari. Instead Ferrari's first mid-engined road car was named after Enzo's ill-fated son, Dino.

"...astounding cornering limits."

"The Dino 246 GT's quad-cam V6 is wonderful, flexible enough to putter around at low speeds but really sings from 3,500 rpm all the way to 7,800 rpm and will happily go way past the red line. It's matched to perfect gear ratios and a transmission that's better the faster you shift it. The mid-engined chassis and wishbones all around mean all the power is easily exploited. In its day, the Dino's cornering limits were astounding and they're still impressive today."

Although never badged as a Ferrari, the Dino interior has unmistakable cues like the gated shifter and large wood-rimmed, alloy-spoked steering wheel.

Milestones

1965 Coachbuilders Pininfarina build the Dino 206 GT Speciale for the Paris Motor Show with four round headlights in an extended nose.

1966 Pininfarina's next show car, the Dino, points the way to the production car, but its V6 engine is mounted longitudinally not transversely.

The Dino 206 Competizione: the last of Pininfarina's show cars.

1967 Definitive Dino 206 GT appears with no Ferrari badges on the Pininfarina stand at the Turin Motor Show.

1969 Engine is changed from an alloy to an iron block, and enlarged to 2.4-liters, while the body is made of steel rather than alloy. The 246 GT has a longer wheelbase than the 206.

1972 246 GT is joined by the GTS. The S stands for Spider or convertible, but it is really a Targa top with a removable roof panel.

Fiat, who built the engine, used it in their own Fiat Dino from 1966 to '75.

UNDER THE SKIN

Ferrari first

The Dino was advanced both in being mid-engined with its transverse V6 and in seeing Ferrari finally switching to rack-and-pinion steering. Otherwise, it is a traditional Ferrari with wishbone suspension and a tubular steel chassis onto which the body (made first in alloy and then in steel) is mounted. A central tunnel helped increase overall stiffness.

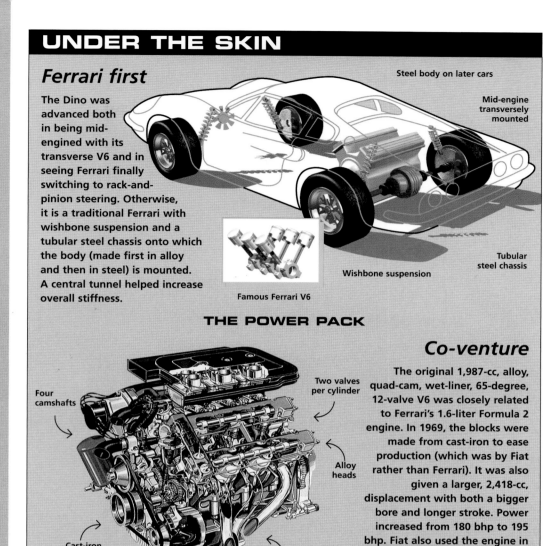

Steel body on later cars

Mid-engine transversely mounted

Tubular steel chassis

Wishbone suspension

Famous Ferrari V6

THE POWER PACK

Four camshafts

Two valves per cylinder

Alloy heads

Cast-iron block

Finned alloy sump

Co-venture

The original 1,987-cc, alloy, quad-cam, wet-liner, 65-degree, 12-valve V6 was closely related to Ferrari's 1.6-liter Formula 2 engine. In 1969, the blocks were made from cast-iron to ease production (which was by Fiat rather than Ferrari). It was also given a larger, 2,418-cc, displacement with both a bigger bore and longer stroke. Power increased from 180 bhp to 195 bhp. Fiat also used the engine in both its original 2.0 and 2.4-liter forms in its front-engined Dino.

Dino 206

To the purist, the first Dino is the best. It has an alloy body rather than the steel body of the later 246. Its engine is made of alloy and closer to a racing motor than the later iron-block 2.4-liter V6. It is less powerful, but makes up for it by being lighter.

The classy yet strong 206 GT has a 2-liter engine and a light alloy body.

Ferrari DINO

The Dino did more than just combine a small race-bred quad-cam V6 in a beautiful lightweight alloy body—it was mid-engined and set new standards of handling for street-legal Ferrari sports cars.

V6 quad-cam engine
By the time this 246 GT was produced, the engine block was made of iron. Ferrari shared the V6 engine with Fiat who used it in its own front-engined Dino.

Front-mounted radiator
Although there appears to be no room for it, the Dino's radiator is mounted in the nose, where it had to be angled to fit under the shallow nose.

Side air vents
Although the radiator is in the front, side air vents are still needed to feed air to the engine and oil cooler.

Alloy wheels
Ferrari used wire wheels from 1947 right up until the 1960s when alloys became standard.

Flying buttress design
Styling the back of a mid-engine car is difficult because it is necessary to leave access space. One solution is to have 'flying buttresses' where the line of the cabin is continued towards the rear of the car, but there's space between the two sides.

Vented disc brakes

Dinos have very effective vented disc brakes and they are the same size on all four wheels because the Dino's weight distribution is almost perfect.

Wishbone suspension

Like most high-performance cars, the Dino uses double wishbones with an anti-roll bar in the front and rear.

Steel bodywork

In 1969, Ferrari switched from alloy bodies to steel. That made the cars noticeably heavier than the original 206 GT but engine size and power were increased to compensate.

Specifications

1971 Ferrari Dino 246 GT

ENGINE

Type: V6
Construction: Cast-iron block and alloy cylinder heads
Valve gear: Two valves per cylinder operated by twin chain-driven overhead cams per bank of cylinders
Bore and stroke: 3.67 in. x 2.36 in.
Displacement: 2,418 cc
Compression ratio: 9.0:1
Induction system: Three Weber 40DCN carburetors
Maximum power: 195 bhp at 5,000 rpm
Maximum torque: 166 lb-ft at 5,500 rpm
Top speed: 148 mph
0-60 mph: 7.3 sec.

TRANSMISSION

Five-speed manual

BODY/CHASSIS

Tubular steel chassis with steel two-door coupe body

SPECIAL FEATURES

Dino's simple door handles help leave the car's beautiful lines uncluttered.

Plastic headlight covers were popular with European manufacturers but became illegal in the U.S. and fell out of fashion.

RUNNING GEAR

Steering: Rack-and-pinion
Front suspension: Double wishbones, coil springs, telescopic shocks and anti-roll bar
Rear suspension: Double wishbones, coil springs, telescopic shocks and anti-roll bar
Brakes: Four-wheel vented discs, 10.6 in. dia.
Wheels: Cast alloy 6.5 in. x 14 in.
Tires: 205/70 VR14

DIMENSIONS

Length: 166.5 in.   **Width:** 67 in.
Height: 45 in.   **Wheelbase:** 92 in.
Track: 55.5 in. (front), 56 in. (rear)
Weight: 2,611 lbs.

ITALY 1966-1972

Fiat **DINO**

In the mid-1960s Ferrari needed a large company to manufacture its Formula 2 V6 engine, while Fiat wanted to produce an up-market sports car with real credibility. The result of the joint partnership is the classic Fiat Dino. Unfortunately the jointly built sports car was never available in the U.S.

"...a high performance hybrid."

"The Dino is a real high performance hybrid. Its V6 engine spins freely to 8,000 rpm with a spine-tingling howl just like a Ferrari. The bigger 2.4-liter engine doesn't sing quite so sweetly as the earlier unit, but it delivers a lot more torque. The iron block also means the engine is quieter than the original 2.0-liter, although the ZF transmission is not one of the slickest units. The full independent suspension ensures balanced handling and a smooth ride."

An attractive feature is the full-length woodgrain dashboard trim.

Milestones

1964 Enzo Ferrari begins talks with Fiat about collaborating on a new sports car powered by a detuned version of Ferrari's 1.5-liter Dino V6 (named after his late son).

1966 Fiat's Dino Spider, with a 160-bhp, 2.0-liter V6 and Pininfarina bodywork, is unveiled at the Turin Motor Show.

The Spider shares its engine with the Ferrari Dino 206/246 series.

1967 The Bertone-styled Fiat Dino Coupe is announced. It has a longer wheelbase and four seats, but is otherwise identical to the Spider.

The Ferrari 246 Dino uses the same engine as the Fiat Spider.

1969 Production of the 2.4-liter Spider and Coupe begins. They are fitted with a more torquey iron-block V6, ZF five-speed transmission, and independent rear suspension. The last Spiders are built in 1972.

UNDER THE SKIN

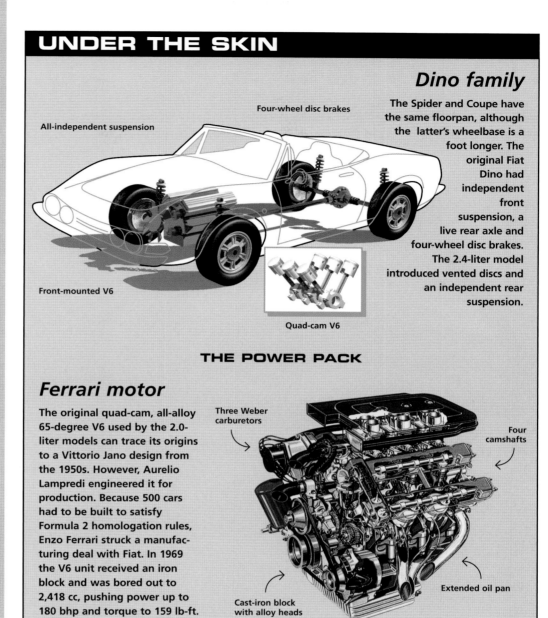

All-independent suspension

Four-wheel disc brakes

Front-mounted V6

Quad-cam V6

Dino family

The Spider and Coupe have the same floorpan, although the latter's wheelbase is a foot longer. The original Fiat Dino had independent front suspension, a live rear axle and four-wheel disc brakes. The 2.4-liter model introduced vented discs and an independent rear suspension.

THE POWER PACK

Ferrari motor

The original quad-cam, all-alloy 65-degree V6 used by the 2.0-liter models can trace its origins to a Vittorio Jano design from the 1950s. However, Aurelio Lampredi engineered it for production. Because 500 cars had to be built to satisfy Formula 2 homologation rules, Enzo Ferrari struck a manufacturing deal with Fiat. In 1969 the V6 unit received an iron block and was bored out to 2,418 cc, pushing power up to 180 bhp and torque to 159 lb-ft.

Three Weber carburetors

Four camshafts

Cast-iron block with alloy heads

Extended oil pan

Bertone Coupe

The Bertone-built Dino Coupe made its debut five months after the Spider. It has more elegant styling and a neater interior, yet is just as quick. Many used Coupes gave up their engines to Ferrari Dinos and are thus rare and desirable today.

Coupes have coachwork by Bertone and a longer wheelbase.

Fiat DINO ▮▮▮

Powered by a Ferrari engine, the Fiat Dino resulted from the requirement to build 500 road cars in order to race in Formula 2. It is one of Fiat's most desirable cars.

Basic cabin
Despite the Spider's up-market pretensions, the interior of the car is surprisingly stark and not unlike that of the much cheaper 124 Spider—another Pininfarina design.

Five-speed transmission
The original transmission in the 2.0-liter models was too fragile for the bigger 2.4-liter engine, and so the later cars use a ZF transmission with closer ratios.

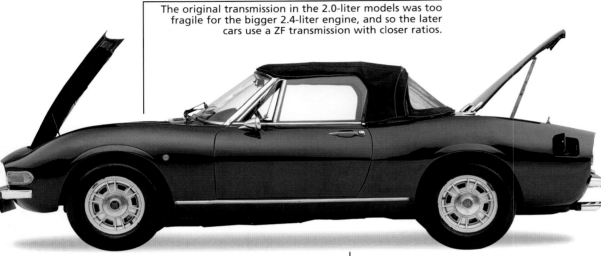

Sophisticated rear suspension
Although the 2.0-liter had a live rear axle, Fiat adopted an independent semi-trailing arm and strut system for the 2.4-liter version, which is also used by the big Fiat 130 sedan. This results in much improved ride and handling.

Pininfarina bodywork
The shapely body of the two-seat Spider was styled and built by Pininfarina of Turin. Fiat supplied the unitary floorpan, which is based on a shortened version of the 2300S Coupe chassis.

Alloy wheels
The Dino's Cromadora alloy wheels are of the knock-off type on the 2.0-liter version, but are conventionally bolted on the later 2.4. The Ferrari Dino 246 GT uses the same design.

Parts bin details
The attractive rear circular lights of the Dino Spider are the same as those fitted to the humble Fiat 850 Coupe.

Specifications

1970 Fiat Dino 2400

ENGINE

Type: V6

Construction: Cast-iron block and alloy heads

Valve gear: Two valves per cylinder operated by two overhead camshafts per cylinder bank

Bore and stroke: 3.64 in. x 2.36 in.

Displacement: 2,418 cc

Compression ratio: 9.0:1

Induction system: Three Weber carburetors

Maximum power: 180 bhp at 6,600 rpm

Maximum torque: 159 lb-ft at 4,600 rpm

Top speed: 130 mph

0-60 mph: 7.7 sec.

TRANSMISSION

ZF five-speed manual

BODY/CHASSIS

Unitary steel chassis with Pininfarina bodywork

SPECIAL FEATURES

Later cars have a five-speed ZF transmission.

Dinos feature cowled headlights with large wraparound turn signal lamps.

RUNNING GEAR

Steering: ZF worm and roller

Front suspension: Wishbones with coil springs and anti-roll bar

Rear suspension: Coil springs with struts, semi-trailing arms and anti-roll bar

Brakes: Girling discs (front and rear)

Wheels: Cromadora alloys, 14-in. dia

Tires: 205/70 14

DIMENSIONS

Length: 161.8 in.   **Width:** 67.6 in.

Height: 50.0 in.   **Wheelbase:** 89.8 in.

Track: 53.9 in. (front), 53.6 in. (rear)

Weight: 2,579 lbs.

Fiat **124 SPIDER**

The Pininfarina-styled Fiat 124 Spider of 1966 became one of the longest-lived and best-selling sports cars of any era. It was blessed with a sophisticated specification for its day.

"...remarkable poise."

"Cynics call the 124 Spider the Italian MGB, but that is doing a disservice to a car that is much more sophisticated than its British rival. The twin-cam engine is peppy and enjoys high revs and hard work. The earlier, smaller engines are the sweetest, but the later, larger units have more torque. The worm-and-peg steering is light, direct and quite high-geared. There is strong initial under-steer, but through faster curves the Spider's poise is remarkable."

All Spiders have smart, comfortable interiors that share their style with other Italian cars.

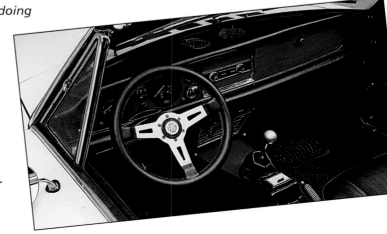

Milestones

1966 The Spider is announced
in 1,438-cc 'AS' form with Pininfarina bodywork, a twin-cam engine and disc brakes.

1969 The BS1 Spider is introduced.
It has a bigger 1,608-cc engine (the 1,438-cc unit is still optional) and a mildly restyled interior.

The Abarth-tuned 124 Spider was a successful rally car.

1972 A CS1 Spider with a
federalized 1,756-cc engine arrives. Big impact bumpers appear on U.S.-market cars for the first time.

The 124 was also available in coupe form.

1979 A new 2.0-liter engine
replaces the smaller 1,608 cc engine.

1982 Pininfarina takes over Fiat production.
The former 124 drop-top becomes known as the Pininfarina Spider Europa. Production ends in 1985.

UNDER THE SKIN

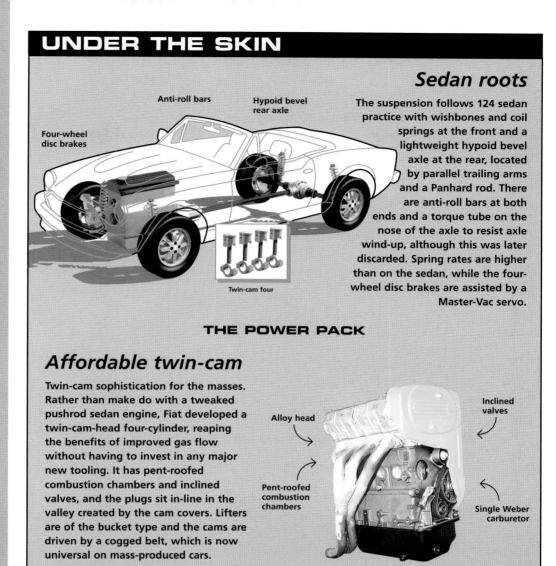

Anti-roll bars

Hypoid bevel rear axle

Four-wheel disc brakes

Twin-cam four

Sedan roots

The suspension follows 124 sedan practice with wishbones and coil springs at the front and a lightweight hypoid bevel axle at the rear, located by parallel trailing arms and a Panhard rod. There are anti-roll bars at both ends and a torque tube on the nose of the axle to resist axle wind-up, although this was later discarded. Spring rates are higher than on the sedan, while the four-wheel disc brakes are assisted by a Master-Vac servo.

THE POWER PACK

Affordable twin-cam

Twin-cam sophistication for the masses. Rather than make do with a tweaked pushrod sedan engine, Fiat developed a twin-cam-head four-cylinder, reaping the benefits of improved gas flow without having to invest in any major new tooling. It has pent-roofed combustion chambers and inclined valves, and the plugs sit in-line in the valley created by the cam covers. Lifters are of the bucket type and the cams are driven by a cogged belt, which is now universal on mass-produced cars.

Alloy head

Inclined valves

Pent-roofed combustion chambers

Single Weber carburetor

Purest form

The Pininfarina styling of the 124 Spider is best displayed on the early chrome-bumpered cars. The later versions with impact-absorbing bumpers clutter the car's lines. Although these cars have smaller engines and less power than later Spiders, they're still fun to drive.

Although overshadowed by Alfa's Spider, the 124 makes a great buy.

Fiat 124 SPIDER

Built for 19 years, mainly for the U.S. market, the 124 Spider brought new levels of sophistication to the affordable sports car class and became an instant classic upon its demise in 1985.

Five-speed transmission

Five-speed transmissions were normally found only in highly exotic cars from the likes of Maserati and Ferrari, but Fiat brought the delights of slick, five-speed driving to a new generation of sports car drivers.

Twin-cam engine

Designed by Aurelio Lampredi, the 124's classic twin-cam engine is smooth and spirited and became the mainstay of Fiat's and Lancia's mid-range sedans in the 1970s and 1980s, growing from 1.4 to 2.0 liters.

Disc brakes

Like the humble 124 sedan—but unlike many other sports cars—the 124 has four-wheel disc brakes with a servo-assisted booster.

Versatile top

When many other sports car drivers were struggling with build-it-yourself tops that resembled tents, the Fiat's could be raised with one hand from the driver's seat.

Pininfarina bodywork

Fiat commissioned Pininfarina to style and build the Spider's steel body. The cars were built on a very large scale at Pininfarina's Turin factory and were later marketed by Pininfarina, too.

Well-located live rear axle

With its lightweight casing, Panhard rod and coil springing, the live axle is able to handle mid-corner bumps extremely well.

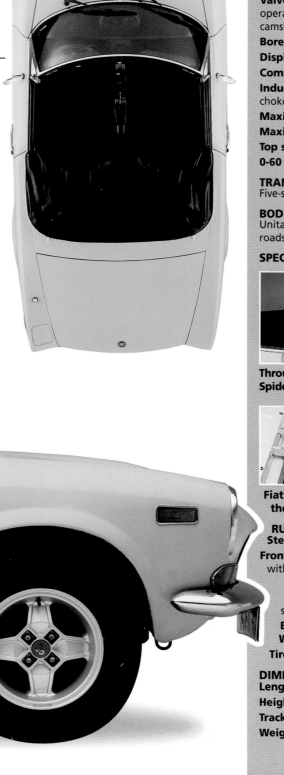

Specifications
1974 Fiat 124 Spider

ENGINE
Type: In-line four-cylinder

Construction: Cast-iron block and alloy cylinder head

Valve gear: Two valves per cylinder operated by twin belt-driven overhead camshafts

Bore and stroke: 3.31 in. x 3.12 in.

Displacement: 1,756 cc

Compression ratio: 8.0:1

Induction system: Single Weber twin-choke carburetor

Maximum power: 93 bhp at 6,200 rpm

Maximum torque: 92 lb-ft at 3,000 rpm

Top speed: 112 mph

0-60 mph: 12.2 sec.

TRANSMISSION
Five-speed manual or three-speed automatic

BODY/CHASSIS
Unitary monocoque construction with steel roadster body

SPECIAL FEATURES

Throughout its production run the Spider retained opening vent windows.

Fiat's lusty twin-cam four provides the power behind the 124 Spider.

RUNNING GEAR
Steering: Worm-and-roller

Front suspension: Double wishbones with coil springs, shocks and anti-roll bar

Rear suspension: Live axle with parallel trailing arms, Panhard rod, coil springs, shocks and anti-roll bar

Brakes: Fiat-Bendix discs, 9.0-in.

Wheels: Alloy, 5 x 13 in.

Tires: 165/70 SR13

DIMENSIONS
Length: 156.3 in.   **Width:** 63.5 in.

Height: 49.3 in.   **Wheelbase:** 89.8 in.

Track: 53.0 in. (front), 52.0 in. (rear)

Weight: 2,540 lbs.

Fiat **130 COUPE**

The Fiat 130 Coupe was one of Pininfarina's classic designs and one of the most influential designs of the 1970s. Few big cars have ever looked so elegant and well balanced.

"...smooth and throaty."

"Although the 130 Coupe is a heavy car with only moderate power, Fiat managed to make it feel lively by giving it useful torque and a responsive automatic transmission. The V6 engine is smooth but with an aggressive exhaust howl. It is more than able to cruise at speeds over 100 mph. For such a large car the handling is extraordinary with very little roll and lots of feel in the steering. In fact, the 130 Coupe could have handled much more power than it was given."

The Fiat 130 Coupe's angular lines are reflected in its interior styling.

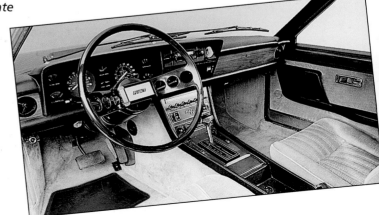

Milestones

1969 The Fiat 130 Sedan debuts at the Geneva show.

The Fiat Dino and 130 Coupes share engines based on Ferrari bottom end designs.

1970 Thanks to new headers and a higher compression ratio, power is increased to 160 bhp.

The Fiat 130 provided the basis for Pininfarina's Coupe body.

1971 130 Coupe is announced at the Geneva Show with a 3.2-liter V6 engine and automatic transmission.

1974 Pininfarina shows four-door and wagon versions of the Coupe but they are never built.

1976 Sedan production ends after 15,000 cars are built.

1977 The Coupe is discontinued after 4,400 cars are made.

UNDER THE SKIN

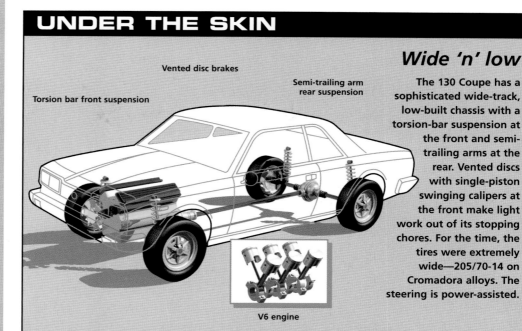

Vented disc brakes

Semi-trailing arm rear suspension

Torsion bar front suspension

V6 engine

Wide 'n' low

The 130 Coupe has a sophisticated wide-track, low-built chassis with a torsion-bar suspension at the front and semi-trailing arms at the rear. Vented discs with single-piston swinging calipers at the front make light work out of its stopping chores. For the time, the tires were extremely wide—205/70-14 on Cromadora alloys. The steering is power-assisted.

THE POWER PACK

Lampredi designed

The 130's V6 engine, with its alloy heads and iron block, was designed by Aurelio Lampredi, the man behind Ferrari's early V12s and the Dino V6 that was fitted to the contemporary Fiat Dino and Ferrari 246 Dino. Although they share some characteristics, the 130 and Dino engines are entirely different. The 130 has single overhead camshafts with toothed beltdrive and the Dino has chain-driven twin overhead camshafts, but the 130's power plant is good for an impressive 165 bhp. In view of the Coupe's 3,500-plus pound curb-weight, however, the result was fairly average performance: 0-60 mph in 11.4 seconds and it topped out at 120 mph.

Hidden classic

Although the 130 sedan's 2.9 engine was admired for its technical finesse, the engine lacks torque and the car proved to be rather gutless. The 3.2-liter version launched in 1971 is much improved, but the 130 sedan never found the success it deserved.

An elegant profile was not enough to put the 130 high on collectors' lists.

Fiat 130 COUPE

Although the Fiat 130 Coupe was futuristic-looking for 1971, its styling pre-empted the angular body shapes associated with 1970s cars. It was also evident that Fiat could actually build high-quality, large cars.

V6 Engine
The 130's strong, free-revving V6 has good torque but that doesn't make the car wildly quick—0-60 mph takes around 11 seconds and it has a top speed of 120 mph.

Automatic transmission
The majority of 130 Coupes have Borg-Warner's Model 12 automatic transmission that tends to make the car a little under-geared and suffer from poor gas mileage, but which suits its smooth personality. A few models use the slick ZF five-speed manual transmission.

Pininfarina badges
The Pininfarina badge means the famous design house didn't just style the body but built it, too. It then sent the completed bodywork to the Rivalta Fiat factory.

Luxurious interior

When it was introduced the 130 Coupe was considered to have one of the most luxurious interiors of any car in the world. It featured thick velour upholstery and real wood trim. Apart from the steering wheel, the dashboard is the same as the one found in the sedan. Because the Coupe is based on the same wheelbase as the sedan, there is plenty of room in the back.

Unique headlights

The 130 Coupe's infamously oblong headlights were never fitted to any other production car.

ENGINE
Type: V6

Construction: Iron block, alloy heads

Valve gear: Single overhead camshaft

Bore and stroke: 4.02 in. x 2.60 in.

Displacement: 3,325cc

Compression ratio: 9.0:1

Induction system: Weber Carburetor

Maximum power: 165 bhp at 5,500 rpm

Maximum torque: 184 lb-ft at 3,400 rpm

Top speed: 120 mph

0-60 mph: 11.4 sec.

TRANSMISSION
Three-speed automatic

BODY/CHASSIS
Unitary monocoque construction with steel, two-door coupe body

SPECIAL FEATURES

The 130 features normal horns for town use and strident air horns for fast, open-road driving.

Shades were fitted in the rear and are mounted on the speaker shelf.

RUNNING GEAR
Steering: Worm-and-roller

Front suspension: Double wishbones with torsion bars, telescopic shock absorbers and anti-roll bar.

Rear suspension: Wishbones and lateral and trailing links with coil springs, telescopic shock absorbers and anti-roll bar.

Brakes: Vented discs, 10.8 in. (front), 10.3 in. (rear)

Wheels: Cromadora cast alloy, 5-stud fixing, 6.5-in. rim

Tires: 205/70 VR14

DIMENSIONS
Length: 190.6 in.   **Width:** 69.3 in.

Height: 54.3 in.   **Wheelbase:** 107.1 in.

Track: 57.8 in. (front and rear)

Weight: 3,528 lbs.

Ford ESCORT RS1600

To further improve what was already a world-class rally car, Ford homologated a Cosworth-engined, 16-valve version of the Escort, and called it the RS1600. The 120-bhp machine was highly successful in competition and was a highly desirable road car.

"...remarkable handling."

"The RS1600 has low, stiff suspension with an old-fashioned leaf-sprung axle. But it does have remarkable handling, with a very direct turn-in and neutral feel, which can change to pronounced oversteer with too much throttle. Steering is so quick, though, that you provoke the oversteer just for fun, but it's easy to get the car back under control. The enjoyment is increased by the eager twin-cam engine and superb gearshift."

The interior of the RS1600 has a more sporty feel to it than the standard Escort.

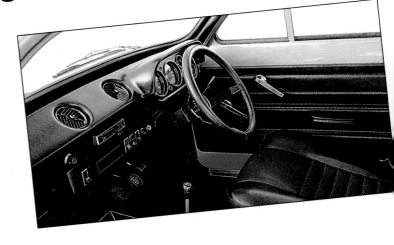

Milestones

1968 Ford replaces the Lotus
Cortina by cramming its running gear into the new, smaller Escort model to produce the Escort Twin Cam. The competition version wins the 1000 Lakes Rally three times and the European Rally Championship in 1968-1969.

The Escort Twin Cam was the precursor of the RS1600.

1970 With a more powerful
Cosworth engine, the RS1600 is produced at Ford's new AVO (Advanced Vehicle Operations) base at South Ockenden in Essex.

The RS Cosworth was the last of the famed homologation Escorts.

1972 Fitted with a lighter
alloy head developed by Brian Hart, an RS1600 driven by Roger Clark is victorious in the British RAC Rally.

1975 A new-shaped Escort
results in a RS1800 model being developed.

UNDER THE SKIN

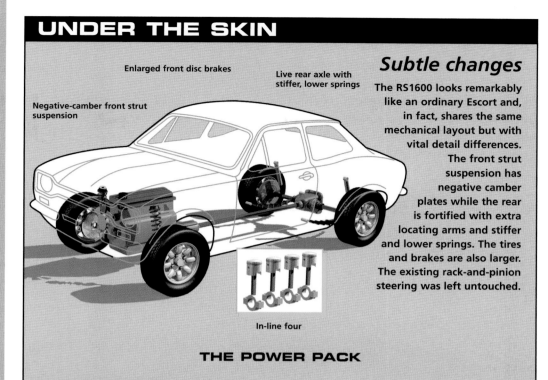

Enlarged front disc brakes

Live rear axle with stiffer, lower springs

Negative-camber front strut suspension

In-line four

Subtle changes

The RS1600 looks remarkably like an ordinary Escort and, in fact, shares the same mechanical layout but with vital detail differences. The front strut suspension has negative camber plates while the rear is fortified with extra locating arms and stiffer and lower springs. The tires and brakes are also larger. The existing rack-and-pinion steering was left untouched.

THE POWER PACK

Cosworth engine

Ford used the Cosworth BDA (Belt-Driven A) engine for the RS1600. A slightly oversquare in-line four-cylinder, it is a development based on the cast-iron block of the Cortina GT engine. The connecting rods and bearings are from the same source, but the crankshaft was tuftrided for strength and the pistons used a new flat-top design. Topping off the bottom end is an all-new alloy cylinder head designed by Cosworth's Keith Duckworth. It features two belt-driven overhead camshafts opening four valves per cylinder and yields a high 10:1 compression ratio.

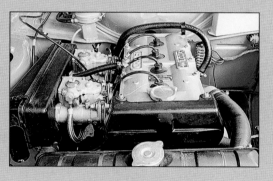

Rare RS

Although the RS1600 was also built in MK II form as the RS Mexico, the earlier street version cars are much more rare. Their excellent road manners, coupled with their simple engineering and touring potential insure that they will always be in high demand.

The RS1600's excellent handling characteristics make it a driver's delight.

Ford ESCORT RS1600

Remarkably, Ford did not make the dramatically faster and better RS1600 look any different than a standard car. Only keen observers would spot the lower ride height, cambered front wheels and tiny RS badges.

Front discs

The RS1600 uses the same braking system as the Escort Twin Cam, which means it has fairly large 9.6-inch diameter front discs. The rear brakes are nine-inch diameter drums, which were considered good enough.

Twin-cam engine

Just as the Lotus twin-cam engine was a development of an existing Ford block, the more powerful BDA engine was a similar approach by Cosworth. The 1.6-liter BDA could easily be bored out to give up to 1.8 liters, or even as much as 2.0 liters.

Rear battery

Shoe-horning a twin-cam engine into the Escort's engine bay meant there was no room for the battery, so it migrated to the rear of the car where it was mounted in the trunk. This had the welcome incidental effect of improving the weight distribution, although the RS1600 still felt too light in the rear.

Flared wheel arches

At first glance it is not obvious, but Ford had to make the wheel arches slightly flared to clear the 165-13 tires. The change can be best seen from the front three-quarter angle.

Strut front suspension

The existing MacPherson-strut front suspension was modified with lower and stiffer springs and struts. In addition, the front wheels were given 1.5 degrees of negative camber to greatly improve front-end grip during hard cornering.

Specifications

1971 Ford Escort RS1600

ENGINE

Type: In-line four-cylinder

Construction: Cast-iron block and alloy cylinder head

Valve gear: Four valves per cylinder operated by twin belt-driven overhead camshafts

Bore and stroke: 3.20 in. x 3.05 in.

Displacement: 1,601 cc

Compression ratio: 10.0:1

Induction system: Two Weber 40 DCOE carburetors

Maximum power: 120 bhp at 6,500 rpm

Maximum torque: 112 lb-ft at 4,000 rpm

Top speed: 114 mph

0-60 mph: 8.3 sec.

TRANSMISSION

Four-speed manual

BODY/CHASSIS

Unitary monocoque construction with steel two-door sedan body

SPECIAL FEATURES

Sporty Escorts can be identified by their two-piece front fenders.

Oil coolers were standard on race-prepped Escort RS1600s.

RUNNING GEAR

Steering: Rack-and-pinion

Front suspension: MacPherson struts with lower control arms and anti-roll bar

Rear suspension: Live axle with semi-elliptic leaf springs, trailing arms and telescopic shock absorbers

Brakes: Discs, 9.6-in. dia. (front), drums 9.0-in. dia. (rear)

Wheels: Pressed-steel disc, 5.5 x 13 in.

Tires: Radial, 165-13

DIMENSIONS

Length: 160.0 in.   **Width:** 61.8 in.

Height: 53.0 in.   **Wheelbase:** 94.5 in.

Track: 50.8 in. (front), 52.0 in. (rear)

Weight: 1,965 lbs.

Ford ESCORT RS2000

The RS badge always means something special on a European Ford and, in the case of the Escort RS2000, it denotes the largest-engined of the overseas Escorts. It looks the part, and its specification allows road drivers to share in the racing exploits the RS Escorts became so famous for.

"...cornering is great fun."

"By today's standards the RS2000 is narrow and upright, but it is quite comfortable. The sub-compact engine feels very lively, and has the sort of carbureted throatiness that is missing in modern-day equivalents. Cornering is great fun thanks to the rear-wheel drive configuration and the amount of power available. While the non-assisted steering feels heavy, the other controls are light and positive; the short-throw gearshift is simply superb."

Equipment levels are generous and the bolstered seats provide great support.

Milestones

1975 The RS2000 Mk2 is announced in March. Production begin at Saarlouis, Germany later in the year.

1976 The RS2000 officially goes on sale in Europe in January and achieves immediate popularity.

The Mk1 and Mk2 Escorts were very successful rally cars.

1978 A Custom pack is offered for the first time as an option. It features Recaro rally seats, bronze-tinted glass and a remote control driver's door mirror. This year also sees a less expensive version with steel wheels.

The phenomenal four-wheel drive Escort Cosworth is the 1990s descendant of the RS2000.

1980 Production ceases as Ford gears up to launch the Mk3 Escort.

UNDER THE SKIN

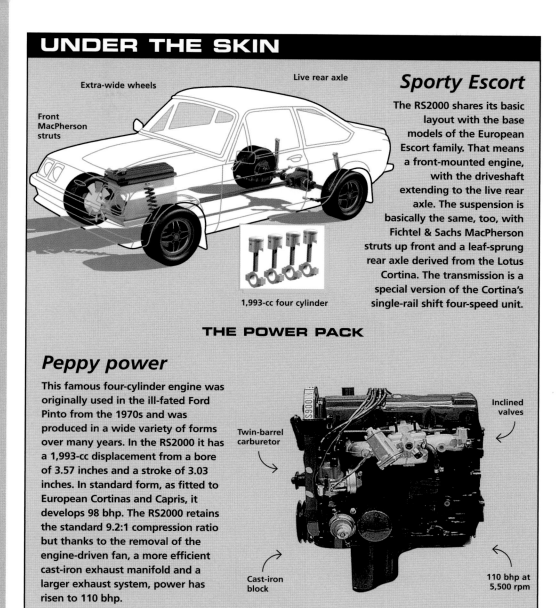

Extra-wide wheels

Live rear axle

Front MacPherson struts

1,993-cc four cylinder

Sporty Escort

The RS2000 shares its basic layout with the base models of the European Escort family. That means a front-mounted engine, with the driveshaft extending to the live rear axle. The suspension is basically the same, too, with Fichtel & Sachs MacPherson struts up front and a leaf-sprung rear axle derived from the Lotus Cortina. The transmission is a special version of the Cortina's single-rail shift four-speed unit.

THE POWER PACK

Peppy power

This famous four-cylinder engine was originally used in the ill-fated Ford Pinto from the 1970s and was produced in a wide variety of forms over many years. In the RS2000 it has a 1,993-cc displacement from a bore of 3.57 inches and a stroke of 3.03 inches. In standard form, as fitted to European Cortinas and Capris, it develops 98 bhp. The RS2000 retains the standard 9.2:1 compression ratio but thanks to the removal of the engine-driven fan, a more efficient cast-iron exhaust manifold and a larger exhaust system, power has risen to 110 bhp.

Twin-barrel carburetor

Cast-iron block

Inclined valves

110 bhp at 5,500 rpm

Custom made

While other Mk2 Escorts might be more powerful, the 'droop-nose' RS2000 looks unique and is very practical to drive. The most desirable models are those with the Custom-trim pack, or the specially-widened X-Pack fiberglass fenders and fat wheels and tires.

The Custom-trim pack, with desirable Recaro 'fish-net' seats adds value.

Ford ESCORT RS2000

Euro-spec Escorts were legendary rally cars in the 1970s and the public wanted a machine that shared some of that pedigree. The distinctive RS2000 was a budget-wise example that quickly achieved cult status.

'Droop-nose'
Ford stylists radically change the shape of the standard European spec model by installing a sloping nose section that neatly matches the hood. It incorporates a black bumper with a deep, purposeful-looking spoiler beneath.

Rear spoiler
Supplementing the spoiler up front is another spoiler on the trunk lid, this time in deformable matte black. It may help to promote rear downforce but the main reason for it is undoubtedly cosmetic.

Quick-shift transmission
One of the best features of the driving experience is the durable transmission. Although the four-speed unit is fairly standard, it is the quality, precision and speed of the short-throw shifter that is such a revelation.

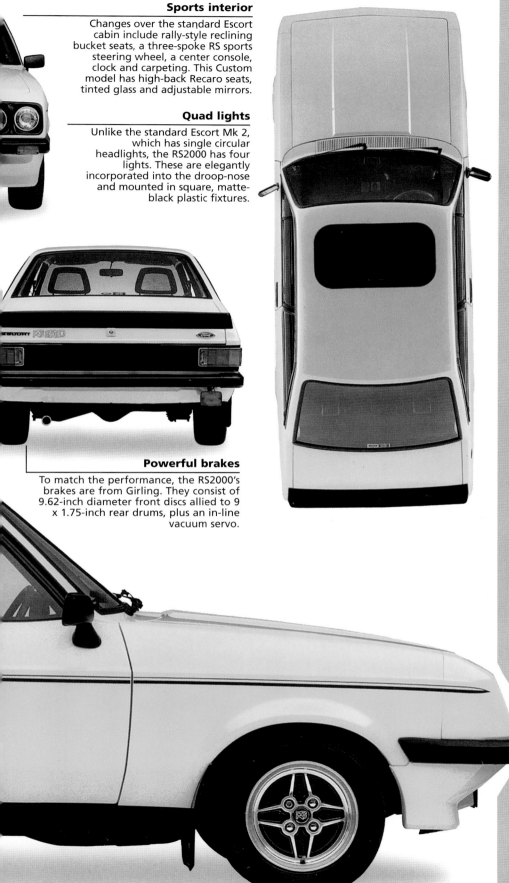

Sports interior

Changes over the standard Escort cabin include rally-style reclining bucket seats, a three-spoke RS sports steering wheel, a center console, clock and carpeting. This Custom model has high-back Recaro seats, tinted glass and adjustable mirrors.

Quad lights

Unlike the standard Escort Mk 2, which has single circular headlights, the RS2000 has four lights. These are elegantly incorporated into the droop-nose and mounted in square, matte-black plastic fixtures.

Powerful brakes

To match the performance, the RS2000's brakes are from Girling. They consist of 9.62-inch diameter front discs allied to 9 x 1.75-inch rear drums, plus an in-line vacuum servo.

Specifications

1979 Ford Escort RS2000

ENGINE

Type: In-line four-cylinder

Construction: Cast-iron block and head

Valve gear: Two valves per cylinder operated by a single camshaft via pushrods and rockers

Bore and stroke: 3.57 in. x 3.03 in.

Displacement: 1,993 cc

Compression ratio: 9.2:1

Induction system: Single Weber twin-barrel carburetor

Maximum power: 110 bhp at 5,500 rpm

Maximum torque: 119 lb-ft at 4,000 rpm

Top speed: 108 mph

0-60 mph: 8.7 sec.

TRANSMISSION

Four-speed manual

BODY/CHASSIS

Integral chassis with steel and plastic two-door sedan body

SPECIAL FEATURES

These four-spoke alloy wheels are used on many RS Fords.

The RS2000's 'droop-nose' front end differentiates it from other Escorts.

RUNNING GEAR

Steering: Rack-and-pinion

Front suspension: MacPherson struts with coil springs, shock absorbers and anti-roll bar

Rear suspension: Live axle with semi-elliptic leaf springs, radius arms and shock absorbers

Brakes: Discs (front), drums (rear)

Wheels: Alloy, 13-in. dia.

Tires: 175/70 HR13

DIMENSIONS

Length: 163.1 in.   **Width:** 61.8 in.

Height: 55.5 in.   **Wheelbase:** 94.5 in.

Track: 50.0 in. (front), 51.0 in. (rear)

Weight: 2,035 lbs.

Ford TORINO COBRA

Ford fielded a larger, more curvaceous Torino for 1970. The Cobra was a bare bones performance version of the sporty Torino GT. With a standard 429 Cobra Jet engine and a Hurst-shifted four-speed, it was a serious racer and owning one was certain to gain you instant respect on the drag strip.

"...traction is excellent."

"The first thing that you notice is the room inside— this is one of the larger muscle intermediates and there are acres of space. Traction off the line is excellent, the Hurst-shifted four-speed is precise and in just 5.9 seconds you're hitting 60 mph. What strikes you even more is the level of refinement—the seats are comfortable and the ride soft and composed. Despite all the weight over the front wheels, the Cobra handles well too, thanks to the wide track."

With a four-speed transmission and a full set of gauges this Torino Cobra means business.

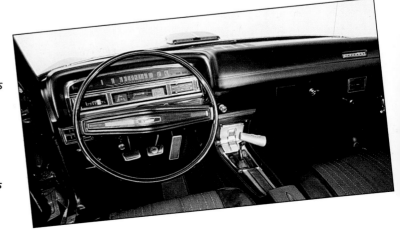

Milestones

1970 Ford releases
a new crop of intermediate-sized cars, which are longer, lower and wider with new streamlined styling. They are now split into two series: the Fairlane 500 and the Torino. The standard sporty machine is the Torino GT. A serious performance version, the Cobra, has exposed headlights and standard 429-cubic inch V8 power.

The Torino GT was the standard sporty Ford intermediate.

1971 Returning
with a facelift, the mid-size line is back for its second and last outing in this form. The Torino Cobra is still offered, although the standard engine is now a 285-bhp, 351-cubic inch small-block.

The Torino was popularized in the TV series Starsky and Hutch.

1972 An all-new
Torino with unitized construction is built this year. A token performance model, the Sports GT fastback, is also offered.

UNDER THE SKIN

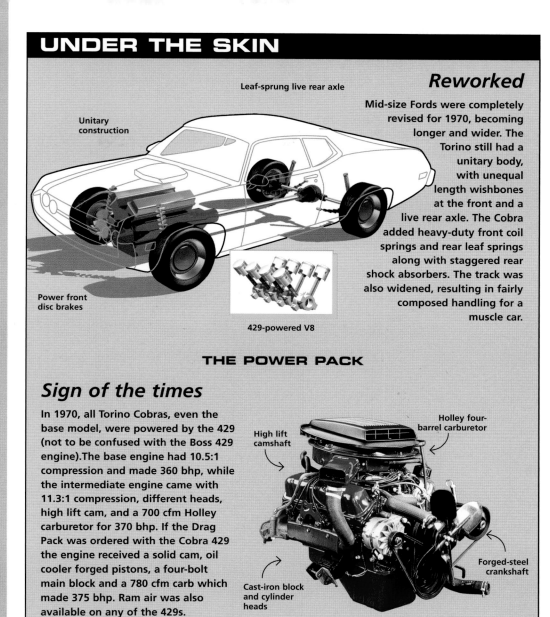

Unitary construction

Leaf-sprung live rear axle

Power front disc brakes

429-powered V8

Reworked

Mid-size Fords were completely revised for 1970, becoming longer and wider. The Torino still had a unitary body, with unequal length wishbones at the front and a live rear axle. The Cobra added heavy-duty front coil springs and rear leaf springs along with staggered rear shock absorbers. The track was also widened, resulting in fairly composed handling for a muscle car.

THE POWER PACK

Sign of the times

In 1970, all Torino Cobras, even the base model, were powered by the 429 (not to be confused with the Boss 429 engine).The base engine had 10.5:1 compression and made 360 bhp, while the intermediate engine came with 11.3:1 compression, different heads, high lift cam, and a 700 cfm Holley carburetor for 370 bhp. If the Drag Pack was ordered with the Cobra 429 the engine received a solid cam, oil cooler forged pistons, a four-bolt main block and a 780 cfm carb which made 375 bhp. Ram air was also available on any of the 429s.

High lift camshaft

Holley four-barrel carburetor

Cast-iron block and cylinder heads

Forged-steel crankshaft

Fully optioned

The 1970 Torino Cobra is, without doubt, the most desirable of these cars. Find one equipped with the 370-bhp 429, Drag Pack and Ram Air and you have one of the muscle era's finest specimens. A good Cobra will set you back $20,000-$30,000 today.

Fast and refined, the Torino Cobra is a cut above many muscle cars.

Ford TORINO COBRA

From any angle, the Torino Cobra has presence. It also has unrivaled handling, comfort and 0-60 mph acceleration. Other muscle cars may be quicker, but few offered so much in a single, tailor-made package.

Wicked 429

In standard form the 429 engine is rated at 360 bhp, although the Cobra Jet version produces 370 bhp thanks to a hotter camshaft, free-flowing cylinder heads and a high-riser intake manifold. The baddest engine option was the 375 bhp version with four-bolt mains, forged pistons, solid cam and larger carburetor. This model happens to be the intermediate model with 370 bhp.

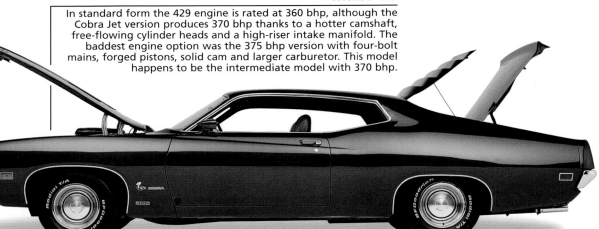

Four-speed transmission

Backing the 429 engine is a standard four-speed transmission, including a Hurst T-shaped shifter. This combination made the Cobra a threat to any car on the street, even with the most average driver behind the wheel.

Beefed-up suspension

Like most muscle machines of its period, the Cobra has standard suspension which has been uprated with a thicker front anti-roll bar and stiffer springs and shocks. The 2-inch wider track results in one of the best-handling muscle cars.

Swoopy styling

The 1970-1971 Torinos are arguably the best-looking, with their fluid styling and fastback roof. Although they look aerodynamic, tests in stock car racing proved that the older 1969 styling was more efficient and therefore Ford continued using 1969 Talladegas on the big NASCAR ovals.

Low rear axle gearing

If equipped with the Drag Pack, Torino Cobras came with either Traction-Lok 3.91:1 rear axle ratio or with the deadly Detroit locker 4.30:1 gears.

Ram Air induction

With the addition of the shaker scoop, the engine became known as the 429 Cobra Jet Ram Air. The scoop attaches directly to the engine's air cleaner.

Specifications

1970 Ford Torino Cobra

ENGINE
Type: V8
Construction: Cast-iron block and heads
Valve gear: Two valves per cylinder operated by pushrods and rockers
Bore and stroke: 4.36 in. x 3.59 in.
Displacement: 429 c.i.
Compression ratio: 11.3:1
Induction system: Single Holley four-barrel carburetor
Maximum power: 370 bhp at 5,400 rpm
Maximum torque: 450 lb-ft at 3,400 rpm
Top speed: 118 mph
0-60 mph: 5.9 sec.

TRANSMISSION
Borg-Warner T10 four-speed with Hurst shifter

BODY/CHASSIS
Unitary steel monocoque with two-door fastback body

SPECIAL FEATURES

The Ram Air induction quickly forced cool air into the carburetor.

A four-speed manual is standard, as is this Hurst T-handle shifter.

RUNNING GEAR
Steering: Recirculating ball
Front suspension: Unequal length wishbones with coil springs, telescopic shock absorbers and anti-roll bar
Rear suspension: Live 9-in. axle with multi-leaf springs and staggered telescopic shock absorbers
Brakes: Discs, 10-in. dia. (front), finned drums, 9-in. dia. (rear)
Wheels: Steel, 15-in. dia.
Tires: ZBF Goodrich Radial T/A, F60-15

DIMENSIONS
Length: 203.6 in.   **Width:** 80.0 in.
Height: 49.3 in.   **Wheelbase:** 117.0 in.
Track: 60.3 in. (front), 58.4 in. (rear)
Weight: 4,000 lbs.

Ford MUSTANG MACH 1

1973 was the final year of the big, original-style Mustang. The pick of the range was the Mach 1. It looked sporty, had special interior trim, competition suspension and standard V8 power. It was one of the most popular of Ford's ponycar range.

"...sporty aspirations."

"A standard 1973 Mustang is a long way from the original 1964 model. It became known as the Mustang that was bigger, heavier and plusher but not really as sporty as its forebearer. The Mach I, with its 302-cubic inch V8 changed that myth. It may not have a sense of urgency to it, but the Mach 1 offers adequate acceleration compared to other 1973 muscle missiles. The competition suspension virtually eliminates body roll, while ride comfort remains soft for a car with sporty aspirations."

The Mach 1's sporty theme extends to the cabin, with extra gauges and tach as standard.

Milestones

1969 The very first Mach 1 performance
SportsRoof model is launched by Ford in response to demand.

A matte-black hood section with an aggressive hood scoop were typical trademarks of the 1969 Mach 1.

1971 The Mustang grows
in all dimensions, addressing previous criticisms of cramped passenger space on early ponycars. There is extra space under the hood, too. Among other options, the 429 Cobra Jet V8 is offered, packing all of 375 bhp.

By 1974, in Mustang II guise, the Mach 1 was built for an environmentally conscious market.

1973 In its last year before it was
replaced by the slimmer, more economical Mustang II (fitting, given the approaching fuel crisis), the Mustang is offered in a range of five variations topped by the sporty Mach 1.

UNDER THE SKIN

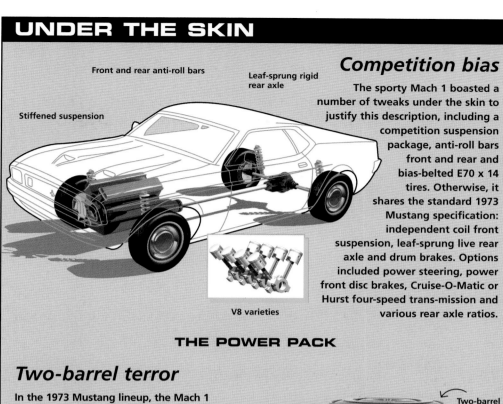

Front and rear anti-roll bars

Leaf-sprung rigid rear axle

Stiffened suspension

V8 varieties

Competition bias

The sporty Mach 1 boasted a number of tweaks under the skin to justify this description, including a competition suspension package, anti-roll bars front and rear and bias-belted E70 x 14 tires. Otherwise, it shares the standard 1973 Mustang specification: independent coil front suspension, leaf-sprung live rear axle and drum brakes. Options included power steering, power front disc brakes, Cruise-O-Matic or Hurst four-speed trans-mission and various rear axle ratios.

THE POWER PACK

Two-barrel terror

In the 1973 Mustang lineup, the Mach 1 was the only model to come with a standard V8. The base V8 was the 302-cubic inch overhead-valve unit, fitted with a Motorcraft two-barrel carburetor. It made 136 bhp. For an extra $128 you could choose the 351-cubic inch Windsor V8 with the two-barrel carb and 156 bhp, or the 351 Cleveland with a two-barrel carb and 154 bhp. Among further options was a four-barrel 351 V8. It made much more power and had large-port cylinder heads and a different intake manifold.

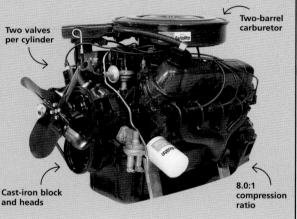

Two valves per cylinder

Two-barrel carburetor

Cast-iron block and heads

8.0:1 compression ratio

Best of breed

Although it was hardly recognizable as a first generation Mustang, the 1973 model, though restyled, was just that. While the Mach 1 isn't the most desirable of the early 1970 Mustangs—the earlier Boss 351 model takes the top honors here—it was still very fast and sporty.

Of all the 1973 Mustangs, the Mach 1 is the most collectable today.

Ford **MUSTANG MACH 1**

The Mach 1 line, which began in 1969, enhanced the sporty qualities of the Mustang, picking up on some of the themes of Carroll Shelby's modifications. The 1973 Mach 1 boasted a variety of enhancements.

Standard V8 power

All Mustangs for 1973 came with a six-cylinder engine as standard except the Mach 1, with its 302-cubic inch V8. Because it had an emissions-restricted output of 136 bhp, ordering one of the optional V8 engines was an attractive choice.

Competition suspension

Justifying its reputation as the sporty member of the Mustang group, the Mach 1 received a standard competition suspension, with heavy-duty front and rear springs and revalved shock absorbers.

SportsRoof style

The Mach 1 was offered in one body style only, a fastback coupe known as the SportsRoof. This is characterized by a near-horizontal rear roof line, in contrast to the cut-away style of the Mustang hardtop coupe. The rear window is tinted on the Mach 1 and a rear spoiler was optional.

Impact bumpers

In 1973 it was federally mandated that all cars had to have 5-mph impact protection bumpers. To try and retain its sporty appearance, the Mach 1's bumpers were painted the same color as the rest of the car.

Choice of hoods

Two hood styles were offered for the Mach 1—one had functional NACA-type ducts the other had non functional duct work. Two-tone hood paint was an option on all Mach 1s.

Specifications

1973 Ford Mustang Mach 1

ENGINE

Type: V8

Construction: Cast-iron block and heads

Valve gear: Two valves per cylinder operated by a single camshaft with pushrods and rocker arms

Bore and stroke: 4.00 in. x 3.00 in.

Displacement: 302 c.i.

Compression ratio: 8.5:1

Induction system: Single Motorcraft two-barrel carburetor

Maximum power: 136 bhp at 4,200 rpm

Maximum torque: 232 lb-ft at 2,200 rpm

Top speed: 110 mph

0-60 mph: 10.4 sec.

TRANSMISSION

Three-speed automatic

BODY/CHASSIS

Unitary monocoque construction with steel two-door coupe body

SPECIAL FEATURES

Fold-down rear seats allow access to the trunk from inside. It also permits more room to carry unusually long items.

The hood scoops took different forms on Mach 1s, but they were always present on all models from 1969 on.

RUNNING GEAR

Steering: Recirculating ball

Front suspension: Wishbones with lower trailing links, coil springs, shock absorbers and anti-roll bar

Rear suspension: Live axle with semi-elliptic leaf springs, shock absorbers and anti-roll bar

Brakes: Discs (front), drums (rear)

Wheels: Steel, 14-in. dia.

Tires: E70 x 14

DIMENSIONS

Length: 189.0 in. **Width:** 74.1 in.

Height: 50.7 in. **Wheelbase:** 109.0 in.

Track: 61.5 in. (front), 59.5 in. (rear)

Weight: 3,090 lbs.

Jaguar **XJ6**

In 1968, the world was amazed by the introduction of the best luxury sedan of the time. Nothing could approach its combination of ride, handling refinement, comfort and style, and certainly none came close on price.

"...beautifully engineered."

"Drive a first generation XJ6 and you'll be amazed at how incredibly modern it feels today. In 1968 it was nothing short of incredible. From the direct rack-and-pinion steering, to the smooth ride and the quiet refinement, everything feels beautifully engineered. All this is allied to handling and roadholding well beyond any contemporary sedan's. The 2.8 liter engine feels a little gutless, but the 4.2 feels swift, even today."

Inside, the XJ6 is extremely well equipped for an early 1970s British sedan.

Milestones

1964 Jaguar boss Sir William Lyons

begins to think about a replacement for the big Mk X sedan and work on the advanced XJ6 design begins.

The Mark VII also relied on the XK straight-six engine.

1968 Launched at London's

Royal Lancaster Hotel in September, the XJ6 goes into production in 4.2-liter and 2.8-liter (180-bhp) forms with either the Jaguar four-speed and overdrive manual transmission or Borg-Warner's three-speed auto. Demand is enormous and owners have to wait up to a year for delivery.

A much modified XJ6 with an all-new engine was launched in 1986.

1973 After over 79,000

Series I cars are made, the new Series II is launched with a raised front bumper, revised grill, and new instrument panel. A 3.4 version of the straight-six engine appears in 1975, as does a two-door coupe.

UNDER THE SKIN

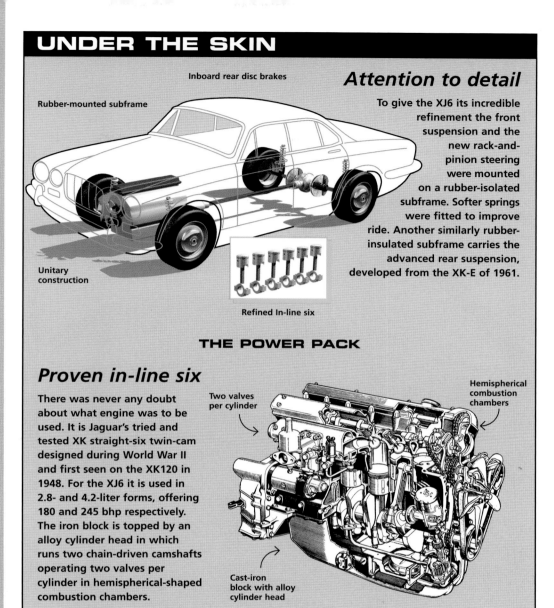

Inboard rear disc brakes

Rubber-mounted subframe

Unitary construction

Refined In-line six

Attention to detail

To give the XJ6 its incredible refinement the front suspension and the new rack-and-pinion steering were mounted on a rubber-isolated subframe. Softer springs were fitted to improve ride. Another similarly rubber-insulated subframe carries the advanced rear suspension, developed from the XK-E of 1961.

THE POWER PACK

Proven in-line six

There was never any doubt about what engine was to be used. It is Jaguar's tried and tested XK straight-six twin-cam designed during World War II and first seen on the XK120 in 1948. For the XJ6 it is used in 2.8- and 4.2-liter forms, offering 180 and 245 bhp respectively. The iron block is topped by an alloy cylinder head in which runs two chain-driven camshafts operating two valves per cylinder in hemispherical-shaped combustion chambers.

Two valves per cylinder

Hemispherical combustion chambers

Cast-iron block with alloy cylinder head

V12 monster

A V12 model followed soon after the XJ6. Powered by a huge 5.3-liter V12 engine, it offered even greater refinement and better performance. The XJ12 continued in production until 1996 and later examples are worth considering.

The XJ12s offer even greater performance and refinement.

Jaguar **XJ6** 🇬🇧

There was nothing that could come remotely close to the XJ6 for the price. This car was so significant that current Jaguar sedans still bear similar styling cues.

Rack-and-pinion steering

Jaguar had been quick to adopt rack-and-pinion steering on its sports and racing cars but the revious large sedan, the huge Mk X, had recirculating ball steering. This was replaced on the XJ6 by sharper and more responsive rack-and-pinion steering.

Twin-cam engine

One of the world's greatest engines powers this milestone sedan. For the XJ6 Series I it was built in 2.8-liter and 4.2-liter forms.

Bolt-on fenders

Although the XJ6 has a modern unitary-construction monocoque, the front fenders can be unbolted for ease of repair. The monocoque is heavily reinforced with box-section cross members while more box-section chassis rails carry the rear subframe.

Inboard rear discs

The rear disc brakes are mounted inboard next to the differential for reduced unsprung weight.

Overdrive transmission

The standard XJ6 transmission is a Borg-Warner three-speed auto, but buyers could opt for Jaguar's four-speed unit with overdrive.

Specifications

1970 Jaguar XJ6 2.8

ENGINE

Type: In-line six

Construction: Iron block and alloy head

Valve gear: Two inclined valves per cylinder operated by twin chain-driven overhead camshafts

Bore and stroke: 3.62 in. x 4.17 in.

Displacement: 2,791 cc

Compression ratio: 9.0:1

Induction system: Two SU carburetors

Maximum power: 180 bhp at 5,500 rpm

Maximum torque: 283 lb-ft at 3,750 rpm

Top speed: 120 mph

0-60 mph: 10.1 sec.

TRANSMISSION

Borg-Warner three-speed auto or Jaguar four-speed plus overdrive manual

BODY/CHASSIS

Unitary construction with four-door body

SPECIAL FEATURES

A four-speed transmission with overdrive offers relaxed high-speed cruising.

The large, upright radiator grill is one of the Mk I's most distinctive features.

RUNNING GEAR

Steering: Rack-and-pinion

Front suspension: Suspension: double wishbones with coil springs, telescopic shock absorbers and anti-roll bar

Rear suspension: Wishbones, trailing arms and double coil spring/shock absorber units per side

Brakes: Discs (front and rear)

Wheels: Steel 15-in. dia.

Tires: Dunlop SP Sport E70VR15

DIMENSIONS

Length: 189.5 in. **Width:** 69.9 in.

Height: 52.8 in. **Wheelbase:** 108.8 in.

Track: 58.0 in. (front), 58.6 in. (rear)

Weight: 3,627 lbs.

Jaguar **XJC**

Few people who drove Jaguar's XJ sedan were in any doubt that this was one of the world's great cars. A two-door coupe version soon followed. However, it was short lived, bowing out after only two years.

"...excellent mid-range power."

"At idle, the V12 engine purrs magically yet will still rev enthusiastically. A very broad torque curve also gives it excellent mid-range power. As for the ride, it would be difficult to find a more comfortable car from the 1970s. A low center of gravity and sophisticated suspension give it good roadholding and can move at a pace that will make you think you are in a smaller car. One of the few drawbacks is the wind noise from the frameless windows."

Sumptuous leather seats and a generous outlay of walnut—this could only be a Jaguar.

Milestones

1973 The new Series 2 XJ range

is launched and a coupe model is displayed—however, it will be another two years before production begins.

The original Series I XJ6 sedan made its debut in 1968, followed by a V12 version in 1972.

1975 Jaguar and Daimler

badged coupe versions of the XJ6 and XJ12 officially enter production.

Jaguar's other two-door coupe of the mid 1970s was the stylish and classic XJS.

1976 Tuning firm Broadspeed

reveals a heavily modified coupe with a 550-bhp V12, Lucas fuel injection and huge disc brakes. Two cars compete in the European Touring Car Championship.

1977 Production of the

XJC comes to an end.

UNDER THE SKIN

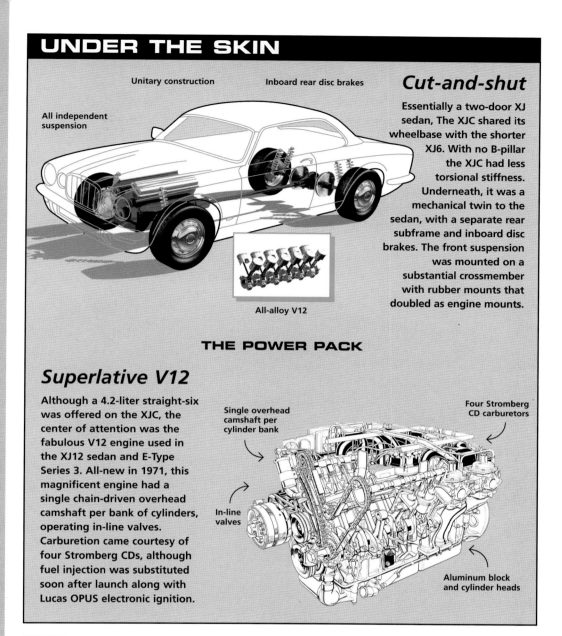

Unitary construction

Inboard rear disc brakes

All independent suspension

All-alloy V12

Cut-and-shut

Essentially a two-door XJ sedan, The XJC shared its wheelbase with the shorter XJ6. With no B-pillar the XJC had less torsional stiffness. Underneath, it was a mechanical twin to the sedan, with a separate rear subframe and inboard disc brakes. The front suspension was mounted on a substantial crossmember with rubber mounts that doubled as engine mounts.

THE POWER PACK

Superlative V12

Although a 4.2-liter straight-six was offered on the XJC, the center of attention was the fabulous V12 engine used in the XJ12 sedan and E-Type Series 3. All-new in 1971, this magnificent engine had a single chain-driven overhead camshaft per bank of cylinders, operating in-line valves. Carburetion came courtesy of four Stromberg CDs, although fuel injection was substituted soon after launch along with Lucas OPUS electronic ignition.

Single overhead camshaft per cylinder bank

Four Stromberg CD carburetors

In-line valves

Aluminum block and cylinder heads

12 cylinders

Of all the XJ range, the two-door coupes are the rarest and most desirable. For ultimate status and refinement, the V12 model is a must, though good ones can be expensive. A badge-engineered Daimler version, the Double-Six Coupe, was also available.

XJCs only came with 4.2- or 5.3-liter engines.

Jaguar **XJC**

Jaguar's speciality is sporty sedans and luxurious sports cars. The XJC was a unique attempt to marry the two in one enticing package. It was elegant, refined, exclusive and—with its V12 engine—a superb cruiser.

Six or twelve cylinders

The XJC used either the old XK straight-six or Jaguar's infamous 5.3-liter V12, found in the final versions of the E-Types. Compared to the six-cylinder XJC, the V12 was much more expensive and rarer—the smaller-engined versions outnumber the V12 by more than three to one.

Short wheelbase

Based on the short wheelbase XJ6 sedan, the coupe was also unique in that it was the only XJ to marry the V12 engine with the 108.8-inch wheelbase chassis.

Long doors

Compared to the XJ sedan, the coupe's doors were four inches longer and substantially heavier. An absence of vent windows also gave it a neater side profile.

Unique roofline

Having a unique roofline gave rise to some problems, particularly wind noise and water leaks. Neither problem was ever properly addressed by Jaguar.

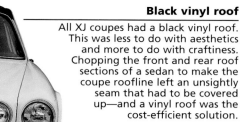

Black vinyl roof

All XJ coupes had a black vinyl roof. This was less to do with aesthetics and more to do with craftiness. Chopping the front and rear roof sections of a sedan to make the coupe roofline left an unsightly seam that had to be covered up—and a vinyl roof was the cost-efficient solution.

Pillarless glass

The opportunity was taken to rid the XJ coupe of a central pillar and so do away with a glass pillar divider. Both front and rear windows could wind away out of sight to allow completely open sides.

Smaller cabin

Although the wheelbase remained the same as the sedan, rear seat room was tighter. Still, compared to most coupe competitors the XJC was very spacious.

Specifications

1976 Jaguar XJ 4.2 C

ENGINE

Type: In-line six-cylinder

Construction: Cast-iron block and head

Valve gear: Two valves per cylinder operated by twin chain-driven overhead camshafts

Bore and stroke: 3.65 in. x 4.17 in.

Displacement: 4,235 cc

Compression ratio: 7.8:1

Induction system: Two SU carburetors

Maximum power: 176 bhp at 4,750 rpm

Maximum torque: 219 lb-ft at 2,500 rpm

Top speed: 139 mph

0-60 mph: 8.8 sec.

TRANSMISSION

Borg Warner three-speed automatic

BODY/CHASSIS

Unitary monocoque construction chassis with two-door steel coupe body

SPECIAL FEATURES

Series III XJs are distinguished by higher mounted bumpers.

All XJC coupes had vinyl roof coverings to hide metal seams.

RUNNING GEAR

Steering: Rack-and-pinion

Front suspension: Double wishbones with coil springs, telescopic shock absorbers and anti-roll bar

Rear suspension: Lower wishbones and radius arms with twin coil springs and telescopic shock absorbers

Brakes: Vented discs (front and rear)

Wheels: Steel or alloy 15-in. dia.

Tires: 205/70 VR15

DIMENSIONS

Length: 189.5 in.   **Width:** 69.3 in.

Height: 54.1 in.   **Wheelbase:** 108.8 in.

Track: 58.0 in. (front), 58.5 in. (rear)

Weight: 3,696 lbs.

Lamborghini COUNTACH

In the early 1970s, wedge-shaped, avant garde styling and mid-mounted V12s paved the way for the modern supercar era. With a 375-bhp, quad-cam V12 and edgy Bertone styling, the Lamborghini Countach was at the forefront of cutting-edge performance.

"...perfectly balanced."

"With its chiseled body and a staggeringly powerful 375 bhp V12, the LP400 Countach was an unbelievable sight and an outstanding performer. With scissor-like doors the Lamborghini is difficult to get into. On the move, its surprisingly light clutch, brakes, steering and gearshift (with its dog-leg first gear) all have the right weight and the chassis is perfectly balanced. The only limits are the driver's skill and bravery."

A cramped driving position is offset by excellent steering and a precise shifter.

Milestones

1968 Famous Italian stylist
Bertone shows a new Alfa Romeo concept car, the Carabo, which inspires the look of the new Lamborghini.

Lamborghini started a supercar revolution with the Miura.

1971 This year's Geneva Show
sees the stunning Countach prototype unveiled. Styled by Bertone under the guidance of Marcello Gandini, the intended powerplant is a 5.0-liter version of Lamborghini's V12.

1974 The 1973 Production is delayed a year
until Lamborghini decides to make the car with a spaceframe chassis instead of a monocoque and a 4.0-liter engine is used.

The ultimate evolution of the Countach is the LP5000.

1978 The first changes
to the basic design includes bigger wheels and tires with larger fenders. Spoilers are also added to the front and rear.

UNDER THE SKIN

Technical marvel

Surprisingly, under the futuristic body is a traditional Italian chassis—an extremely complicated spaceframe network of steel tubes. The chassis turns into a cradle behind the cabin to hold the longitudinal, rear-mounted engine behind the transmission. A driveshaft then goes back under the engine to the rear differential. Double wishbone suspension is used all around and twin coil spring/shock units are fitted to the rear.

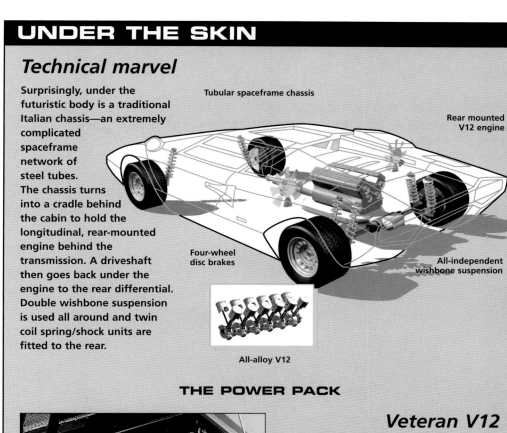

Tubular spaceframe chassis

Rear mounted V12 engine

Four-wheel disc brakes

All-independent wishbone suspension

All-alloy V12

THE POWER PACK

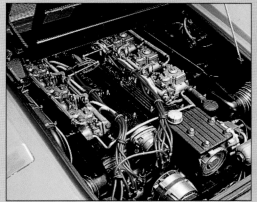

Veteran V12

Lamborghini already had an engine waiting for the Countach—the Bizzarrini-designed V12 dating back to the early 1960s. It is a very oversquare (3.23 inches x 2.44 inches) 4.0-liter powerplant, constructed around an alloy block and cylinder heads with dry cast-iron liners. Each bank of cylinders carries twin, duplex, chain-driven, overhead camshafts, operating two valves per cylinder in hemispherical combustion chambers. Six Weber twin-barrel carburetors provide the necessary fuel.

Purest form

To some enthusiasts, the original LP400 Countach with its clean lines devoid of the spoilers and fender extensions of later versions is the most desirable. Only 150 of these cars were built between 1974 and 1978. Good examples are very hard to find.

The 375-bhp, V12 LP400 is the purest-looking Countach.

Lamborghini COUNTACH 🇮🇹

Forget the later Countach models with their wild spoilers and huge wheel arches, it's the very first car—a masterpiece designed by Marcello Gandini—that has the purest lines.

Upright opening doors

One of the car's most dramatic features is the door design. Because of its unusually large sills, the doors swing upward and are held in position with a gas pressurized shock on each door.

V12 engine

When Ferruccio Lamborghini decided to start making cars, his aim was to outdo Ferrari, so it was almost inevitable that his cars had V12 engines. The engine was developed in the Miura and Espada. It is an all-alloy, 4.0-liter quad-cam with six Weber carburetors.

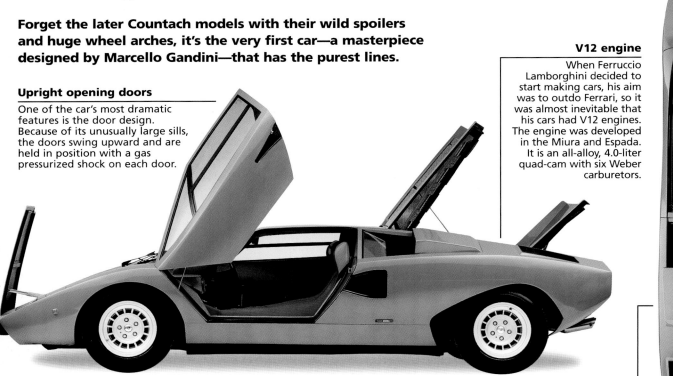

Side-mounted radiators

Keeping a huge mid-mounted V12 cool is a potential problem. Lamborghini uses two radiators mounted to the sides of the engine right behind the cockpit. However, overheating can still be a problem in stop-and-go traffic.

Alloy body

Years before the Acura NSX boasted about it, the Countach had bodywork made in alloy as a weight-saving measure. The panels are all unstressed over a tubular chassis.

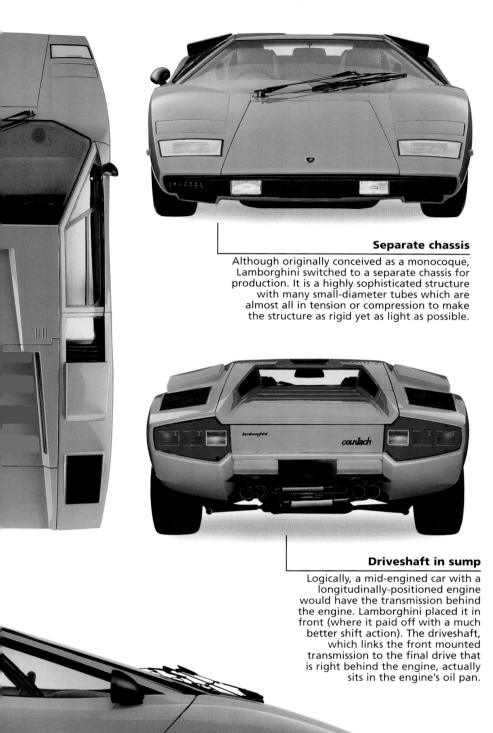

Separate chassis

Although originally conceived as a monocoque, Lamborghini switched to a separate chassis for production. It is a highly sophisticated structure with many small-diameter tubes which are almost all in tension or compression to make the structure as rigid yet as light as possible.

Driveshaft in sump

Logically, a mid-engined car with a longitudinally-positioned engine would have the transmission behind the engine. Lamborghini placed it in front (where it paid off with a much better shift action). The driveshaft, which links the front mounted transmission to the final drive that is right behind the engine, actually sits in the engine's oil pan.

Specifications

1976 Lamborghini Countach LP400

ENGINE
Type: V12
Construction: Alloy block and heads
Valve gear: Two valves per cylinder operated by twin overhead camshafts per cylinder bank
Bore and stroke: 3.23 in. x 2.44 in.
Displacement: 3,929 cc
Compression ratio: 10.5:1
Induction system: Six Weber 45 DCOE sidedraft carburetors
Maximum power: 375 bhp at 8,000 rpm
Maximum torque: 266 lb-ft at 5,000 rpm
Top speed: 180 mph
0-60 mph: 5.5 sec.

TRANSMISSION
Five-speed manual

BODY/CHASSIS
Separate tubular-steel chassis with two-door two-seat alloy and fiberglass body

SPECIAL FEATURES

The tiny door handles are hidden in the ducts to avoid spoiling the lines.

Vents atop the rear fenders help keep the engine bay as cool as possible.

RUNNING GEAR
Steering: Rack-and-pinion
Front suspension: Double wishbones with coil springs, telescopic shock absorbers and anti-roll bar
Rear suspension: Double wishbones with radius arms, twin coil spring/shock absorber units and anti-roll bar
Brakes: Vented discs (front and rear)
Wheels: Alloy, 7.5 x 14 in. (front), 9.5 x 14 in. (rear)
Tires: Michelin XWX radial, 205/70 VR14 (front), 215/70 VR15 (rear)

DIMENSIONS
Length: 163.0 in.   **Width:** 74.4 in.
Height: 42.1 in.   **Wheelbase:** 96.5 in.
Track: 59.1 in. (front), 59.8 in. (rear)
Weight: 3,020 lbs.

Lancia FULVIA COUPE

Often described as the last of the real Lancias, the beautiful and well-engineered Fulvia Coupe was also a big seller for the company because it had a jewel of a V4 engine and sharp front-wheel drive handling. It remains highly regarded by enthusiasts today.

"...much more modern."

"The light, airy interior afforded by the generous glass area makes the Fulvia feel much more modern than it really is. The dash is well laid out and the controls are perfectly placed. The little V4 fires up without a problem and pulls well on the road once it's spinning beyond 4,500 rpm. Front-wheel drive and excellent suspension give great road-holding with a touch of understeer. The five-speed transmission is sweet, and the disc brakes are powerful."

The Fulvia's dashboard is simple and well laid out but still oozes Italian style.

Milestones

1963 Lancia introduces its new small
sedan, the Fulvia. It uses a 1.1-liter V4 engine and front-wheel drive.

Fulvia HFs proved to be competent rally cars.

1965 The new Coupe variant is
launched. It has crisp in-house styling and shares its mechanicals with the sedan. The 1.2-liter engine gives 80 bhp.

The spiritual successor to the Fulvia was the Beta coupe.

1967 A larger 1.3-liter engine peps up the
Fulvia's performance.

1968 A 1.6-liter engine becomes available
with up to 132 bhp.

1976 Production comes to an end after
more than 140,000 Fulvias have been built.

UNDER THE SKIN

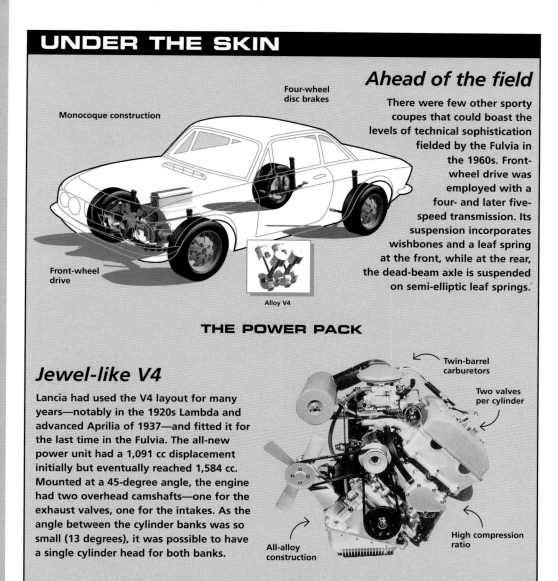

Monocoque construction

Four-wheel disc brakes

Front-wheel drive

Alloy V4

Ahead of the field

There were few other sporty coupes that could boast the levels of technical sophistication fielded by the Fulvia in the 1960s. Front-wheel drive was employed with a four- and later five-speed transmission. Its suspension incorporates wishbones and a leaf spring at the front, while at the rear, the dead-beam axle is suspended on semi-elliptic leaf springs.

THE POWER PACK

Jewel-like V4

Lancia had used the V4 layout for many years—notably in the 1920s Lambda and advanced Aprilia of 1937—and fitted it for the last time in the Fulvia. The all-new power unit had a 1,091 cc displacement initially but eventually reached 1,584 cc. Mounted at a 45-degree angle, the engine had two overhead camshafts—one for the exhaust valves, one for the intakes. As the angle between the cylinder banks was so small (13 degrees), it was possible to have a single cylinder head for both banks.

Twin-barrel carburetors

Two valves per cylinder

High compression ratio

All-alloy construction

Full house

There is a huge range of different Fulvia Coupe variants. Earlier cars are considered the most desirable, but anything wearing the coveted HF badge commands quite a premium over lesser models. All, however, are valuable today.

Early HF models can be distinguished by their lack of bumpers.

Lancia FULVIA COUPE

The top of the Fulvia range is the Coupe 1.6 HF. Its larger, tuned engine can produce up to 132 bhp, and it was campaigned successfully in rallying, taking the 1972 world title.

Wider wheels

Six-inch wide alloy wheels are fitted to the 1.6 HF necessitating distinctive plastic fender flares to cover them.

V4 engine

Lancia fitted its last V4 engine to the Fulvia. It started out with 1,091 cc and 58 bhp but eventually grew to 1,584 cc and 132 bhp.

Beam axle

The rear beam axle is suspended on semi-elliptic leaf springs and has extra location provided by a Panhard rod.

Five-speed transmission

Launched in 1968, the 1.6-liter HF was always fitted with a five-speed transmission as standard. The rest of the Fulvia range made do with a four-speeder until the Series 2 was launched in 1969.

Steel and alloy panels

The HF is lighter than the other production Fulvia Coupes, thanks to the use of alloy body panels and Plexiglas windows.

Quad headlights

The Fulvia Coupe was always fitted with quad headlights. The larger, inner pair on this car indicate that it is a Fulvia Rallye 1.6 HF. On later Series 2 cars, the outer pair is raised to comply with light height regulations.

Specifications
1970 Lancia Fulvia 1.6 HF

ENGINE
Type: V4
Construction: Alloy block and head
Valve gear: Two valves per cylinder operated by two overhead camshafts
Bore and stroke: 3.23 in. x 2.95 in.
Displacement: 1,584 cc
Compression ratio: 10.5:1
Induction system: Two Solex carburetors
Maximum power: 115 bhp at 6,000 rpm
Maximum torque: 113 lb-ft at 4,500 rpm
Top speed: 112 mph
0-60 mph: 9.0 sec.

TRANSMISSION
Five-speed manual

BODY/CHASSIS
Unitary monocoque construction with steel two-door coupe body

SPECIAL FEATURES

A distinctive feature of the Fulvia is the center-mounted hood vent.

The Fulvia's V4 engine is slightly inclined toward the left.

RUNNING GEAR
Steering: Worm-and-sector
Front suspension: Unequal length wishbones with a transverse leaf spring, telescopic shock absorbers and anti-roll bar
Rear suspension: Beam axle with semi-elliptic leaf springs, Panhard rod, telescopic shock absorbers and anti-roll bar
Brakes: Discs (front and rear)
Wheels: Alloy, 5 x 14 in.
Tires: 165 SR-14

DIMENSIONS
Length: 156.5 in.   **Width:** 61.2 in.
Height: 51.2 in.   **Wheelbase:** 91.7 in.
Track: 54.7 in. (front), 52.6 in. (rear)
Weight: 1,874 lbs.

Land Rover RANGE ROVER

Nothing less than a masterstroke, the Range Rover was the world's first luxury 4x4 vehicle. As well as being one of the most capable off-roaders ever seen, it boasted a high-quality ride, a practical interior and luxurious equipment. It remained the one to beat for the next two decades.

"...excellent 4x4 performance."

"The driving qualities of the Range Rover really sold it to the public, because it's just as happy on the road as it is off it. The torquey V8 engine provides enough pull for excellent 4x4 performance and also enables it to cruise happily at 90 mph. The ride is superb, thanks to compliant coil springs and damping all around. On difficult surfaces the Range Rover has virtually no peers. It can climb steep hills and handle impossibly slippery surfaces."

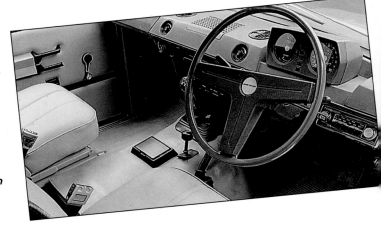

The inside of the Range Rover is more suited to dress shoes than muddy boots.

Milestones

1970 A truly innovative new 4x4
vehicle: that's the conclusion of the world's press on the launch of the Range Rover.

The Land Rover was the forerunner to the Range Rover.

1981 A four-door
bodyshell is added to the range.

1985 Fuel injection
and a four-speed automatic arrive.

1986 A 2.4-liter turbo-diesel engine joins
the V8 powerplant.

The new Range Rover, which made its debut in 1994, had a tough act to follow.

1987 The Range Rover goes on sale in the
U.S. and proves an instant hit.

1994 An all-new Range Rover is launched,
but the old model continues in production for one more year as the Range Rover Classic.

UNDER THE SKIN

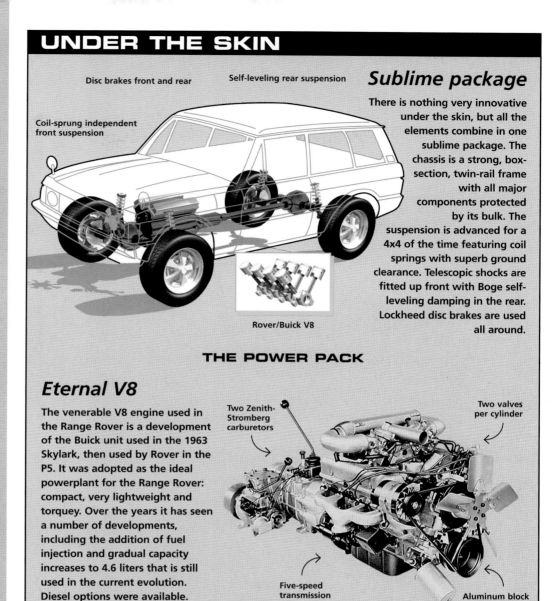

Disc brakes front and rear

Self-leveling rear suspension

Coil-sprung independent front suspension

Rover/Buick V8

Sublime package

There is nothing very innovative under the skin, but all the elements combine in one sublime package. The chassis is a strong, box-section, twin-rail frame with all major components protected by its bulk. The suspension is advanced for a 4x4 of the time featuring coil springs with superb ground clearance. Telescopic shocks are fitted up front with Boge self-leveling damping in the rear. Lockheed disc brakes are used all around.

THE POWER PACK

Eternal V8

The venerable V8 engine used in the Range Rover is a development of the Buick unit used in the 1963 Skylark, then used by Rover in the P5. It was adopted as the ideal powerplant for the Range Rover: compact, very lightweight and torquey. Over the years it has seen a number of developments, including the addition of fuel injection and gradual capacity increases to 4.6 liters that is still used in the current evolution. Diesel options were available.

Two Zenith-Stromberg carburetors

Two valves per cylinder

Five-speed transmission

Aluminum block and heads

001 testbed

The Range Rover featured is chassis number 001. Virtually handbuilt before official production started, the car was used as a testbed for components. Found in a barn, it has been meticulously restored to the original spec, including an authentic tool kit.

The off-road ability of the Range Rover was unmatched by its rivals.

Land Rover **RANGE ROVER**

The surprising thing about the Range Rover is not that it was voted the best 4x4 in the world by numerous magazines, but that it was still winning such awards more than 20 years after it was launched.

V8 engine

A detuned (low-compression) version of the perennial Rover/Buick V8 engine powers the Range Rover. Its lightness allows excellent weight distribution and its power and torque are perfect for its intended role.

Live floating axles

Both axles are live and floating, mainly for reasons of ground-clearance and simplicity. Coil springs are fitted front and rear, with Woodhead shocks up front and a Boge Hydromat self-leveling damper strut at the rear. This is because, although the Range Rover has perfect 50:50 weight distribution, the rear end, in some cases, sagged under heavy loads.

Permanent four-wheel drive

Unlike the Land Rover, the four-wheel drive system is permanently engaged, with a special Salisbury differential eliminating windup. The two-speed transfer gear shares the same casing as the main transmission, with a large difference between high and low speeds (2.83 to 1).

Luxurious feel

Compared to the 4x4 standards of its day, this was a very luxurious truck. Although the first Range Rovers had PVC trim and rubber floormats, the seats were well padded and there was an attractive, well-laid-out dash. As the years passed, the Range Rover grew steadily more luxurious, gaining leather upholstery, wood trim, air conditioning, air suspension and so on.

Excellent ground clearance

The lowest point on the Range Rover sits 7 inches above the ground, well out of the way of rocks and ruts. Most of the vulnerable components, such as the transmission and fuel tank, are situated well within the chassis frame for protection. The suspension itself is fairly soft, with up to 8 inches of travel.

Specifications

1970 Land Rover Range Rover

ENGINE

Type: V8

Construction: Aluminum block and heads

Valve gear: Two valves per cylinder operated by a single camshaft with pushrods and rockers

Bore and stroke: 3.50 in. x 2.80 in.

Displacement: 3,528 cc

Compression ratio: 8.5:1

Induction system: Two Zenith-Stromberg carburetors

Maximum power: 130 bhp at 5,000 rpm

Maximum torque: 205 lb-ft at 3,000 rpm

Top speed: 99 mph

0-60 mph: 12.9 sec.

TRANSMISSION

Four-speed manual driving all four wheels

BODY/CHASSIS

Separate chassis with steel and aluminum two-door station wagon body

SPECIAL FEATURES

Early Range Rovers came with a simple four-speed transmission as standard.

The V8 engine was detuned to optimize off-road performance.

RUNNING GEAR

Steering: Recirculating-ball

Front suspension: Live axle with leading arms, Panhard rod, coil springs and shock absorbers

Rear suspension: Live axle with A-bracket, radius arms, self-leveling strut, coil springs and shock absorbers

Brakes: Discs (front and rear)

Wheels: Steel, 16-in. dia.

Tires: 205 x 16

DIMENSIONS

Length: 176.0 in.   **Width:** 70.0 in.

Height: 70.0 in.   **Wheelbase:** 100.0 in.

Track: 58.5 in. (front and rear)

Weight: 3,864 lbs.

Lincoln CONTINENTAL MK V

Looking almost exactly like its Mastodon predecessor, the Mark V was in reality a much lighter car. It was still huge, however, but proved that even in the energy-conscious 1970s, some buyers still wanted big, luxury coupes.

"...glitz on four wheels."

"An appropriate description of the Mark V is perhaps 'glitz on four wheels.' Smooth velour upholstery and woodgrain trim take you back to the late-1970s disco era. Softly sprung, the Mark V pitches and wallows over bumpy roads and leans through corners. Although a smog-controlled engine lies under the hood, this Lincoln is still effortless to drive and never runs out of breath. It is big on the outside but feels intimate once you are inside."

The 1978 Diamond Jubilee edition has real ebony woodgrain and unique upholstery.

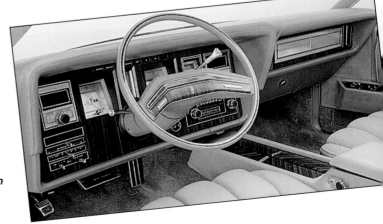

Milestones

1977 Although it looks almost the same as the Mk IV, the Continental Mk V is much lighter and has more trunk space. The standard engine is downsized to a 400-cubic inch unit, although the big 460 remains an option. Sales of the new coupe total 80,321, much better than the old Mk IV.

The first and most prestigious of all Continental coupes was the 1956-1957 Mark IIs.

1978 Celebrating Ford's 50th Anniversary, Lincoln rolls out a special Diamond Jubilee edition Mk V with unique paint and commemorative exterior and interior trim.

The crisp, clean 1968-71 Mk III was the first personal luxury Continental since the 1956 Mk II.

1979 The 460-cubic inch engine option is dropped and a Collector's Edition replaces the Diamond Jubilee model. In its final season, 75,939 Continental Mk Vs are built.

UNDER THE SKIN

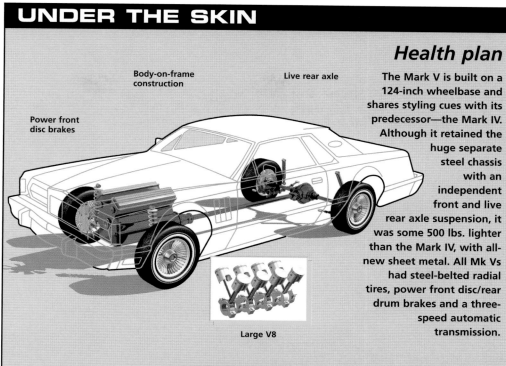

Body-on-frame construction

Power front disc brakes

Live rear axle

Large V8

Health plan

The Mark V is built on a 124-inch wheelbase and shares styling cues with its predecessor—the Mark IV. Although it retained the huge separate steel chassis with an independent front and live rear axle suspension, it was some 500 lbs. lighter than the Mark IV, with all-new sheet metal. All Mk Vs had steel-belted radial tires, power front disc/rear drum brakes and a three-speed automatic transmission.

THE POWER PACK

Massive V8 power

By the mid-1970s the automotive landscape was changing. Even so, the Continental Mk V was still powered by large-displacement engines: a standard 400-cubic inch V8 with 166 bhp or Lincoln's monster 460-cubic inch engine. This huge engine, an outgrowth of the 1950s vintage 430, was rated at just 210 bhp, due in part to a restrictive intake manifold, a single catalytic convertor and exhaust, plus a low 8.0:1 compression ratio. It was not available in 1979 models.

A lot for little

A popular car in the late 1970s, the Continental Mk V is not a favored collector's car, which means reason-ably priced examples can be easily found. Its blocky styling may not win you over initially, but it has a special character that modern cars cannot match.

Mk Vs were only built for three model years but they sold respectably.

Lincoln CONTINENTAL MK V

In an era where disco music and three-piece leisure suits were all the rage, the Continental Mk V with its designer trim and luxury gadgets was the perfect set of wheels for the upper-middle class.

Anniversary celebration

The Diamond Jubilee edition, offered exclusively for 1978, was distinguished by special Diamond Blue or Jubilee Gold metallic paint, body colored bumper strips, special opera windows and a lavish Valino vinyl covering on the trunk lid cove.

Mammoth V8

As one of the largest engines ever built, the 460-cubic inch V8 may have only had 210 bhp, but with 357 lb-ft of torque it was ideal for comfortable cruisers like the Mk V. Tough emissions regulations meant that this engine was not available on Mk Vs sold in California.

Steel-belted tires

By the mid-1970s, radial tires were a virtual industry standard. All Lincoln Mk Vs rode on Michelin BSW 225/230x15 steel-belted radials. Finned aluminum wheels were standard on the 1978 Diamond Jubilee edition.

Sure Track brakes

Sure Track four-wheel disc brakes were available as a $296 option in 1978. It was a smart add-on, especially in view of the Mk V's torquey engine and massive 2-ton curb weight.

Five-mph bumpers

From 1974, all cars were required to be able to withstand 5-mph shunts without sustaining damage. The Mk V has hefty steel bumpers mounted on hydraulic rams. They are pushed inward upon impact and bounce back to their original position.

Tall gearing

With corporate average fuel economy becoming an important part of the automotive industry, the Mk V was offered with tall rear axle ratios in an attempt to improve its gas mileage. A set of 2.75:1 rear gears were fitted to 400-powered cars, while those with the big 460 got even taller 2.50:1 cogs.

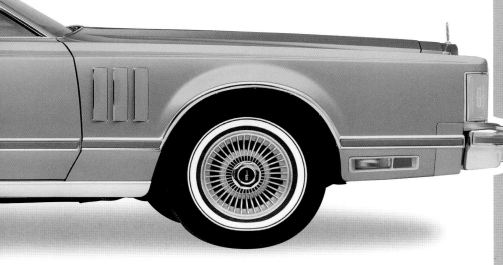

Specifications

1978 Lincoln Continental Mk V

ENGINE

Type: V8

Construction: Cast-iron block and heads

Valve gear: Two valves per cylinder operated by a single block-mounted camshaft with pushrods and rocker arms

Bore and stroke: 4.36 in. x 3.85 in.

Displacement: 460 c.i.

Compression ratio: 8.0:1

Induction system: Motorcraft 4350 four-barrel carburetor

Maximum power: 210 bhp at 4,200 rpm

Maximum torque: 357 lb-ft at 2,200 rpm

Top speed: 118 mph

0-60 mph: 9.8 sec.

TRANSMISSION

Select-Shift Cruise-O-Matic automatic

BODY/CHASSIS

Separate steel chassis with two-door coupe body

SPECIAL FEATURES

These non-functional fender air extractors are unique to the Mk V.

Even the hood ornament is color-coded on the Diamond Jubilee edition.

RUNNING GEAR

Steering: Recirculating ball

Front suspension: Unequal length A-arms with coil springs, telescopic shock absorbers and anti-roll bar

Rear suspension: Live axle, leaf springs and telescopic shock absorbers

Brakes: Discs (front), drums (rear)

Wheels: Cast-aluminum, 15-in. dia.

Tires: Michelin BSW 225/230 x 15

DIMENSIONS

Length: 230.3 in.   **Width:** 79.7 in.

Height: 54.7 in.   **Wheelbase:** 122.4 in.

Track: 63.2 in. (front), 62.6 in. (rear)

Weight: 4,567 lbs.

Lotus ELITE/ECLAT

The Elite and its sister, the Eclat, retained the Lotus flair for handling yet were more sophisticated, stylish and expensive than any earlier Lotus sports car. The four-seater sports coupes were also very practical.

"..finely balanced."

"Enthusiasts buy Lotus sports cars for one reason—their exquisite handling. Using the traditional backbone chassis, the Elite/Eclat displays all the virtues of the earlier Elan. Turn-in is crisp, the steering is communicative and the suspension taut enough to prevent significant body roll. Around corners it is finely balanced, and the engine is a gem, revving smoothly but with great strength. The driving position is tight, but for a four-seater with pure-bred manners, it has few peers."

The tight fitting cabin is very functional and, unusual for a sports car, can easily seat four.

Milestones

1974 Lotus launches its new
Elite. Its striking cutoff, wedge-shaped styling is designed by Oliver Winterbottom.

The Elite's styling was rigid and unusual for the 1970s.

1975 A fastback
version, the Eclat, is launched and is planned to sell at a lower price than the Elite.

1980 With the S2.2, the engine size is
expanded to 2,174 cc and it has a new transmission and deeper chin spoiler.

As a transition, the Excel was first sold as the Eclat Excel.

1982 The Elite body
shape is dropped, leaving only the Eclat Excel. Its name is changed to simply Excel. The tiny sports car continues in production until 1989.

UNDER THE SKIN

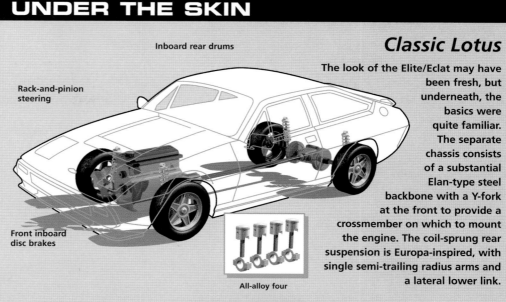

Inboard rear drums

Rack-and-pinion steering

Front inboard disc brakes

All-alloy four

Classic Lotus

The look of the Elite/Eclat may have been fresh, but underneath, the basics were quite familiar. The separate chassis consists of a substantial Elan-type steel backbone with a Y-fork at the front to provide a crossmember on which to mount the engine. The coil-sprung rear suspension is Europa-inspired, with single semi-trailing radius arms and a lateral lower link.

THE POWER PACK

All-new twin-cam

The Elite was the first Lotus to receive the then new 907 engine. With sturdy yet light aluminum-alloy construction, it uses four valves per cylinder—an atypical exercise at the time—and has twin overhead camshafts with solid lifters. With twin Zenith or Dellorto carburetors, the 1,973-cc engine initially developed 155 bhp, and later 160 bhp. In 1980, the engine was expanded to 2.2 liters and became known as the 912 engine. Power output remained the same but torque was drastically improved.

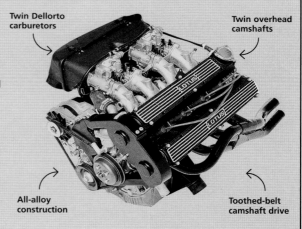

Twin Dellorto carburetors

Twin overhead camshafts

All-alloy construction

Toothed-belt camshaft drive

Torquey S2.2

As launched, the Elite and Eclat were available in a number of variations with different model codes and special options. For a more unique driving experience, the later S2.2 has torquier performance from its 2.2-liter engine and a much improved five-speed transmission.

The special edition Eclat Riviera has a lift-out roof panel.

Lotus ELITE/ECLAT

Moving Lotus firmly upmarket, the Elite and the later Eclat cast the company's first use of its fresh, 2.0-liter, twin-cam engine. In addition to the sophisticated engine, the sporty Lotus also receives a revised body.

Injection molding

A new fiberglass process was used for the Elite and Eclat, inspired by Colin Chapman's experience with boats. This was Vacuum-Assisted Resin Injection, in which fiberglass was laid into molds and the air expelled as the resin mix was injected.

New twin-cam engine

Although it had been seen before in the Jensen-Healey, the Elite was the first Lotus to get the 907 powerplant. At 1,973 cc (later 2,174 cc), it was larger and more powerful than previous Lotus engines.

In-house styling

The Elite and Eclat were known for their extraordinary wedge-shaped styling. They are the work of Oliver Winterbottom of Lotus and feature a complex interplay of very aerodynamically efficient curves and straight lines

Award-winning safety

Steel beams in the doors satisfied U.S. safety legislation and helped win the Elite the prestigious international Don Safety Award.

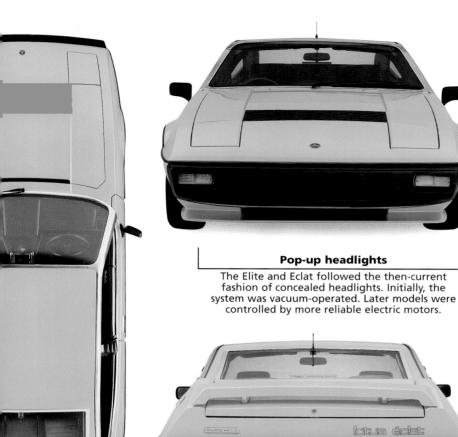

Pop-up headlights

The Elite and Eclat followed the then-current fashion of concealed headlights. Initially, the system was vacuum-operated. Later models were controlled by more reliable electric motors.

Luxurious interior

Giorgetto Giugiaro's ItalDesign orchestrated the interior's design. Like most Lotus cars, it is configured around a substantial center tunnel to clear the backbone chassis, but it succeeds in appearing light and airy. The cockpit is much more luxurious than previous Lotus cars.

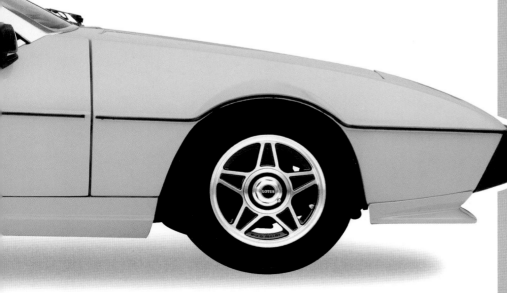

Specifications
1980 Lotus Eclat Riviera

ENGINE
Type: In-line four-cylinder
Construction: Aluminum block and head
Valve gear: Four valves per cylinder operated by twin overhead camshafts
Bore and stroke: 3.75 in. x 3.00 in
Displacement: 2,174 cc
Compression ratio: 9.4:1
Induction system: Two Dellorto twin-choke carburetors
Maximum power: 160 bhp at 6,500 rpm
Maximum torque: 160 lb-ft at 5,000 rpm
Top speed: 125 mph
0-60 mph: 9.7 sec

TRANSMISSION
Five-speed manual

BODY/CHASSIS
Separate backbone chassis with fiberglass two-door coupe body

SPECIAL FEATURES

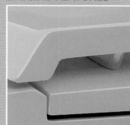

A rear deck spoiler breaks up the Eclat's straight and long fastback lines.

Alloy wheels are a standard requirement at this level—this five-spoke design is particularly effective.

RUNNING GEAR
Steering: Rack-and-pinion
Front suspension: Double wishbones with coil spring/shock absorber units and anti-roll bar
Rear suspension: Semi-trailing arms with lower links, fixed driveshafts and coil spring/shock absorber units
Brakes: Discs (front), drums (rear)
Wheels: Alloy, 14-in. dia.
Tires: 205/60 x 14

DIMENSIONS
Length: 175.5 in. **Width:** 71.5 in.
Height: 47.5 in. **Wheelbase:** 98.0 in.
Track: 58.5 in. (front), 59.0 in. (rear)
Weight: 2,540 lbs.

Maserati **INDY**

Designed to combine supercar looks and performance in a car that could hold four people, the Indy did the job and was one of the most respected high-speed cruisers of the 1970s.

"...high-speed stability."

"High-speed stability was important and even at over 150 mph there's no front end lift. The Indy is in its element on fast, open roads where the stiff shock absorbers work well and the live axle is no handicap. It's a different story on smaller roads, however. It's a bit unwieldy, but there are no nasty surprises with the handling, which is well balanced with slight understeer and minimal roll through corners. In the wet, however, the back slides easily."

The Indy's interior is well laid out and comfortable for grand touring.

Milestones

1949 Wilbur Shaw
wins the Indianapolis 500 in a Maserati 8CTF and repeats the win the following year.

1969 Twenty years
later Maserati takes inspiration from Shaw's wins by calling its new car the Indy. It appears first with the 260-bhp, 4.2-liter and the optional 330-bhp, 4.7-liter V8 engines. It is a Vignale-styled 2+2 coupe.

The Indy uses the same engine as the legendary Ghibli.

1973 The 335-bhp,
4.9-liter V8 is added to the range. Maserati settles on the larger engine size for the last of the Indy line.

The Khamsin replaced the Indy but was less successful.

1974 Production
ceases after more than 1,100 cars have been sold, making the Indy a real success story for Maserati.

UNDER THE SKIN

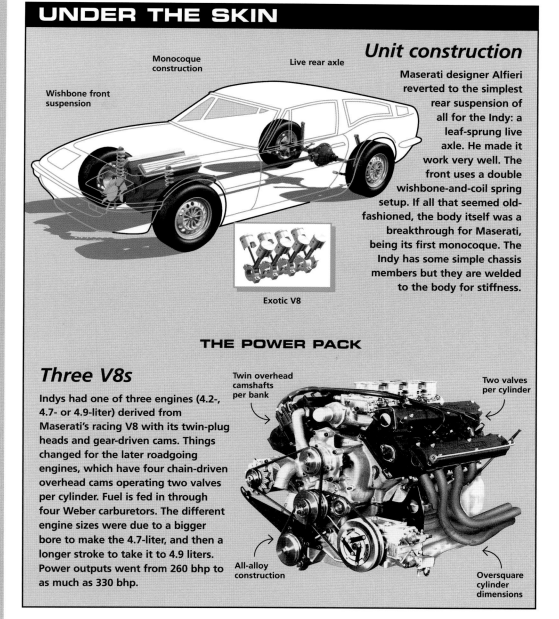

Monocoque construction

Live rear axle

Wishbone front suspension

Unit construction

Maserati designer Alfieri reverted to the simplest rear suspension of all for the Indy: a leaf-sprung live axle. He made it work very well. The front uses a double wishbone-and-coil spring setup. If all that seemed old-fashioned, the body itself was a breakthrough for Maserati, being its first monocoque. The Indy has some simple chassis members but they are welded to the body for stiffness.

Exotic V8

THE POWER PACK

Three V8s

Indys had one of three engines (4.2-, 4.7- or 4.9-liter) derived from Maserati's racing V8 with its twin-plug heads and gear-driven cams. Things changed for the later roadgoing engines, which have four chain-driven overhead cams operating two valves per cylinder. Fuel is fed in through four Weber carburetors. The different engine sizes were due to a bigger bore to make the 4.7-liter, and then a longer stroke to take it to 4.9 liters. Power outputs went from 260 bhp to as much as 330 bhp.

Twin overhead camshafts per bank

Two valves per cylinder

All-alloy construction

Oversquare cylinder dimensions

Revised Indy

The revised post-1973 Indy is the best. It has the 4.9-liter V8, along with an improved ZF transmission and revised power-assisted steering. At the same time, a high-pressure brake system was added and the suspension settings were altered to improve the handling.

Post-1973 Indys are much improved over earlier models.

Maserati **INDY** ⬛⬛

**The Indy was a blend of the old and new, the advanced and the crude.
The new was the switch to a monocoque design without a chassis, advanced
was the quad-cam engine, but old-fashioned was the sprung rear axle.**

V8 engine

The Indy's engine is a descendent of Maserati's
racing V8. The same engine was also used in the
Ghibli and the mid-engined Bora.

Vented discs

The Indy is both fast and heavy and
so the brakes needed to be large.
Maserati fitted 11.6-inch diameter
vented discs up front and 10.7-inch
discs at the rear.

Live axle

Previous Maseratis had de Dion axles or a
well-located live axle with coil springs and
radius arms. But the Indy has simple semi-
elliptic leaf springs with radius arms to
help locate the axle.

Rear hatchback

Maserati wanted the Indy to be a practical
supercar so it has an opening rear hatch.
Because of the sloping back of the car, though,
only 6.6 cubic feet of luggage can be carried.
An optional cover could be ordered to keep
the luggage out of sight.

Pop-up lights

One oddity of the Indy's pop-up lights is that even if the driver just wants side lights on to indicate his presence, the headlight pods have to be raised.

Twin fuel tanks

Fuel is carried in two tanks, one on each side at the rear, with a total capacity of 26 gallons. There is a switch inside the car to change from one tank to the other and the fuel gauge is adjusted accordingly.

Unitary construction

All previous Maseratis had been built using a separate chassis, but the Indy marked the move to unitary construction where the body takes the place of the chassis. It was an interim design though, retaining some vestigial chassis elements onto which the body was welded.

Specifications

1972 Maserati Indy

ENGINE

Type: V8

Construction: Alloy block and heads

Valve gear: Two valves per cylinder operated by four overhead camshafts

Bore and stroke: 3.70 in. x 3.35 in.

Displacement: 4,719 cc

Compression ratio: 8.8:1

Induction system: Four Weber carburetors

Maximum power: 330 bhp at 5,000 rpm

Maximum torque: 325 lb-ft at 4,000 rpm

Top speed: 155 mph

0-60 mph: 7.5 sec.

TRANSMISSION

ZF five-speed manual

BODY/CHASSIS

Unitary steel construction with two-door four-seater hatchback body

SPECIAL FEATURES

The Indy's pop-up headlight units contain two lights each.

The large glass area is a distinctive part of the Indy's Vignale styling.

RUNNING GEAR

Steering: Recirculating ball

Front suspension: Wishbones with coil springs, telescopic shock absorbers and anti-roll bar

Rear suspension: Live axle with semi-elliptic leaf springs, telescopic shock absorbers and anti-roll bar

Brakes: Vented discs, 11.6-in. dia. (front)10.72 in. (rear)

Wheels: Alloy 7.5 x 14.0 in.

Tires: 205 x 14

DIMENSIONS

Length: 186.6 in.   **Width:** 69.2 in.

Height: 48.0 in.   **Wheelbase:** 102.5 in.

Track: 58.2 in. (front), 53.5 in. (rear)

Weight: 3,465 lbs.

Maserati **BORA**

The Bora marked Maserati's move into the modern world in the early 1970s. It was the company's first mid-engined supercar and was designed to compete with exotic mid-engined rivals from Ferrari and Lamborghini.

"...mid-engined V8 performer."

"Almost an Italian muscle car rather than a supercar, the Bora has a lot in common with the De Tomaso, employing a big V8 engine instead of a high-revving 12 cylinder engine. The V8 has masses of torque and powers the Bora to 100 mph in just 15 seconds. The car cruises comfortably at high speeds, but its stiff springing results in a hard ride. Although it has very responsive steering, it takes a brave driver to throw the Bora around."

The Bora's interior is comfortable, but unfortunately it has hard-to-read instruments.

Milestones

1968 Citroën becomes
Maserati's major shareholder and gives the firm financial strength to consider exciting new models. Maserati agrees to build two mid-engined cars, the V6 Merak and V8 Bora.

1971 The Bora
makes its world debut at the Geneva Show in March, and enters production soon after.

Maserati's 4.7-liter V8 also powers the beautiful Ghibli.

1974 Long after
being sold in Europe, the Bora is finally made suitable for the American market. The larger 4.9-liter V8 satisfies the more stringent emissions and safety requirements.

Smaller than the Bora, the Merak features V6 power.

1980 Production of
the Bora finally comes to an end.

UNDER THE SKIN

Old and new

Chassis construction is a mix of monocoque and a separate body-on-the-frame. The center and front sections are a folded steel monocoque, but the rear is a tubular steel structure carrying the longitudinally mid-mounted engine, transmission, and suspension. The entire rear of the car can be detached for maintenance.

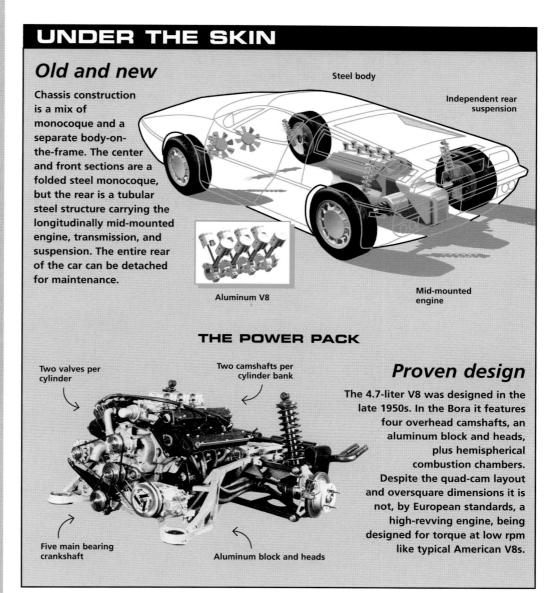

Steel body

Independent rear suspension

Aluminum V8

Mid-mounted engine

THE POWER PACK

Two valves per cylinder

Two camshafts per cylinder bank

Five main bearing crankshaft

Aluminum block and heads

Proven design

The 4.7-liter V8 was designed in the late 1950s. In the Bora it features four overhead camshafts, an aluminum block and heads, plus hemispherical combustion chambers. Despite the quad-cam layout and oversquare dimensions it is not, by European standards, a high-revving engine, being designed for torque at low rpm like typical American V8s.

Bigger engine

In 1974 a bigger, 4.9-liter version of the V8 was used in Boras destined for the U.S. The larger engine was required to satisfy economy and emissions laws. Available in European trim from 1976, it produces 10 bhp extra and naturally offers more performance.

Although it had a long production run, only 570 Boras were built.

143

Maserati BORA 🇮🇹

The Bora, which is the Italian name for a strong wind, has a slippery shape and slices through the air at speeds of up to 160 mph thanks to its 310 bhp quad-cam V8 engine.

V8 engine

The Bora's V8 engine is as large as a typical American V8 of the time but is made of alloy instead of cast-iron and has four overhead camshafts. It is a more complicated but exciting way of producing 310 bhp from 4.7 liters.

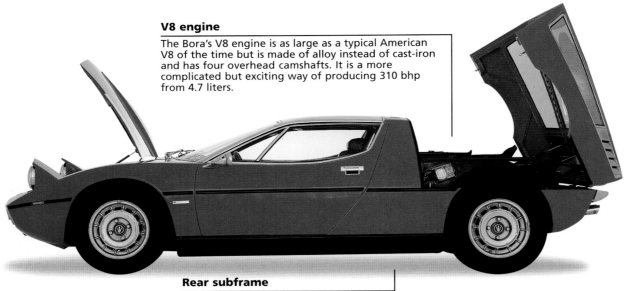

Rear subframe

At the rear, a welded-up square tube structure is used to support the engine, transmission and rear suspension.

Early alloy bodies

The very first Boras were produced with hand-crafted alloy bodies, a skill Maserati was well versed in. Standard production Boras, however, have steel bodies.

Transmission behind engine

German manufacturers ZF supplied the transmission, which is mounted behind the engine toward the tail of the car. This requires a longer and more complicated gear linkage.

Vented discs

Both front and rear brakes are discs, as is common on Italian supercars of the 1970s. They are also vented to improve cooling and to prevent fade.

Aerodynamic shape

Even though the Bora never went anywhere near a wind tunnel, designer Giorgetto Giugiaro achieved a drag coefficient of just 0.30.

Front-mounted radiator

Unlike later mid-engined cars, the Bora has a front-mounted radiator with electric fans.

Specifications
1973 Maserati Bora

ENGINE
Type: V8
Construction: Light alloy block and heads
Valve gear: Two inclined valves per cylinder operated by four chain-driven overhead camshafts via bucket tappets
Bore and stroke: 3.69 in. x 3.35 in.
Displacement: 4,719 cc
Compression ratio: 8.5:1
Induction system: Four Weber DCNF/14 downdraft carburetors
Maximum power: 310 bhp at 6,000 rpm
Maximum torque: 325 lb-ft at 4,200 rpm
Top speed: 160 mph
0-60 mph: 6.5 sec.

TRANSMISSION
Five-speed ZF manual

BODY/CHASSIS
Steel unitary construction front sections with square-tube rear frame; steel two-door coupe body

SPECIAL FEATURES

The flat rear end or 'Kamm tail' was a popular feature on 1970s supercars.

The Bora was an early Giorgetto Giugiaro design.

RUNNING GEAR
Steering: Rack-and-pinion
Front suspension: Double wishbones with coil springs, telescopic shocks and anti-roll bar
Rear suspension: Double wishbones with coil springs, telescopic shocks and anti-roll bar
Brakes: Vented discs (front and rear), with Citroën high-pressure hydraulics
Wheels: Alloy, 7.5 in. x 15 in.
Tires: Michelin 215/70 VR15

DIMENSIONS
Length: 170.4 in.   **Width:** 68.1 in.
Height: 44.6 in.   **Wheelbase:** 102 in.
Track: 58 in. (front), 57 in. (rear)
Weight: 3,570 lbs.

Maserati **MERAK**

As an answer to Ferrari's highly successful Dino, Maserati produced the V6 Merak. It was an unusual sports car but was extraordinarily handsome and solid as well.

"...sharp oversteer."

"The gutsy V6 engine behind you may not have sounded as good as a Ferrari powerplant, but it does provide good acceleration. The gearing allows for very comfortable cruising as well as spirited 0-60 mph acceleration. The strangest thing about driving it is the on-off brake feel, which takes some getting used to. Handling is typical of a mid-engined car: initial understeer followed by sharp oversteer can be controlled with power, but it's tricky to drive at the limit."

Well trimmed seats and creature comforts make the cabin a pleasant environment.

Milestones

1972 Maserati launches the Merak, a junior version of its Bora supercar.

The Citroën SM shared parts with the Merak including the V6 and transmission.

1975 As Citroën pulls out of Maserati, Alejandro De Tomaso steps in. A more powerful Merak SS with a 220 bhp engine is released. Other changes include the adoption of the Bora's dash for all Meraks.

The Merak was based on the V8 powered Bora and shared its inner structure.

1980 The Merak is withdrawn from the U.S. market.

1982 Production of the Bora ends though some leftover cars continue to be sold into 1983.

UNDER THE SKIN

Bora basis

The structure of the Merak from the roof forward was inherited from the V8 Bora, which meant a steel unitary chassis with a rear subframe, and Ingeniere Alfieri's superb all-independent suspension by wishbones and coil springs. The Citroen influence can be felt in the hydraulically operated power clutch and braking systems, plus the five-speed transmission, which was also shared with the Citroen SM.

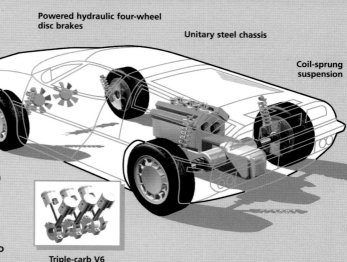

Powered hydraulic four-wheel disc brakes

Unitary steel chassis

Coil-sprung suspension

Triple-carb V6

THE POWER PACK

Under the influence

When the Merak was conceived, Maserati was owned by Citroën, which dictated the choice of powerplant: the V6 from SM, which was effectively a Maserati engine with two cylinders and a slice off the end. With a displacement of 2,965 cc, triple carburetors and dual overhead camshafts per bank, it's certainly a potent powerplant, developing 190 bhp (182 bhp in the U.S. due to strict emissions controls). A more powerful V6 arrived in 1974 in Europe, as part of the Merak SS. With bigger carburetors and a higher 9.0:1 compression ratio it produced a healthy 220 bhp. In Italy, an affordable 1,999-cc V6 engine with 159 bhp was offered.

SS supercar

The more powerful, and rarer, SS version is the most desirable for collectors and driving enthusiasts. It elevates this small rocket ship into true junior supercar territory rather than being merely a swift sports car.

The sporty Merak SS offers buyers excellent value.

Maserati MERAK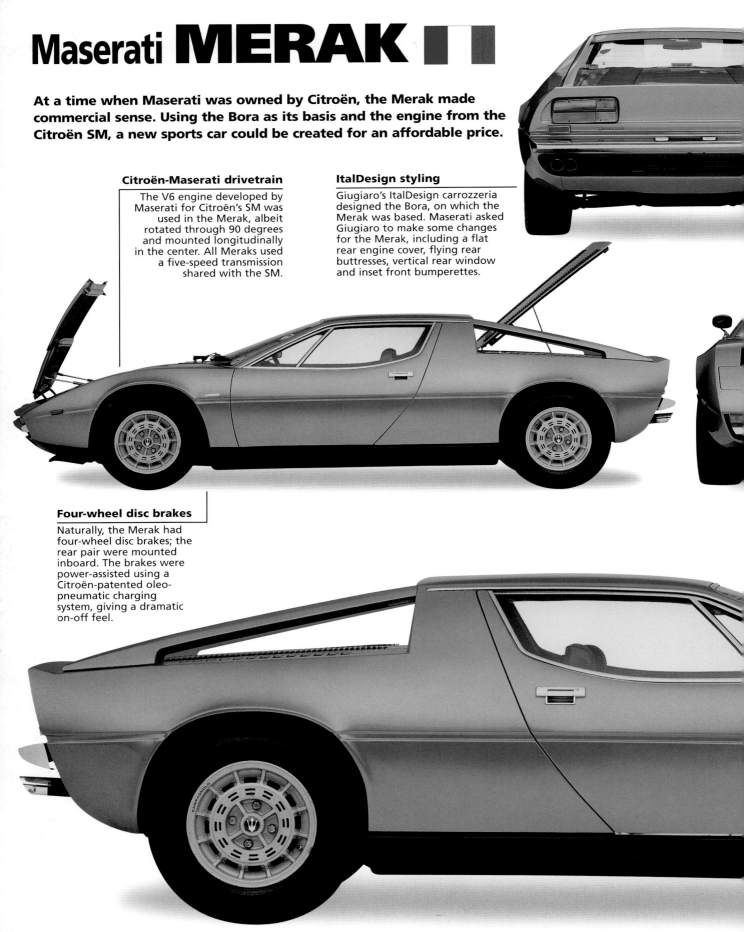

At a time when Maserati was owned by Citroën, the Merak made commercial sense. Using the Bora as its basis and the engine from the Citroën SM, a new sports car could be created for an affordable price.

Citroën-Maserati drivetrain

The V6 engine developed by Maserati for Citroën's SM was used in the Merak, albeit rotated through 90 degrees and mounted longitudinally in the center. All Meraks used a five-speed transmission shared with the SM.

ItalDesign styling

Giugiaro's ItalDesign carrozzeria designed the Bora, on which the Merak was based. Maserati asked Giugiaro to make some changes for the Merak, including a flat rear engine cover, flying rear buttresses, vertical rear window and inset front bumperettes.

Four-wheel disc brakes

Naturally, the Merak had four-wheel disc brakes; the rear pair were mounted inboard. The brakes were power-assisted using a Citroën-patented oleo-pneumatic charging system, giving a dramatic on-off feel.

Concealed headlights

Like the Bora, the Merak features pop-up headlights. This enabled a low nose profile while at the same time satisfying height requirements for lighting in the U.S.

2+2 accommodation

Officially, the Merak is classed as a 2+2, unlike the strictly two-seater Bora. However, the packaging restrictions of the midmounted engine mean that space in the rear is extremely tight, even for children.

Citroën hydraulics

The Merak was designed around certain Citroën hydraulic components, including the clutch and brakes. The result was quite an unusual driving experience compared to other Italian exotics of the 1970s.

Specifications

1977 Maserati Merak SS

ENGINE

Type: V6

Construction: Aluminum block and heads

Valve gear: Two valves per cylinder operated by chain-driven dual overhead camshafts

Bore and stroke: 3.61 in. x 2.95 in.

Displacement: 2,965 cc

Compression ratio: 8.5:1

Induction system: Three Weber 44DNCF carburetors

Maximum power: 182 bhp at 6,000 rpm

Maximum torque: 180 lb-ft at 4,000 rpm

Top speed: 141 mph

0-60 mph: 9.1 sec.

TRANSMISSION

Five-speed manual

BODY/CHASSIS

Unitary monocoque construction with steel two-door coupe body

SPECIAL FEATURES

Because the nose has a low, wedged shape, the headlights had to pop up to reach regulation height.

The long and angled side glass styling is all part of the Merak's appeal.

RUNNING GEAR

Steering: Rack-and-pinion

Front suspension: Double wishbones with coil springs, shock absorbers and anti-roll bar

Rear suspension: Double wishbones with coil springs, shock absorbers and anti-roll bar

Brakes: Discs (front and rear)

Wheels: Alloy, 15-in. dia.

Tires: 205/70 (front), 215/70 (rear)

DIMENSIONS

Length: 180.0 in. **Width:** 69.6 in.

Height: 44.6 in. **Wheelbase:** 102.3 in.

Track: 58.0 in. (front), 56.9 in. (rear)

Weight: 3,185 lbs.

Mercedes **450 SEL 6.9**

Big, powerful luxury sedans are what Mercedes-Benz is most famous for. In its day the 450 SEL had only one peer—the company's own 6.9-liter model with its mighty V8 engine and ultra-soft ride. With a price tag that was more than twice as much as its rivals, the 450 SEL 6.9 was a very expensive machine.

"...a very satisfying drive."

"It doesn't take long for the superb qualities of the 6.9 to emerge. There's a terrific surge of power offering performance that seems unnatural for a car of this size. And it's all delivered in an unusually refined manner through an excellent automatic transmission. The steering has all the benefits of low-speed maneuverability but still has a reassuring feel at higher speeds. This car offers a very satisfying drive over a broad range of areas."

The 6.9 has power windows and steering, air-conditioning, cruise control and a sunroof.

Milestones

1975 Three years after the demise of the 300 SEL 6.3, Mercedes-Benz launches a belated successor in the shape of the 450 SEL 6.9.

The 450 SEL 6.9 replaced Mercedes' previous luxury hot rod, the 300 SEL 6.3.

1977 The 6.9 reaches the U.S. market.

The luxury S Class superseded the old 450 SEL 6.9.

1980 Production of the 6.9 ends and the entire S-Class range is replaced. The 6.9 has done its job by establishing a reputation for Mercedes-Benz as a master of the top-level sport luxury cars. The new S-Class range is set for the success that is to follow.

UNDER THE SKIN

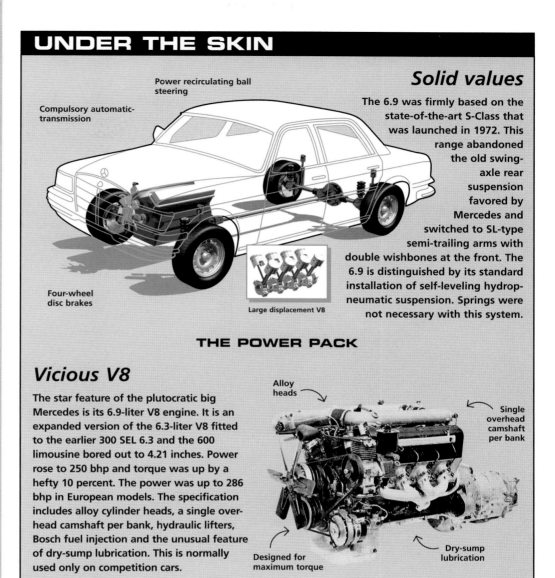

Power recirculating ball steering

Compulsory automatic-transmission

Four-wheel disc brakes

Large displacement V8

Solid values

The 6.9 was firmly based on the state-of-the-art S-Class that was launched in 1972. This range abandoned the old swing-axle rear suspension favored by Mercedes and switched to SL-type semi-trailing arms with double wishbones at the front. The 6.9 is distinguished by its standard installation of self-leveling hydropneumatic suspension. Springs were not necessary with this system.

THE POWER PACK

Vicious V8

The star feature of the plutocratic big Mercedes is its 6.9-liter V8 engine. It is an expanded version of the 6.3-liter V8 fitted to the earlier 300 SEL 6.3 and the 600 limousine bored out to 4.21 inches. Power rose to 250 bhp and torque was up by a hefty 10 percent. The power was up to 286 bhp in European models. The specification includes alloy cylinder heads, a single overhead camshaft per bank, hydraulic lifters, Bosch fuel injection and the unusual feature of dry-sump lubrication. This is normally used only on competition cars.

Alloy heads

Single overhead camshaft per bank

Designed for maximum torque

Dry-sump lubrication

Top quality

The 6.9 holds a hallowed place in Mercedes-Benz history. With the exception of the 600 limousine, it was the Stuttgart car maker's finest offering during the 1970s. It still holds a strong fascination for collectors, but you'll need to ensure that it has been well maintained.

A 6.9 is typically worth 50 percent more than a standard 450 SEL.

Mercedes **450 SEL 6.9**

Many automobile road testers believed that the 450 SEL 6.9 was the best car in the world when it was new. Its huge V8 endowed it with sports car-humbling performance and its elegantly engineering made it a real driver's car.

6.9-liter engine

At 6,834 cc, the V8 motor was easily the largest produced by Mercedes-Benz since 1945. In Europe the output was 286 bhp, though in the U.S., emissions restrictions knocked 36 bhp off that figure.

Vacuum central locking

The main advantage of Mercedes-Benz's vacuum-operated central locking system over conventional power setups is that it was extremely quiet. It was also more reliable in service.

Four-wheel disc brakes

The 450 SEC 6.9 takes full advantage of four-wheel disc brakes. There are 10.9-inch vented discs up front and 11.0-inch solid discs at the rear while a vacuum servo provides power assistance. Along with other S-Class models, the 450 SEC 6.9 became one of the first cars to be offered with ABS. It was introduced as an option in 1979.

Split air-conditioning

The driver and front passenger have separate temperature controls so that a different ambience can be created on each side of the cabin.

Self-leveling suspension

The 6.9 has standard self-leveling suspension, using a system of hydropneumatics. Remote gas-filled reservoirs are connected to the struts, so whatever the load, the ride height is always maintained. A switch on the fascia can also alter the ride height smoothing out even the roughest terrain.

ENGINE
Type: V8
Construction: Cast-iron block and aluminum cylinder heads
Valve gear: Two valves per cylinder operated by a single overhead camshaft per bank
Bore and stroke: 4.21 in. x 3.74 in.
Displacement: 6,834 cc
Compression ratio: 8.0:1
Induction system: Bosch mechanical fuel injection
Maximum power: 250 bhp at 4,000 rpm
Maximum torque: 360 lb-ft at 2,500 rpm
Top speed: 140 mph
0-60 mph: 7.1 sec.

TRANSMISSION
Three-speed automatic

BODY/CHASSIS
Unitary monocoque construction with steel four-door sedan body

SPECIAL FEATURES

Like other 1970s Mercedes, the 450 SEL has the trademark ribbed taillights.

The V8 engine has a very large bore and is capable of revving quite high.

RUNNING GEAR
Steering: Recirculating ball
Front suspension: Double wishbones with hydropneumatic struts and anti-roll bar
Rear suspension: Semi-trailing arms with hydropneumatic struts and anti-roll bar
Brakes: Discs (front and rear)
Wheels: Alloy, 14-in. dia.
Tires: 215/70 VR14

DIMENSIONS
Length: 210.0 in.   **Width:** 73.6 in.
Height: 55.5 in.   **Wheelbase:** 116.5 in.
Track: 59.9 in. (front), 59.3 in. (rear)
Weight: 4,390 lbs.

Mercury COUGAR ELIMINATOR

A true performance Cougar emerged in 1969 and continued through 1970. Available with a long list of sports options, it posed a considerable threat to the established muscle cars both on the street and at the drag strip. Despite its potential, the Eliminator is often overlooked by enthusiasts today.

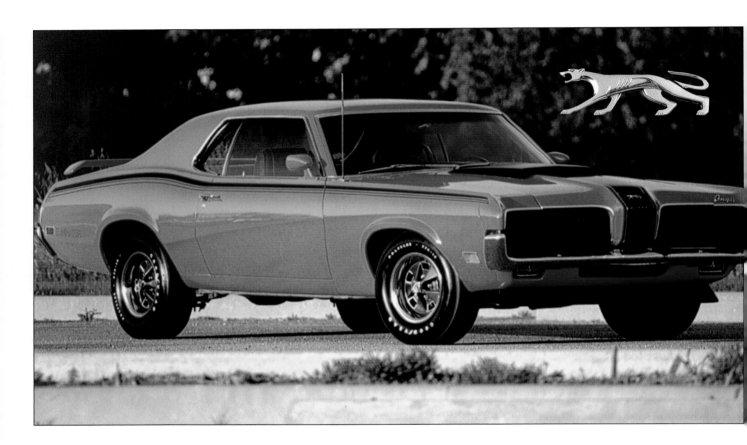

"...a gentleman's muscle car."

"With its wood-rimmed steering wheel and full instrumentation, the Cougar appears to be a gentleman's muscle car. Starting up the monster 428 engine reveals a totally different character. The big engine demands high-octane fuel and concentration on the open road. Its greatest asset is the huge amount of mid-range torque. A drag racer's dream, it is enough to humble any would-be challenger. It's quick enough to run the ¼ mile in 14.1 seconds."

This Eliminator has base model trim and is fitted with vinyl seats instead of leather ones.

Milestones

1967 Two years after
Mustang, Mercury launches its own pony car, the Cougar. It features a distinctive front end with a razor-style grill and hidden headlights. Initially it is offered only as a hardtop.

Mercury's other 1969 muscle car was the Cyclone. This one is a Spoiler II.

1969 After minor updates
for 1968, the Cougar is restyled the following year and a convertible is now offered. A high performance model, the Eliminator, is launched mid-year and is available with a host of extra performance options, and was painted with 'high impact' exterior colors such as yellow blue, and orange.

The Cougar share the 302 and 428 engines with the Mustang.

1970 The Eliminator
returns for its second and final season. Its body restyling is more refined than the 1969 model. Just over 2,000 cars are sold and the model is dropped after only two years of production.

UNDER THE SKIN

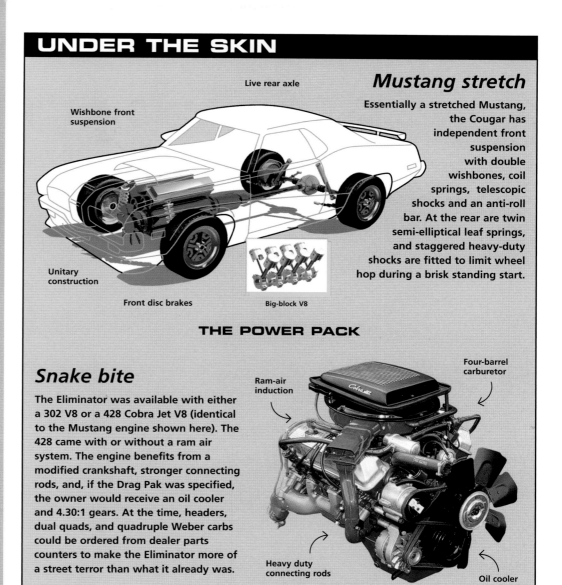

Live rear axle

Wishbone front suspension

Mustang stretch
Essentially a stretched Mustang, the Cougar has independent front suspension with double wishbones, coil springs, telescopic shocks and an anti-roll bar. At the rear are twin semi-elliptical leaf springs, and staggered heavy-duty shocks are fitted to limit wheel hop during a brisk standing start.

Unitary construction

Front disc brakes

Big-block V8

THE POWER PACK

Snake bite
The Eliminator was available with either a 302 V8 or a 428 Cobra Jet V8 (identical to the Mustang engine shown here). The 428 came with or without a ram air system. The engine benefits from a modified crankshaft, stronger connecting rods, and, if the Drag Pak was specified, the owner would receive an oil cooler and 4.30:1 gears. At the time, headers, dual quads, and quadruple Weber carbs could be ordered from dealer parts counters to make the Eliminator more of a street terror than what it already was.

Ram-air induction

Four-barrel carburetor

Heavy duty connecting rods

Oil cooler

Street racer
Since the Eliminator is longer and heavier than the Mustang, it is able get more grip and harness the power from the mighty 428 V8. Though the engine had a factory rating of 335 bhp it actually made closer to 410. The lower rating was to fool insurance companies.

The 1970 Eliminator is offers more refined body panels than the 1969 car.

Mercury COUGAR ELIMINATOR

This is Mercury's version of the high-performance Mustang. More refined than its baby brother, it still keeps the Ford heritage with bright paint, side stripes, spoilers, a hood scoop, and big block power.

Staggered shocks

Axle tramp can be a serious problem with smaller-sized performance Fords from this era, especially those with big engines. The Cougar Eliminator has staggered rear shock absorbers to help overcome this problem.

'High Impact' paintwork

'High Impact' exterior colors was the order of the day in 1970. The Cougar was available in bright blue, yellow and Competition Orange as seen here.

Cobra Jet engine

The Eliminator is available with either the 290-bhp Boss 302 or the more stout 428 Cobra Jet with a conservatively rated 335 bhp. This example is powered by the larger 428, often thought of as one of the finest muscle car engines ever produced.

Interior trim

Although more luxurious than the Mustang, the Eliminator is a base model Cougar and has vinyl upholstery. Full instrumentation is standard and includes a tachometer.

Drag Pak

This Eliminator is garnished with the legendary 'Drag Pak' option, which includes the 428 Super Cobra Jet engine, an oil cooler, and ultra-low rear-end gearing (3.91:1 or 4.30:1). This makes the Cougar one of the fastest accelerating muscle cars.

Restyled front

For 1970 the Cougar received a revised front grill with vertical bars and a more pronounced nose. The tail panel was also slightly altered.

Sequential turn indicators

The rear indicators, which are also combined with the brake lights, flash in sequence when the driver flicks the lever. These are also found on contemporary Shelby Mustangs.

Specifications
1970 Mercury Cougar Eliminator

ENGINE
Type: V8
Construction: Cast-iron block and heads
Valve gear: Two valves per cylinder operated by pushrods and rockers
Bore and stroke: 4.0 in. x 3.5 in.
Displacement: 428 c.i.
Compression ratio: 10.6:1
Induction system: Four-barrel carburetor
Maximum power: 335 bhp at 5,200 rpm
Maximum torque: 440 lb-ft at 3,400 rpm
Top speed: 106 mph
0-60 mph: 5.6 sec

TRANSMISSION
C-6 Cruise-O-Matic

BODY/CHASSIS
Steel monocoque two-door coupe body

SPECIAL FEATURES

The headlights are concealed behind special 'flip-up' panels.

A rear Cougar spoiler is standard Eliminator equipment.

RUNNING GEAR
Steering: Recirculating ball
Front suspension: Unequal length wishbones with coil springs, telescopic shocks and anti-roll bar
Rear suspension: Semi-elliptical multi-leaf springs with staggered rear telescopic shocks
Brakes: Discs (front), drums (rear)
Wheels: Styled steel, 5 x 14 in.
Tires: F60-14 Goodyear Polyglas GT

DIMENSIONS
Length: 191.6 in.   **Width:** 77.6 in.
Height: 52.8 in.   **Wheelbase:** 111 in.
Track: 60 in. (front), 60 in. (rear)
Weight: 3,780 lbs.

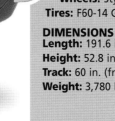

MGB **GT V8**

Fitting a Rover V8 into the MGB was a great idea, one famously tried by engine tuner Ken Costello. Later, in 1973, MG tried it. The result was a high-performing sports car that doubled as a top-notch grand tourer.

"...a fine period GT."

"Flexibility is the keynote with the MGB GT V8. Its big-capacity engine chugs willingly from very low revs and delivers a strong punch through the gears. Although cruising at speed is relaxed, some aspects of the car betray the age of the basic design. The ride quality suffers because of harder springing, plus oversteer and traction can be problems due to the V8's power and torque. In other respects, however, this is a fine period GT car."

Wood and leather, the hallmarks of a British sports car, grace the MGB V8's interior.

Milestones

1973 British Leyland takes note

of the many specialist MGB V8 conversions and launches its own B GT V8.

The smallest member of the MG family was the Midget.

1974 In common with other MGBs,

new rubber bumpers are used, and the ride height is raised to conform with U.S. federal laws.

The V8 finally made its way into the roadster body in 1992, when the MG RV8 was launched.

1976 After disappointing sales,

the V8 model is withdrawn. The four-cylinder MGB lasts for another four years, however.

1980 After an incredibly long

production run, the final MGBs are built at British Leyland's Abingdon factory.

UNDER THE SKIN

Leaf-sprung live rear axle

Stiffer front springs

Power brakes

All-alloy V8

Beefed-up 'B'

The MGB GT V8 can trace its origins right back to the 1955 MGA, whose combination of wishbone front suspension with coil springs and lever-arm shocks and a live rear axle with semi-elliptic leaf springs was pretty effective. The suspension pickup points were altered to gain an extra inch of height over the regular GT. A brake servo, electric cooling fans and an oil cooler are included in the package.

THE POWER PACK

Lightweight V8

British Leyland had tried fitting a larger engine into an MGB before—the MGC of 1967-1969 had a straight-six unit. But shoehorning in the ex-Buick V8 gave much more satisfactory results. As fitted to the MGB GT, it runs a low compression ratio (shared with the version used in the Range Rover) and two SU carburetors. Maximum power is 137 bhp and torque is 193 lb-ft. An all-alloy unit, it is a little heavier than the cast-iron four-cylinder engine and does not upset the car's weight distribution or balance.

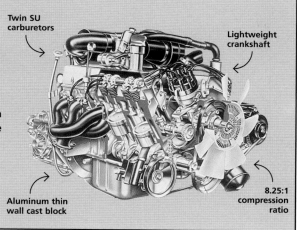

Twin SU carburetors

Lightweight crankshaft

Aluminum thin wall cast block

8.25:1 compression ratio

Early is better

To some, the GT V8 is the best MGB of all. It was never offered in ragtop form, but the torquey engine more than makes up for this. Early chrome-bumper models are more collectable, but the later rubber-bumper cars can be picked up for a lot less money.

The rubber-bumper MGB GT V8s are more affordable than earlier cars.

MGB **GT V8**

The MGB GT V8 should have been a greater success than it was. Yet this Rover V8-engined MG was the most satisfying to drive of all the 'B' family—beefy, relaxed and still reasonably sporty.

V8 engine

The installation of a slightly detuned all-alloy Rover V8 engine in the MGB GT bodyshell resulted in a well-balanced grand touring machine.

Overdrive transmission

The four-speed manual transmission came standard with a Laycock overdrive on top gear. This alters the ratio of the direct-drive (1:1) fourth gear to 0.82:1.

Classic body shape

The basic body shape of the GT was unchanged for the V8. This was not a bad thing, as the shape was timeless, thanks to its good proportions and practical flavor.

Comfortable interior

The roomy cabin of the 2+2 MGB is little altered, although it has smaller instruments and a speedometer calibrated to 140 mph. Standard equipment includes tinted windows, twin door mirrors and a heated rear window. The only option was inertia reel seatbelts.

Ideal weight distribution

By mounting the engine far back in the engine bay, a near-perfect 50:50 weight distribution is achieved.

Stiffened suspension

Although the suspension layout is identical to that of the (rather antiquated) MGB, the spring rates are adjusted at the rear to compensate for the extra torque.

Specifications
1973 MGB GT V8

ENGINE
Type: V8

Construction: Aluminum block and heads

Valve gear: Two valves per cylinder operated by a single camshaft

Bore and stroke: 3.50 in. x 2.80 in.

Displacement: 3,528 cc

Compression ratio: 8.25:1

Induction system: Two SU carburetors

Maximum power: 137 bhp at 5,000 rpm

Maximum torque: 193 lb-ft at 2,900 rpm

Top speed: 125 mph

0-60 mph: 8.6 sec

TRANSMISSION
Four-speed manual with overdrive

BODY/CHASSIS
Unitary monocoque construction with steel two-door coupe body

SPECIAL FEATURES

The all-alloy V8 weighs little more than the four-cylinder unit.

Unique wheels help distinguish the V8 from lesser-engined MGBs.

RUNNING GEAR
Steering: Rack-and-pinion

Front suspension: Double wishbones with coil springs, shock absorbers and anti-roll bar

Rear suspension: Live axle with semi-elliptic leaf springs and shock absorbers

Brakes: Discs (front), drums (rear)

Wheels: Alloy, 14-in. dia.

Tires: 175/70 HR14

DIMENSIONS
Length: 154.7 in. **Width:** 60.0 in.

Height: 50.0 in. **Wheelbase:** 91.0 in.

Track: 49.0 in. (front), 49.3 in. (rear)

Weight: 2,387 lbs.

NSU **RO80**

It was a brave move by NSU to build one of the most advanced sedans in the world. Powered by a rotary engine and using a semi-automatic transmission, it ruined the small company before the car was perfected.

"...the ride is wonderful."

"The first culture shock is the NSU's semi-automatic transmission; rest your hand on the shifter by mistake and the clutch disengages and the engine winds up, but if you use it properly the clutchless shift is simple and reliable. Like all rotary engines, the Ro80 loves to rev up toward its 7,000 rpm redline. Typically for a Wankel, you have to rev it hard for acceleration. For its time, the Ro80 set new standards in handling and road-holding abilities. At high speeds it's immensely stable and the Ro80 can hustle along country roads at high speed."

Unlike the avant-garde nature of the body styling and mechanicals, the Ro80 cabin has a 1960s design.

Milestones

1964 NSU produces
the tiny Bertone-bodied Spider to gain experience with rotary engines.

1966 Spider proves
good enough to win the German Hillclimb Championship and its class in the German GT Championship. About 2,000 Spiders are eventually sold.

Ro80's shape was highly advanced for its day.

1967 Debut of the
new Ro80 at the Frankfurt Show, using a larger, twin-rotor, version of the Wankel rotary engine producing 115 bhp.

1968 Rotor-tip wear
starts putting Ro80 engines out of operation at just 15,000 miles.

1969 Rotary engine
redesigned, with a single spark plug per rotor, transistorized ignition, and better rotor sealing. Audi-NSU is acquired by VW.

1977 Sales of the
Ro80 fall so low that VW stops production, even though the car is the group's executive flagship.

UNDER THE SKIN

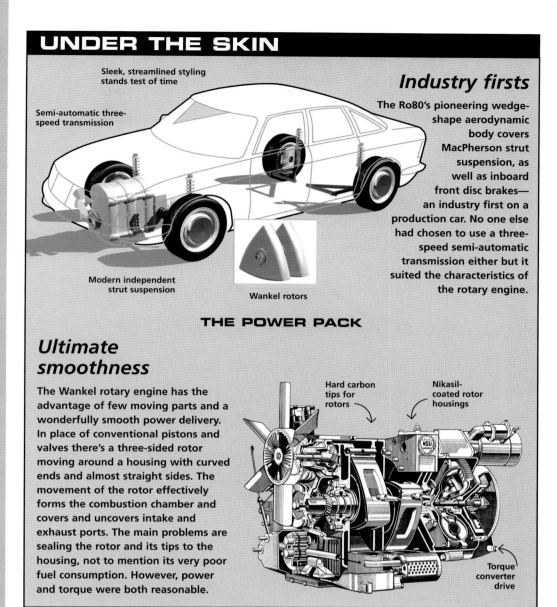

Sleek, streamlined styling stands test of time

Semi-automatic three-speed transmission

Modern independent strut suspension

Wankel rotors

Industry firsts

The Ro80's pioneering wedge-shape aerodynamic body covers MacPherson strut suspension, as well as inboard front disc brakes—an industry first on a production car. No one else had chosen to use a three-speed semi-automatic transmission either but it suited the characteristics of the rotary engine.

THE POWER PACK

Ultimate smoothness

The Wankel rotary engine has the advantage of few moving parts and a wonderfully smooth power delivery. In place of conventional pistons and valves there's a three-sided rotor moving around a housing with curved ends and almost straight sides. The movement of the rotor effectively forms the combustion chamber and covers and uncovers intake and exhaust ports. The main problems are sealing the rotor and its tips to the housing, not to mention its very poor fuel consumption. However, power and torque were both reasonable.

Hard carbon tips for rotors

Nikasil-coated rotor housings

Torque converter drive

Durability

By the end of production life in the late-1970s, the mechanical problems had been overcome. Where the original engines sometimes failed by 15,000 miles, later models could exceed more than 100,000 miles. Most collectors invariably choose later built Ro80s.

With engine troubles solved, the comfortable Ro80 became quite a catch.

NSU **RO80**

There are few cars designed in the 1960s which still look and feel modern. If only NSU had fully developed the rotary engine properly before production, it might have succeeded.

Power steering

With the Ro80 being so nose-heavy and designed for the luxury market, power assistance had to be included to make the steering lighter.

MacPherson strut suspension

The Ro80 was designed to be very comfortable and has MacPherson struts at the front. Much more unusually, it has them at the rear, too.

Rotary engine

Many manufacturers, including GM, evaluated the idea of rotary engines, but only NSU and Mazda put it into production. The Ro80's 995 cc is equivalent to a 1,990 cc conventional engine.

Inboard front discs

To reduce unsprung weight, the front discs are mounted inboard alongside the transmission.

Wider front track

The front track is wider than the rear as more weight is carried on the front. A wider track helped handling and roadholding.

Semi-automatic transmission

Although Mazda always used conventional transmissions with its rotary engines, NSU opted for a three-speed semi-automatic. This did little to help the dreadful fuel consumption.

Aerodynamic shape

The NSU's shape was developed in the wind tunnel at Stuttgart Technical University. The result was a wedge shape with a drag coefficient of 0.33.

Specifications
1974 NSU Ro80

ENGINE
Type: Rotary twin
Construction: Alloy rotor housing
Valve gear: Single exhaust and inlet port per rotor covered and uncovered as the rotor passes
Compression ratio: 9.0:1
Induction system: Single Solex 32 DT ITS carburetor
Maximum power: 115 bhp at 5,500 rpm
Maximum torque: 121 lb-ft at 4,500 rpm
Top speed: 110 mph
0-60 mph: 13.4 sec

TRANSMISSION
Three-speed semi-automatic with torque converter

BODY/CHASSIS
Steel monocoque with four-door sedan body

SPECIAL FEATURES

Alloy wheels were not common on sedans in the 1960s and 1970s. The optional cast-alloy wheels on this car are typical of 1970s styling.

The origins of the Ro80 name are quite simple—'Ro' stands for rotary engine, 80 is the car's design number.

RUNNING GEAR
Steering: Rack-and-pinion
Front suspension: MacPherson struts, lower wishbones and anti-roll bar
Rear suspension: MacPherson struts and semi-trailing arms
Brakes: Four-wheel discs, 11.1 in. dia. (front), 10.7 in. dia. (rear)
Wheels: Steel or optional alloy, 5 in. x 14 in.
Tires: 175SR14

DIMENSIONS
Length: 190 in.   **Width:** 69.5 in.
Height: 55.5 in.   **Wheelbase:** 112.7 in.
Track: 58.5 in. (front), 56.5 in. (rear)
Weight: 2,695 lbs.

Front heavy
Although the rotary engine is very compact, it is mounted ahead of the front axle line helping to give the Ro80 a front-heavy weight distribution of 63/37 front to rear.

Rear disc brakes
In the late-1960s rear drum brakes were common on most cars, but the Ro80 benefitted from four-wheel discs.

Opel **MANTA**

In the late 1960s, Opel set out to transform its dull family-car image. An important weapon in that fight came in the shape of the fast, fine-handling and attractive Manta, which was an instant success.

"...immediate throttle response."

"Mantas have the performance to match their looks. Maximum power may be only 75 bhp, but the engine is smooth and has lots of low-down torque giving immediate throttle response. The four-speed transmission is quick in action and the clutch is light. Its best feature is the way it handles: almost neutral with mild understeer. The steering is accurate and there is next to no roll, even through quick corners."

Black vinyl bucket seats and deeply set gauges convey a true 1970s feel. An automatic transmission was an option.

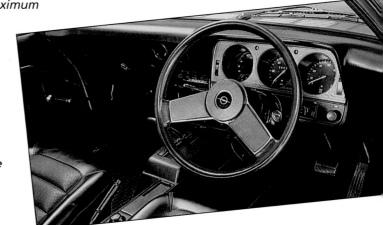

Milestones

1970 In September, Opel introduces some serious competition for the fast-selling Ford Capri with its new two-door Manta. Two engines are used: an 80-bhp 1.6-liter and the more powerful 1.9-liter four-cylinder with an extra 10 bhp.

The sportiest Opel prior to the Manta was the 1968-1973 GT.

1972 The first significant change comes

with the introduction of the Berlinetta version, which has a vinyl roof and the option of a three-speed automatic.

The Mk II Manta GT/E remained in production until 1988.

1974 Broadspeed in England produces

a Turbo Manta, building approximately 50 of the 125-mph models with a deep front spoiler and alloy wheels.

1975 It is the end of the road

for the first Manta, which is replaced by the longer Mk II.

UNDER THE SKIN

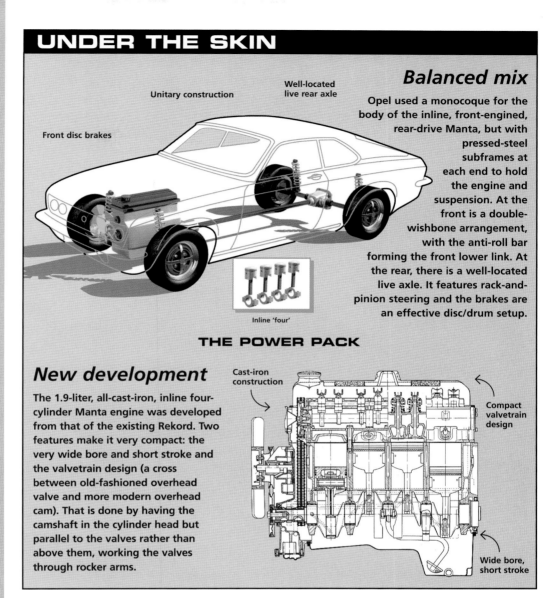

Front disc brakes

Unitary construction

Well-located live rear axle

Inline 'four'

THE POWER PACK

Balanced mix

Opel used a monocoque for the body of the inline, front-engined, rear-drive Manta, but with pressed-steel subframes at each end to hold the engine and suspension. At the front is a double-wishbone arrangement, with the anti-roll bar forming the front lower link. At the rear, there is a well-located live axle. It features rack-and-pinion steering and the brakes are an effective disc/drum setup.

New development

The 1.9-liter, all-cast-iron, inline four-cylinder Manta engine was developed from that of the existing Rekord. Two features make it very compact: the very wide bore and short stroke and the valvetrain design (a cross between old-fashioned overhead valve and more modern overhead cam). That is done by having the camshaft in the cylinder head but parallel to the valves rather than above them, working the valves through rocker arms.

Cast-iron construction

Compact valvetrain design

Wide bore, short stroke

Turbo option

Fastest and most collectible of all early Mantas is one of the rare Turbo versions produced for Dealer Opel Team by UK specialist Ralph Broad's Broadspeed firm. It has a Holset turbo blowing through the carburetor to give 156 bhp.

Broadspeed conversion models are rare but can easily reach 125 mph.

Opel MANTA

Opel was very clever with the Manta's design. It is a very stylish two-door coupe—almost a fastback—but despite the exaggerated slope to the rear roofline, it is still easily big enough for four people.

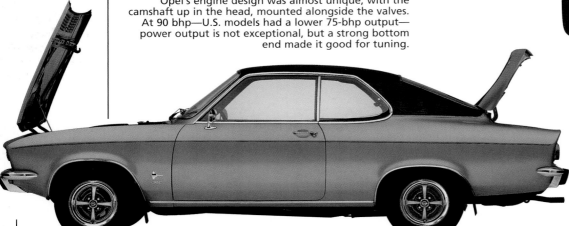

Four-cylinder engine

Opel's engine design was almost unique, with the camshaft up in the head, mounted alongside the valves. At 90 bhp—U.S. models had a lower 75-bhp output—power output is not exceptional, but a strong bottom end made it good for tuning.

Rack-and-pinion steering

A superior part of the Manta's engineering was the adoption of rack-and-pinion steering. Although it is fairly high geared (taking 4 turns lock to lock), it still feels relatively quick to sporty drivers.

Four-speed transmission

With a good spread of power and torque, the Manta could get by with a four-speed transmission and a cable-operated, rather than hydraulic, clutch. It was not until the the 1980s that Mantas were offered with five speeds from the factory.

Four headlights

Important styling features are the quad circular headlights and narrow front grill design. These give it the appearance of a miniature muscle car and undoubtedly helped sales.

Live axle

Opel took a lot of trouble to make the live-axle suspension as good as possible, so it is located by trailing links, a Panhard rod, a torque tube and an anti-roll bar.

Steel wheels

Although the Manta was meant to be a sporty car, Opel gave it ordinary pressed-steel wheels with 5.5-inch wide rims. The Broadspeed turbo conversions done in England did, however, feature alloy wheels.

Specifications
1971 Opel
Manta Rallye

ENGINE
Type: Inline four-cylinder
Construction: Cast-iron block and head
Valve gear: Two valves per cylinder operated by a single head-mounted camshaft with rockers
Bore and stroke: 3.66 in. x 2.75 in.
Displacement: 1,897 cc
Compression ratio: 7.6:1
Induction system: Single Solex two-barrel carburetor
Maximum power: 90 bhp at 5,100 rpm
Maximum torque: 108 lb-ft at 2,800 rpm
Top speed: 102 mph
0-60 mph: 11.2 sec.

TRANSMISSION
Four-speed manual

BODY/CHASSIS
Unitary monocoque construction with front and rear subframes and steel coupe body

SPECIAL FEATURES

A vinyl roof accentuates the lines of the swoopy Manta GT coupe.

Rear taillights mimic those found on the contemporary Chevy Corvette.

RUNNING GEAR
Steering: Rack-and-pinion
Front suspension: Double wishbones with coil springs, telescopic shock absorbers and anti-roll bar
Rear suspension: Live axle with trailing arms, coil springs, telescopic shock absorbers, Panhard rod and roll bar
Brakes: Discs (front), drums (rear)
Wheels: Pressed-steel disc, 5.5 x 13 in.
Tires: Radial, 185/70 HR13

DIMENSIONS
Length: 176.1 in. **Width:** 64.3 in.
Height: 53.3 in. **Wheelbase:** 95.8 in.
Track: 52.4 in. (front), 52.0 in. (rear)
Weight: 2,150 lbs.

Peugeot **504 CABRIOLET**

Combining reliable French mechanicals with stylish, Italian-built bodywork, the Peugeot 504 Cabriolet represents the best of both worlds. It was one of the most civilized open cars of its generation.

"...broad band of torque."

"The fuel injected four-cylinder engine installed in most of the 504 Coupes and Cabriolets might sound uninspired, yet it manages to move the car along on a healthy broad band of torque so you never feel the need to rev it hard. The gear shift is a little notchy but positive in action and allied to a light, well-cushioned clutch. The car has good manners, too. The best thing about the 504 is the ride; a fine combination of firm damping and soft springs."

By the mid-1970s, Peugeot had earned a reputation for supportive, comfortable seats.

Milestones

1969 Early cars have a
1,796-cc 404 injection engine and column hand brake. In 1970, a 2.0-liter model with a new hood scoop appears.

The 504 sedan became the staple diet of the French middle class.

1974 The Mk 2 model is
distinguished by long, single headlights, flush door handles and one-piece back lights. It appears first as a carburetor-fed, 2.6-liter PRV V6, then the 2.0-liter four-cylinder is reintroduced when the V6 fails to sell in sufficient numbers during the fuel crisis.

Production of the smaller 304 Cabriolet ran from 1970 to 1975.

1978 Color-coded bumpers
are fitted on all models.

1982 The interior is more
upmarket, including different dials and a veneer dash. Production ends in 1983.

UNDER THE SKIN

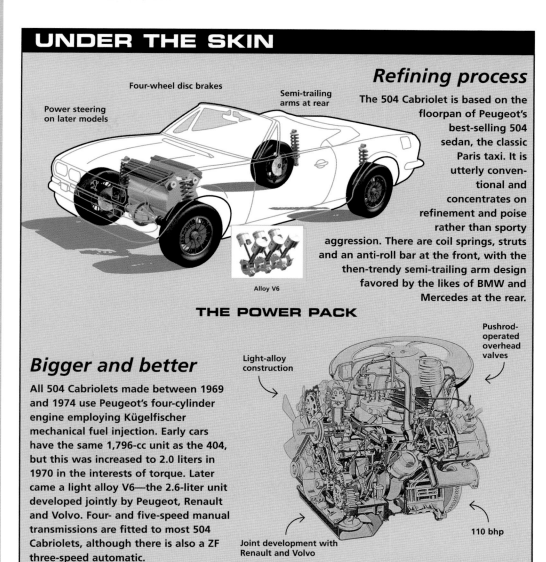

Four-wheel disc brakes

Power steering on later models

Semi-trailing arms at rear

Alloy V6

Refining process

The 504 Cabriolet is based on the floorpan of Peugeot's best-selling 504 sedan, the classic Paris taxi. It is utterly conventional and concentrates on refinement and poise rather than sporty aggression. There are coil springs, struts and an anti-roll bar at the front, with the then-trendy semi-trailing arm design favored by the likes of BMW and Mercedes at the rear.

THE POWER PACK

Bigger and better

All 504 Cabriolets made between 1969 and 1974 use Peugeot's four-cylinder engine employing Kügelfischer mechanical fuel injection. Early cars have the same 1,796-cc unit as the 404, but this was increased to 2.0 liters in 1970 in the interests of torque. Later came a light alloy V6—the 2.6-liter unit developed jointly by Peugeot, Renault and Volvo. Four- and five-speed manual transmissions are fitted to most 504 Cabriolets, although there is also a ZF three-speed automatic.

Light-alloy construction

Pushrod-operated overhead valves

Joint development with Renault and Volvo

110 bhp

Franco-Italian bond

Peugeot has an association with the Italian stylist and coachbuilder Pininfarina that goes back to the early 1950s and the handsome 403 sedan. There are coupe and cabriolet versions of this model too, with bodywork actually produced in Italy at Pininfarina's Turin factory. Today, Pininfarina styling is still found on some modern Peugeots.

Clean, elegant lines are the hallmark of classic Pininfarina design.

Peugeot **504 CABRIOLET**

Smooth and comfortable, the handsome Pininfarina-styled 504 Cabriolet has a sophisticated rather than sporty image. It was a long-lived model with few direct rivals, though rust has depleted its numbers dramatically.

Dependable four-cylinder

Most 504s have Peugeot's rugged in-line four-cylinder engine fitted. It is reliable and has endured, but it lacks aggressive character: it is a cruiser rather than a sprinter.

Refined suspension

Few open-top cars ride as well as the 504 Cabriolet, which mixes firm damping with soft springs. Road noise is minimal and the car is remarkably free of cowl shake, even by today's standards.

Pininfarina badging

These badges in front of the rear wheel cutouts indicate that the 504 was built as well as styled by Pininfarina at the company's factory in Turin, alongside the fixed-head coupe version.

Smooth, elegant profile

The timeless, good-looking shape of the 504 was penned by Pininfarina in the late 1960s. There is an individuality about that firm's designs of the time—you can see styling hints of the Fiat Dino and 124 Spider.

Excellent top

The 504's top looks handsome when up, and, perhaps more important, it folds neatly out of sight, leaving a clean side profile.

Left-hand drive only

The 504 Cabriolet left the factory with the steering wheel on the left-hand side only, although a few models, like this one, were converted to right hand drive for the British market by a specialist company. These RHD exports ceased in 1974.

Comfortable interior

The 504 has big sedan style seats with soft cushions that hug the torso and make for a comfortable ride.

Specifications
Peugeot 504 Cabriolet

ENGINE
Type: In-line four-cylinder
Construction: Iron block and alloy head
Valve gear: Two valves per cylinder operated by a single camshaft via pushrods and rockers
Bore and stroke: 3.46 in. x 3.19 in.
Displacement: 1,971 cc
Compression ratio: 8.3:1
Induction system: Kügelfischer mechanical fuel injection
Maximum power: 110 bhp at 5,600 rpm
Maximum torque: 131 lb-ft at 3,000 rpm
Top speed: 111 mph
0-60 mph: 12.0 sec.

TRANSMISSION
Five-speed manual or four-speed automatic

BODY/CHASSIS
Steel monocoque two-door convertible

SPECIAL FEATURES

Mark 1 models are distinguished by their four-light front end design.

Pronounced cowl scoops gather air for the ventilation system.

RUNNING GEAR
Steering: Rack-and-pinion
Front suspension: MacPherson struts with coil springs, telescopic shock absorbers and anti-roll bar
Rear suspension: Semi-trailing arms, coil springs, telescopic shock absorbers and anti-roll bar
Brakes: Discs, 10.75-in. dia. (front and rear)
Wheels: Steel, 4.35 x 14 in.
Tires: Michelin XAS, 175/70 HR14

DIMENSIONS
Length: 172.0 in.   **Width:** 67.0 in.
Height: 55.0 in.   **Wheelbase:** 100.4 in.
Track: 58.7 in. (front), 56.3 in. (rear)
Weight: 2,685 lbs.

Plymouth **SUPERBIRD**

Developed from the budget Road Runner coupe, the Superbird was designed to defeat Ford's Talladegas in NASCAR superspeedway races. Shortly after Plymouth's powerful rocket appeared, NASCAR had changed the rules, and Superbirds were only allowed to race the 1970 season.

"...NASCAR racing warrior."

"Plymouth built more than 1,935 Superbirds as a follow up to Dodge's less-than-victorious 1969 Daytonas that were designed to slaughter Ford's Talladegas. The strikingly similar looking Superbird proved to be a NASCAR racing warrior. The aluminum wing, flush mounted rear window, Hemi engine, and 18-inch metal nose cone all added up to victory in 1970. In race trim at speeds in excess of 190 mph, the Superbird's nose cone actually added more weight to the front wheels, while the rear wing had to be properly adjusted or the rear tires would wear prematurely."

Stock Superbirds had typical Plymouth interiors with only the necessary gauges, console and shifter.

Milestones

1963 Chrysler decides
to take on Ford in NASCAR. As owners of Plymouth and Dodge, they had the 426-cubic inch Hemi V8 engine, whose power should have been enough to guarantee supremacy.

1964-68 Power alone
is not enough. On stock car ovals, Ford's supremacy continues because their cars have better aerodynamics.

1969 Dodge Charger
Daytona appears with a rear wing giving downforce to keep the car on the track at 200 mph speeds. They win 18 NASCAR races this year. Unfortunately, Ford takes home more than 30.

The Superbirds proved their worth on the superspeedways.

1970 Superbird has
better aerodynamics than the Dodge Charger and wins 21 races (including the Daytona 500) and beating Ford. Not very many people liked its unusual styling, so many were stripped of their wings and nose cones and turned back into Road Runners just so Plymouth could sell them.

1971 NASCAR rules,
designed to keep racing equal, impose a 25 percent engine volume restriction on rear-winged cars, which spells the end of the Superbird in competition.

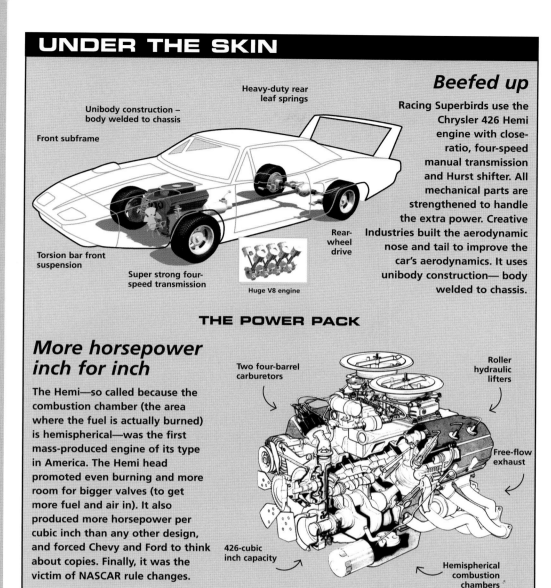

UNDER THE SKIN

Heavy-duty rear leaf springs

Unibody construction – body welded to chassis

Front subframe

Torsion bar front suspension

Super strong four-speed transmission

Huge V8 engine

Rear-wheel drive

Beefed up

Racing Superbirds use the Chrysler 426 Hemi engine with close-ratio, four-speed manual transmission and Hurst shifter. All mechanical parts are strengthened to handle the extra power. Creative Industries built the aerodynamic nose and tail to improve the car's aerodynamics. It uses unibody construction— body welded to chassis.

THE POWER PACK

More horsepower inch for inch

The Hemi—so called because the combustion chamber (the area where the fuel is actually burned) is hemispherical—was the first mass-produced engine of its type in America. The Hemi head promoted even burning and more room for bigger valves (to get more fuel and air in). It also produced more horsepower per cubic inch than any other design, and forced Chevy and Ford to think about copies. Finally, it was the victim of NASCAR rule changes.

Two four-barrel carburetors

Roller hydraulic lifters

Free-flow exhaust

426-cubic inch capacity

Hemispherical combustion chambers

Vinyl Top

Did you ever notice that all Superbirds had vinyl tops? Plymouth was in a hurry to homologate these cars for NASCAR racing. Instead of properly doing the body work around the flush mounted rear window, it just hid the rough body work with a vinyl top.

The fender scoops cover a cut out giving better tire clearance at high speeds.

Plymouth SUPERBIRD

The Superbird could achieve over 200 mph on the race track using the vital downforce generated by the huge rear wing. Even the tamer street version could easily reach 140 mph.

Roll cage
The NASCAR version used a tubular roll cage welded to the frame that stiffened it tremendously as well as protected the driver at 200 mph.

Rear suspension
Asymmetric rear leaf springs (the front third was stiffer than the rear two-thirds) helped locate the rear axle.

Four-speed transmission
Heavy-duty four-speed Chrysler model 883 was the strongest transmission available at the time.

Standard steel wheels
Steel wheels are still standard in NASCAR—wider 9.5 inch x 15 inch are used now, 15 inch x 7 inch when the Superbird ran. All NASCAR tires then were bias ply with inner tubes.

Live rear axle
Dana-built rear axle was originally intended for a medium-duty truck. Even in drag racing, the mighty Hemi could break it.

High-mounted rear wing
The rear wing provided downforce at the rear. Its angle was adjustable—too much and the increased force would shred the tires.

Front suspension

Front torsion bars resulted in better front suspension than competitors.

Cowl induction

Carburetor intake air was picked up from the high-pressure area at the base of the windshield—called cowl induction.

Aerodynamic nose

The nose was designed to lower drag and increase top speed while adding downforce—it actually put more weight on the front as speed increased.

Specifications
1970 Plymouth Superbird

ENGINE
Type: Hemi V8
Construction: Cast-iron block and heads; hemispherical combustion chambers
Valve gear: Two valves per cylinder operated by single block-mounted camshaft
Bore and stroke: 4.25 in. x 3.74 in.
Displacement: 426 c.i.
Compression ratio: 12:1
Induction system: Two four-barrel carbs, aluminum manifold
Maximum power: 425 bhp at 5,000 rpm
Maximum torque: 490 lb-ft at 4,000 rpm
Top speed: 140 mph
0-60 mph: 6.1 sec.

TRANSMISSION
Torqueflite three-speed auto plus torque converter or Mopar 883 four-speed manual

BODY/CHASSIS
Steel channel chassis welded to body with bolted front subframe

SPECIAL FEATURES

Front spoiler overcomes front-end lift.

The rear wing's height means it operates in less-disturbed airflow.

RUNNING GEAR
Steering: Recirculating ball steering, power-assisted on road cars
Front suspension: Double wishbones with torsion bars and telescopic shocks
Rear suspension: Live axle with asymmetric leaf springs and telescopic shocks
Brakes: Vented discs 11 in. dia. (front), drums 11 in. dia. (rear)
Wheels: Steel disc, 7 in. x 15 in.
Tires: Goodyear 7.00/15

DIMENSIONS
Length: 218 in.   **Width:** 76.4 in.
Wheelbase: 116 in.
Height: 59.4 in. (including rear wing)
Track: 59.7 in. (front), 58.7 in. (rear)
Weight: 3,841 lbs.

Plymouth **DUSTER 340**

At the end of the 1960s the Chrysler Corporation attempted to create a new entry-level muscle car. This was achieved by combining the powerful 340-cubic inch V8 with a light, two-door version of the Plymouth Valiant bodyshell to create the high-performance Duster 340.

"...a budget street racer."

"The Duster 340, Plymouth's budget muscle machine, is in essence a down-sized Road Runner. The 340-cubic inch V8 provides smooth power delivery and is capable of embarrassing drivers of other high-performance cars. Combined with a Torqueflite automatic transmission, it makes the Duster a perfect low-cost street racer. Standard front disc brakes provide exceptional stopping power, and the torsion bar suspension is extremely rugged."

Like all Plymouth cars, the Duster's interior is simple but very functional.

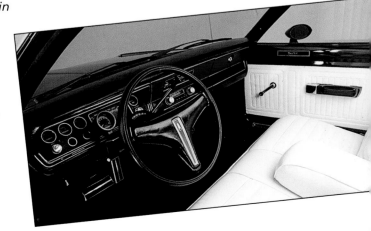

Milestones

1970 Plymouth division introduces its Valiant-based Duster 340, with a swoopy coupe body and a high-power V8. With 275 bhp and a $3,300 list price, it is one of the best muscle car bargains of the year.

In 1971 Dodge introduced a Duster clone, the Demon 340.

1971 Performance is unchanged, but the appearance is updated with the addition of a vertical bar grill, vivid graphics and an optional hood with huge '340' script.

The Challenger T/A was also powered by a 340-cubic inch V8 but it used three two barrels.

1972 New power and emissions regulations take their toll and power is at 230 bhp.

1974 The Duster 340 is replaced by the Duster 360 with a larger V8 producing 245 bhp. Performance Dusters are retired after 1976.

UNDER THE SKIN

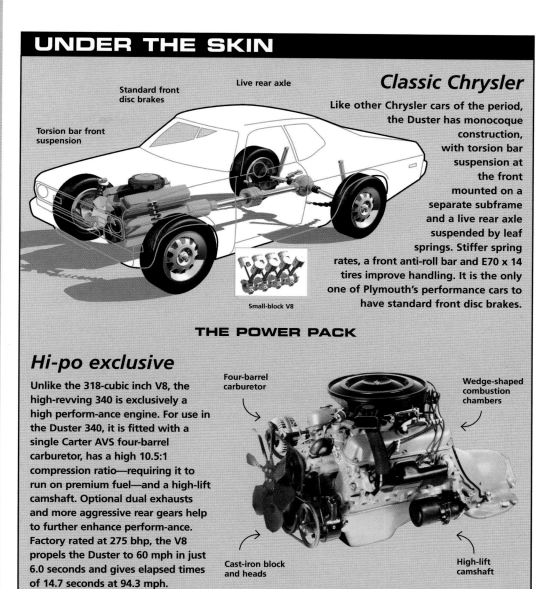

Standard front disc brakes

Live rear axle

Torsion bar front suspension

Small-block V8

Classic Chrysler

Like other Chrysler cars of the period, the Duster has monocoque construction, with torsion bar suspension at the front mounted on a separate subframe and a live rear axle suspended by leaf springs. Stiffer spring rates, a front anti-roll bar and E70 x 14 tires improve handling. It is the only one of Plymouth's performance cars to have standard front disc brakes.

THE POWER PACK

Hi-po exclusive

Unlike the 318-cubic inch V8, the high-revving 340 is exclusively a high perform-ance engine. For use in the Duster 340, it is fitted with a single Carter AVS four-barrel carburetor, has a high 10.5:1 compression ratio—requiring it to run on premium fuel—and a high-lift camshaft. Optional dual exhausts and more aggressive rear gears help to further enhance perform-ance. Factory rated at 275 bhp, the V8 propels the Duster to 60 mph in just 6.0 seconds and gives elapsed times of 14.7 seconds at 94.3 mph.

Four-barrel carburetor

Wedge-shaped combustion chambers

Cast-iron block and heads

High-lift camshaft

A good buy

The original Duster 340s are the most understated. 1971 editions retain all the performance credentials, but feature louder graphics. After 1971 performance is noticeably reduced, but today, at around $5,000 a good Duster 340 is an excellent buy.

In their day the Duster 340s were a good muscle car buy.

Plymouth DUSTER 340

Although sometimes viewed as little more than a coupe version of the Valiant, the Duster 340 combined light weight, Mopar V8 power and heavy-duty suspension at a very attractive price.

V8 engine

The 340-cubic inch V8 is one of Detroit's most tractable small-blocks of the muscle car era. With hydraulic lifters and a single four-barrel carburetor, it is easy to tune and its 275 bhp was more than adequate for street races.

Performance tires

The Duster 340 came with standard Goodyear Polyglas E70 x 14 tires and Rallye wheels, although this example has been fitted with period aftermarket wheels and later Jetzon Revenger 15-inch radials.

Optional transmissions

The standard transmission is a three-speed manual, but a four-speed or the excellent TorqueFlite automatic were available as options.

Loud graphics

From 1971 the Duster 340 was given larger side stripes with a 340 script carried on the rear quarter panels. Two different hoods were available—one with fake scoops and the other with a large 340 script.

Rear axle ratios

At the rear, the live axle is suspended by leaf springs. Standard rear gearing is 3.23:1, although shorter gears and a Sure Grip limited-slip differential were also available.

Power steering

In base form the Duster 340 has manual steering, although the optional power set-up at extra cost was a sensible choice. Very light by today standards, it nevertheless makes the Duster easy to maneuver, especially at lower speeds.

Specifications
1971 Plymouth Duster 340

ENGINE
Type: V8
Construction: Cast-iron block and heads
Valve gear: Two valves per cylinder operated by a single camshaft via pushrods, rockers and hydraulic lifters
Bore and stroke: 4.03 in. x 3.30 in.
Displacement: 340 c.i.
Compression ratio: 10.5:1
Induction system: Single Carter four-barrel carburetor
Maximum power: 275 bhp at 5,000 rpm
Maximum torque: 340 lb-ft at 3,200 rpm
Top speed: 120 mph
0-60 mph: 6.0 sec.

TRANSMISSION
Three-speed TorqueFlite automatic

BODY/CHASSIS
Unitary steel construction with two-door coupe body

SPECIAL FEATURES

An optional matt-black hood introduced in 1971 includes '340' in large script.

The 340-cubic inch V8 was previously used in the Dart and the 'Cuda.

RUNNING GEAR
Steering: Recirculating ball
Front suspension: Double wishbones with longitudinal torsion bars, telescopic shocks and anti-roll bar
Rear suspension: Live axle with semi-elliptic leaf springs and telescopic shocks
Brakes: Ventilated discs, 10.5-in. dia. (front), drums, 9-in. dia. (rear)
Wheels: Cragar, 5.5 x 15 in.
Tires: Jetzon Revenger, 70 x 15

DIMENSIONS
Length: 192 in.   **Width:** 71.6 in.
Height: 52.7 in.   **Wheelbase:** 108 in.
Track: 57.5 in. (front), 55.5 (rear)
Weight: 3,500 lbs.

Pontiac **GTO**

Generally acknowledged as the first factory-built muscle car, the name was borrowed from Ferrari where it stood for Gran Turisomo Omologato. Now its one of the top collectible cars of its era.

"...All attitude and performance."

"While many can argue which muscle car was the fastest, nicest or most powerful, only one can be the first—that's the Pontiac GTO. In 1964, when John Z. DeLorean installed a 389-cubic inch V8 in Pontiac's intermediate Tempest cars, he created a legend, not to mention an American automotive trend that would ripple for the next eight years. By 1971, the GTO was all about attitude as well as performance. Styled with the Judge™ option, and powered by a huge 455-cubic inch High Output engine with Ram-Air induction, the GTO had the sound and fury of real steel."

This GTO has the optional hood-mounted tachometer that is visible through the windshield.

Milestones

1968 The GTO receives another major restyling. The wheelbase is shortened from 115 to 112 inches. The new body uses rubber Endura bumpers and hidden headlights are a popular option. Its 400-cubic inch V8 retains 360 bhp in both the HO and Ram Air versions. Midyear, Pontiac replaces the Ram Air engine with a Ram Air II.

The 1965 GTO was a tough act to follow by 1971.

1969 The Judge is an attempt to revive GTO sales. It features a sharp rear spoiler, stripes and badging. Standard engine is the Ram Air III 400 V8 engine, but for and extra $390 the 370 bhp Ram Air IV engine becomes available.

1970 GTOs are again restyled. This is the most refined version yet. The Judge is still available and so is the Ram Air IV engine. A huge 455 V8 is also offered, but isn't popular.

1971 Poor sales in 1970 force the Judge option to be dropped after selling 357 hardtops and 17 convertibles. The top engine is a 455 V8 with 355 bhp.

1972 GTO becomes an option on the Le Mans.

UNDER THE SKIN

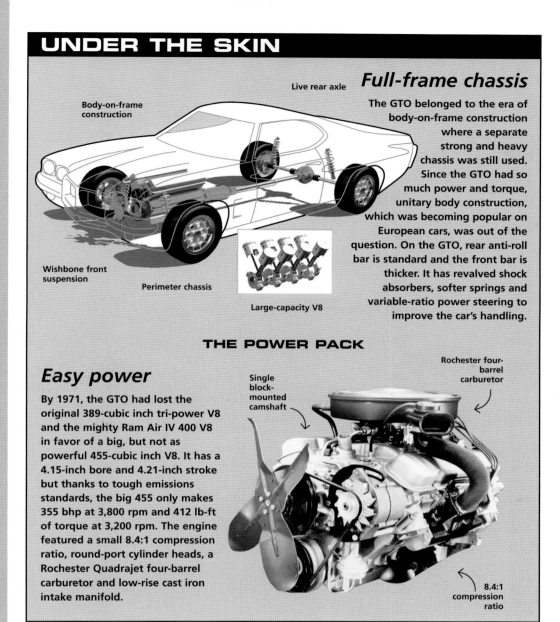

Body-on-frame construction

Live rear axle

Wishbone front suspension

Perimeter chassis

Large-capacity V8

Full-frame chassis

The GTO belonged to the era of body-on-frame construction where a separate strong and heavy chassis was still used. Since the GTO had so much power and torque, unitary body construction, which was becoming popular on European cars, was out of the question. On the GTO, rear anti-roll bar is standard and the front bar is thicker. It has revalved shock absorbers, softer springs and variable-ratio power steering to improve the car's handling.

THE POWER PACK

Easy power

By 1971, the GTO had lost the original 389-cubic inch tri-power V8 and the mighty Ram Air IV 400 V8 in favor of a big, but not as powerful 455-cubic inch V8. It has a 4.15-inch bore and 4.21-inch stroke but thanks to tough emissions standards, the big 455 only makes 355 bhp at 3,800 rpm and 412 lb-ft of torque at 3,200 rpm. The engine featured a small 8.4:1 compression ratio, round-port cylinder heads, a Rochester Quadrajet four-barrel carburetor and low-rise cast iron intake manifold.

Single block-mounted camshaft

Rochester four-barrel carburetor

8.4:1 compression ratio

Rare Judge

One of the rarest GTOs is the 1971 Judge convertible. Unfortunately, the Judge option was dropped midway through the 1971 model year and only 17 convertibles were built. This pristine Judge is equipped with a High Output 455-cubic inch V8.

This rare GTO is one of only 17 Judge convertibles made in 1971.

Pontiac **GTO**

The GTO set the infamous John DeLorean on the road to success at GM and virtually invented the muscle car, giving seemingly ordinary Tempests the performance to embarrass any sports car.

Ram Air

From 1965, all GTOs had an optional Ram Air system. By pulling a knob inside the cabin, hood vents would open and fed the carburetor with fresh, cool air.

High Output 455 V8

By 1971, the biggest and most powerful V8 you could order in the GTO was the High Output 455-cubic inch V8 with 355 bhp.

Servo front brakes

While the Le Mans range—which shared much of its hardware with the GTO—had unassisted drum brakes all around, the GTO models have front discs giving excellent results.

TH400 Automatic transmission

While the M-22 close-ratio manual four-speed was the racer's choice of transmissions, the TH400 automatic was easier in traffic and just as capable of delivering the power to the rear axles.

Positraction rear axle

Since these cars deliver a lot of power, a positraction rear axle was a popular option. For maximum acceleration, GTOs differentials were available with up to 4.33:1 gearing.

"Judge" graphics

If you wanted to get noticed, the Judge was the car to have. If the huge wing didn't make a loud enough statement, the multicolored graphics sure did.

Wishbone front suspension

There are no surprises with the front suspension which features double wishbones with a thick anti-roll bar, coil springs and revalved shocks.

Wider wheels

To improve cornering and road holding, the GTO has wider wheels than the base Le Mans models. This car carries optional 'Honeycomb' wheels.

Rear anti-roll bar

The rear suspension needed all the help it could get to stop the car's body roll around corners. Its standard rear anti-roll bar greatly improve the way the GTO handles.

Specifications
1971 Pontiac GTO Judge

ENGINE
Type: V8
Construction: Cast-iron block and heads
Valve gear: Two valves per cylinder operated by single block-mounted camshaft via pushrods, rockers and hydraulic lifters
Bore and stroke: 4.15 in. x 4.21 in.
Displacement: 455 c.i.
Compression ratio: 8.4:1
Induction system: Single Rochester four-barrel carburetor
Maximum power: 335 bhp at 4,800 rpm
Maximum torque: 412 lb-ft at 3,200 rpm
Top speed: 108 mph
0-60 mph: 7.0 sec.

TRANSMISSION
Turbo 400 Hydra-Matic automatic

BODY/CHASSIS
Perimeter chassis with two-door coupe or two-door convertible bodywork

SPECIAL FEATURES

Optional hood-mounted, 8,000-rpm tachometer was first introduced in 1967.

The large vents on the hood are for the Ram Air system feeding fresh air to the four-barrel carburetor.

RUNNING GEAR
Steering: Variable-ratio power-assisted recirculating ball
Front suspension: Double wishbones with coil springs, revalved shocks and anti-roll bar
Rear suspension: Live axle with trailing radius arms, upper oblique torque arms, coil springs, revalved shocks and anti-roll bar
Brakes: Discs (front) and drums (rear)
Wheels: Honeycombs 14 in. x 7 in.
Tires: G60 x 14

DIMENSIONS
Length: 205.1 in.   **Width:** 76.7 in.
Height: 52 in.   **Wheelbase:** 112 in.
Track: 61 in. (front), 60 in. (rear)
Weight: 3,894 lbs.

Pontiac **FIREBIRD**

The second-generation Firebird is one of Pontiac's most successful cars ever and it remained in production for 11 years. Perhaps the purest and best-performing cars are the early-1970s Firebird Formulas.

"...plenty of low-end power."

"While most muscle cars were scrapped by 1972, Pontiac refused to let go. It continued to charge hard with the popular ponycar. Those who wanted attention bought the Trans Am, but the more sedate looking Formula shared its power. The Formula has a 400-cubic inch V8 under its dual-scooped hood. Although power in the 1973 model is down because of the government's strict emissions regulations, this car is still very quick and has plenty of low-end power."

In 1973, Formulas had plush bucket seats and a sporty center console.

Milestones

1970 The second-generation
Firebird makes its debut in February. It is longer, lower and wider, with an Endura flexible nose. Four models are available: Firebird, Esprit®, Formula and Trans Am. The latter two are the performance models.

The first-generation Firebird made its debut in February 1967.

1973 The last of
the true muscle Firebirds appear as the 455 Super Duty Formula and the Trans Am.

1974 A facelift for the
second-generation Firebird introduces new front and rear styling to satisfy crash requirements.

The 1979 model was the most popular year, with 211,000 Firebirds being sold.

1979 This is the last year
for the 400- and 403-cubic inch V8s. The 400-cubic inch V8 was the more powerful engine and was used with a 4-speed transmission, while the lower performance 403 V8 was used with an automatic.

UNDER THE SKIN

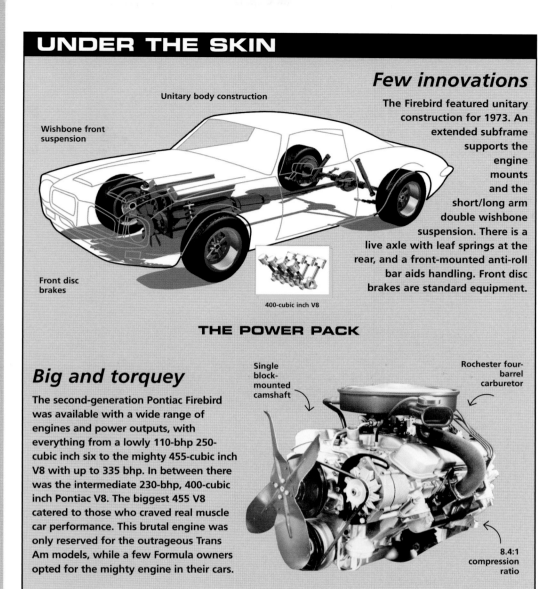

Unitary body construction

Wishbone front suspension

Front disc brakes

400-cubic inch V8

Few innovations

The Firebird featured unitary construction for 1973. An extended subframe supports the engine mounts and the short/long arm double wishbone suspension. There is a live axle with leaf springs at the rear, and a front-mounted anti-roll bar aids handling. Front disc brakes are standard equipment.

THE POWER PACK

Big and torquey

The second-generation Pontiac Firebird was available with a wide range of engines and power outputs, with everything from a lowly 110-bhp 250-cubic inch six to the mighty 455-cubic inch V8 with up to 335 bhp. In between there was the intermediate 230-bhp, 400-cubic inch Pontiac V8. The biggest 455 V8 catered to those who craved real muscle car performance. This brutal engine was only reserved for the outrageous Trans Am models, while a few Formula owners opted for the mighty engine in their cars.

Single block-mounted camshaft

Rochester four-barrel carburetor

8.4:1 compression ratio

Fiery flagship

The flagship of the Firebird line in 1973 was the Trans Am. Apart from spoilers, decals and a shaker hood scoop, it is mechanically identical to the 455 Formula. The toughest engine available in 1973 was the 455-cubic inch Super Duty, with 310 bhp.

1970-1973 Firebirds are the cleanest-looking second-generation models.

Pontiac **FIREBIRD**

For those who did not have the money to buy the Trans Am but still wanted performance, the Formula was a good choice. It had the same mechanics as its more renowned stablemate.

400-cubic inch engine

This large bore 400-cubic inch engine features 8.4:1 compression cast-iron pistons, large chamber D-port cylinder heads with 2.11-inch intake and 1.77-inch exhaust valves, a low lift hydraulic camshaft and a Rochester Quadrajet.

Steel wheels

Firebirds have steel Pontiac Rally wheels as standard, although special 'honeycomb' wheels were available at extra cost.

Separate rear bumper

In contrast to the front color-coded, impact-absorbing Endura nose, there is still a traditional-style chrome bumper at the rear. The last year for this very clean rear-end styling was 1973.

Limited-slip differential

Standard equipment with the four-speed manual transmission is the limited-slip differential. It was much easier to offer this as an aid to traction than to re-engineer the Firebird with independent rear suspension.

Optional air-conditioning
Unlike its import rivals, even the lowest model of the Firebird could be ordered with air-conditioning as an option.

Impact-absorbing nose
Pontiac was one of the first companies to introduce impact-absorbing bumpers. The Firebird has one of the cleanest nose profiles of any 1973 car.

Specifications
1973 Pontiac Firebird Formula 400

ENGINE
Type: V8
Construction: Cast-iron block and heads
Valve gear: Two valves per cylinder operated by a single block-mounted camshaft, pushrods and rockers
Bore and stroke: 4.13 in. x 3.74 in.
Displacement: 400 c.i.
Compression ratio: 8.4:1
Induction system: Single Rochester 7043263 four-barrel carburetor
Maximum power: 230 bhp at 4,400 rpm
Maximum torque: 177 lb-ft at 3,200 rpm
Top speed: 118 mph
0-60 mph: 9.4 sec.

TRANSMISSION
Four-speed manual

BODY/CHASSIS
Steel monocoque with ladder-type front chassis rails and two-door coupe body

SPECIAL FEATURES

Twin hood scoops are unique to the high-performance Formula model.

Rally II wheels are standard equipment on the Formula and optional on lesser models.

RUNNING GEAR
Steering: Recirculating ball
Front suspension: Double unequal length wishbones, with coil springs, telescopic shocks and anti-roll bar
Rear suspension: Live axle with semi-elliptic leaf springs, telescopic shocks and anti-roll bar
Brakes: Discs, 11-in. dia. (front), drums (rear)
Wheels: Steel disc, 7 in. x 14 in.
Tires: F70-14

DIMENSIONS
Length: 191.5 in. **Width:** 73.4 in.
Height: 50.4 in. **Wheelbase:** 108.1 in.
Track: 61.6 in. (front), 61.6 in. (rear)
Weight: 3,766 lbs.

Pontiac TRANS AM SD455

By 1974, only GM could offer anything even vaguely approaching the performance machines of the late 1960s and early 1970s, with the Chevrolet Corvette and the more powerful Pontiac Trans Am SD-455.

"...raucous take-offs."

"The 1974 Trans Am was strictly 'old school' American muscle in the performance and handling departments. Like its predecessors a decade earlier, it was great in a straight line. The massive 455-cubic inch engine plays a part in the car's front-heavy handling, although it gives fantastic midrange acceleration. Standard disc brakes up front and a limited-slip differential for raucous take-offs are major plus points."

There is a comfortable feel to the interior, which is unmistakably 1970s.

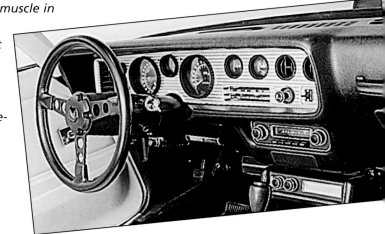

1967 Pontiac
introduces the Firebird, t shares its basic shell with the Chevrolet Camaro, which debuted a few months earlier. Both are aimed at the 'pony market' created by the Mustang.

Chevrolet dropped the Camaro in 1975, leaving the Trans Am as GM's only muscle car.

1969 The Trans Am
is offered for the first time in the Firebird lineup as the top-of-the-line performance Firebird. Standard was the Ram Air III, 335 bhp 400 HO engine.

The Trans Am had a bold redesign for 1979.

1974 First major
body and engineering restyle for the Firebird/Trans Am series.

1976 Last year of
the Pontiac 455-c.i. engine, only available in the Trans Am as a limited edition.

UNDER THE SKIN

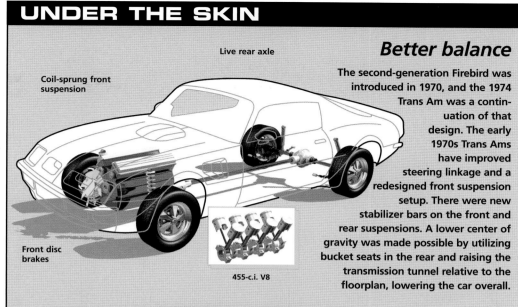

Coil-sprung front suspension

Live rear axle

Front disc brakes

455-c.i. V8

Better balance

The second-generation Firebird was introduced in 1970, and the 1974 Trans Am was a continuation of that design. The early 1970s Trans Ams have improved steering linkage and a redesigned front suspension setup. There were new stabilizer bars on the front and rear suspensions. A lower center of gravity was made possible by utilizing bucket seats in the rear and raising the transmission tunnel relative to the floorplan, lowering the car overall.

THE POWER PACK

Super-Duty punch

Pontiac's Super Duty 455 was the last bastion of big-cube power for the performance enthusiast. With a compression ratio of 8.4:1, output was down as the first of the mandatory emissions controls began to sap power. Nonetheless, the engine still sported all the performance features of the soon-to-be-gone muscle car era. This includes a lot of displacement, four-bolt mains, forged-aluminum pistons and an 800-cfm Quadrajet carb. There was even built-in provision for dry-sump lubrication. Earlier 1974 cars make use of the Ram IV camshaft and are capable of 310 bhp; later 1974 cars do not and are rated at 290 bhp.

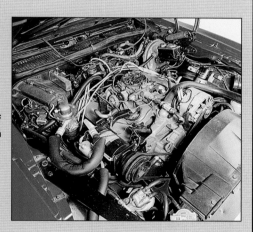

Last of its kind

If you wanted a muscle car in 1974, there was only one choice: the Trans Am SD-455. Big-block Camaros had been discontinued and MOPAR, the purveyor of some of the hot muscle car property, had pulled the plug on performance.

For 1974, Pontiac gave the Trans Am new front-end treatment.

Pontiac **TRANS AM SD455**

Pontiac Firebirds were offered in four series for 1974: Firebird, Esprit, Formula and Trans Am. The 455-SD engine could be ordered only in the Formula and the Trans Am. Super-Duty equipped Formulas are the rarest.

Special dash

Trans Ams featured a special steering wheel, a faux metal dash and a rally gauge cluster, which included a clock and dash-mounted tachometer. As a sign of the times, a new 'fuel economy' gauge was introduced later in the year.

LSD

Standard on the Trans Am was a limited-slip differential, ensuring minimal wheelspin and consistent launches.

New tires

For 1974, all General Motors cars had to use steel-belted radials. Hence, the old Firestone Wide-Oval F60-15 bias-belted tires were replaced with new Firestone 500 F60 x 15 steel-belted radials.

'Soft' bumpers

New for 1974 was a soft bumper treatment front and rear, utilizing molded urethane foam. These were faced with black rubber front bars to absorb parking bumps.

Scoops galore

Pontiac made sure that the Trans Am looked aggressive and powerful with flared wheel arches and front fender air extractors. The menacing-looking, rear-facing Shaker hood scoop finishes off the whole effect with SD-455 decals on the side.

Restyled rear end

The rear-end treatment includes a full-width rear spoiler. Taillights are wider, in a horizontal casing, giving a more integrated appearance.

Specifications
1974 Trans Am SD455

ENGINE
Type: V8

Construction: Cast-iron cylinder block and cylinder head

Valve gear: Two valves per cylinder

Bore and stroke: 4.15 in. x 4.21 in.

Displacement: 455 c.i.

Compression ratio: 8.4:1

Induction system: 800-cfm Quadrajet four-barrel carburetor

Maximum power: 310 bhp at 4,000 rpm

Maximum torque: 390 lb-ft at 3,600 rpm

Top speed: 132 mph

0-60 mph: 5.4 sec

TRANSMISSION
Three-speed automatic M40 Turbo Hydramatic

BODY/CHASSIS
Steel unibody construction

SPECIAL FEATURES

The SD-455 logos are seen only on Trans Ams and Formulas.

A holographic applique on the dash perfectly reflects mid-1970s style.

RUNNING GEAR
Steering: Variable-ratio, ball-nut

Front suspension: A-arms with coil springs and telescopic shock absorbers

Rear suspension: Live rear axle with leaf springs and telescopic shock absorbers

Brakes: Discs (front), drums (rear)

Wheels: Steel, 15-in. Rally II

Tires: F60 x 15 (raised white letters) Firestone steel belted

DIMENSIONS
Length: 196.0 in.   **Width:** 73.4 in.

Height: 50.4 in.   **Wheelbase:** 108.0 in.

Track: 61.6 in. (front), 60.3 in. (rear)

Weight: 3,655 lbs.

Pontiac CAN AM

Although it is often said that performance died during the 1970s, there were some bright spots. In 1977, Pontiac dropped a 400-cubic inch V8 into the LeMans™ to create the Can Am, a limited production sports coupe.

"...something different."

"Based on the mid-1970s LeMans, the Can Am has a low-set driving position and feels wide on the road. The interior may be bland, but the floor shifter at the end of your right hand indicates something different is going on. The 400 V8 works best at low rpm, and while not fast on paper, the Can Am still feels quick. A nice surprise is the handling—stiffer springs and anti-roll bars, along with radial tires give assuring grip."

Velour upholstery and every gauge one could imagine come standard in all Can Ams.

Milestones

1973 Pontiac fields a restyled intermediate line, now called LeMans. Convertibles and hardtop coupes are not offered, but pillared sedans, coupes and wagons are. This is also the last year for the A-body GTO™.

Pontiac's popular Trans Am™ also used 400- or 403-cubic inch V8s.

1975 Pontiac drops its only surviving performance intermediate, the Grand Am™, after sales reach only 10,769.

Pontiac's original muscle car, the GTO was also based on the midsize LeMans.

1977 In an attempt to inject more performance into its lineup, Pontiac offers the Can Am, based on the LeMans Sport. It has big V8 power, handling suspension and white paint with orange and black graphics. A downsized LeMans arrives for 1978 on a 108.1-inch wheelbase. The sporty Can Am does not return.

UNDER THE SKIN

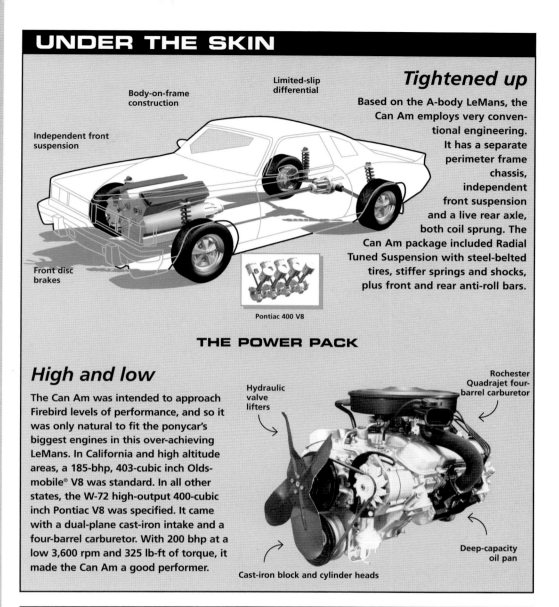

Body-on-frame construction

Limited-slip differential

Independent front suspension

Front disc brakes

Pontiac 400 V8

Tightened up

Based on the A-body LeMans, the Can Am employs very conventional engineering. It has a separate perimeter frame chassis, independent front suspension and a live rear axle, both coil sprung. The Can Am package included Radial Tuned Suspension with steel-belted tires, stiffer springs and shocks, plus front and rear anti-roll bars.

THE POWER PACK

High and low

The Can Am was intended to approach Firebird levels of performance, and so it was only natural to fit the ponycar's biggest engines in this over-achieving LeMans. In California and high altitude areas, a 185-bhp, 403-cubic inch Oldsmobile® V8 was standard. In all other states, the W-72 high-output 400-cubic inch Pontiac V8 was specified. It came with a dual-plane cast-iron intake and a four-barrel carburetor. With 200 bhp at a low 3,600 rpm and 325 lb-ft of torque, it made the Can Am a good performer.

Hydraulic valve lifters

Rochester Quadrajet four-barrel carburetor

Deep-capacity oil pan

Cast-iron block and cylinder heads

White warrior

The Can Am was built only for 1977 and just 3,177 examples left the factory. It may be slower than its 1960s forebears, but thanks to a 400-cubic inch engine packing 200 bhp in top condition, it is undoubtedly a high performance bargain.

Today, good Can Ams can be bought for a very reasonable price.

Pontiac CAN AM

Fitting a huge engine in a mid-range coupe was the muscle car concept in its purest form. Although not the quickest, one road tester claimed the Can Am was "the strongest thing to come from Motown in years."

Biggest V8

In 1977, the 400 was the biggest engine offered by Pontiac. With a four-barrel carburetor and 200 bhp, it was potent too, and enabled Can Am drivers to flog their machines down the ¼-mile in a shade over 17 seconds.

Driver-oriented interior

Although it is essentially a LeMans, the Can Am has a driver-oriented Grand Prix instrument panel, with large circular gauges that are angled toward the driver.

Live axle

Most American production cars of the 1970s had front-mounted engines, with a live rear axle. Can Ams came with a 10-bolt rear end with a Safe-T-Track limited-slip differential. For economy, 3.23:1 was the shortest ratio offered.

Five-mph bumpers

Beginning in 1973, all manufacturers who sold cars in the U.S. had to comply with federal regulations which required heftier bumpers to withstand low-speed shunts. After a low-speed impact they bounce back to their original position.

All automatics

Though two different engines were available in the Can Am, only one transmission was available—a TH350 three speed automatic. The transmission included a 2.52 first gear for spirited standing starts.

Chassis enhancements

Stiffer coil springs, shocks with improved damping and front and rear anti-roll bars were offered as part of the RTS (Radial Tuned Suspension) package, along with 15-inch wheels.

Cosmetic enhancements

Because performance was a scarce commodity in the 1970s, Detroit dressed up its 'hot' offerings. This included a trunk spoiler, shaker hood scoop, plus a white body and wheels.

Specifications
1977 Pontiac Can Am

ENGINE
Type: V8
Construction: Cast-iron block and heads
Valve gear: Two valves per cylinder operated by a single camshaft with pushrods and hydraulic lifters
Bore and stroke: 4.12 in. x 3.75 in.
Displacement: 400 c.i.
Compression ratio: 8.0:1
Induction system: Rochester Quadrajet four-barrel carburetor
Maximum power: 200 bhp at 3,600 rpm
Maximum torque: 325 lb-ft at 2,400 rpm
Top speed: 120 mph
0-60 mph: 8.6 sec

TRANSMISSION
TurboHydramatic three speed automatic

BODY/CHASSIS
Steel perimeter chassis with separate two-door coupe body

SPECIAL FEATURES

Vents over the quarter windows add a sporty look to this 1970s hot rod.

Chrome-plated exhaust tips, as seen here, were a popular dealer option.

RUNNING GEAR
Steering: Recirculating ball
Front suspension: Unequal length A-arms with coil springs, telescopic shock absorbers and anti-roll bar
Rear suspension: Live axle with lower control arms, coil springs, telescopic shock absorbers and anti-roll bar
Brakes: Discs (front), drums (rear)
Wheels: Cast-steel, 7 x 15 in.
Tires: Goodyear Polysteel, GR70-15

DIMENSIONS
Length: 208.0 in.   **Width:** 77.0 in.
Height: 52.7 in. **Wheelbase:** 112.0 in.
Track: 61.6 in. (front), 61.1 in. (rear)
Weight: 4,140 lbs.

Pontiac TRANS AM

With the outrageous Firebird decal taking center stage on the hood, the 1978 Trans Am naturally lends itself to extreme modifications and competition in quarter-mile racing. Best of all, however, is that this car's suspension setup makes it ideal for autocrossing, too.

"...thunderous roar."

"The comfortable bucket seats and CD player inside the Trans Am create a relaxing atmosphere. That is, until you turn the ignition! The thunderous roar of the engine is accompanied by a squeal of the tires as you drop the clutch and leap forward with considerable force. The suspension has been stiffened and it shows— this car grips and corners without excessive roll. However, push it too hard and the back will come around, putting you in a lurid slide."

The modified interior of this Trans Am pays great attention to comfort.

Milestones

1969 Pontiac releases its first model to carry the name Trans Am, a Polar White-with-blue-stripes version of the Firebird.

Trans Ams were given a major facelift for the 1978 model year.

1970 The Trans Am becomes a model in its own right.

1974 The first major restyle for the Trans Am sees a new sloping front, which incorporates bumpers conforming to new federal crash legislation.

The last of the 400/403 Trans Ams were built in 1979.

1977 Another nose change sees the adoption of twin headlights.

1982 A new Trans Am with a sleeker body and pop-up headlights replaces the classic shape of the outgoing version.

UNDER THE SKIN

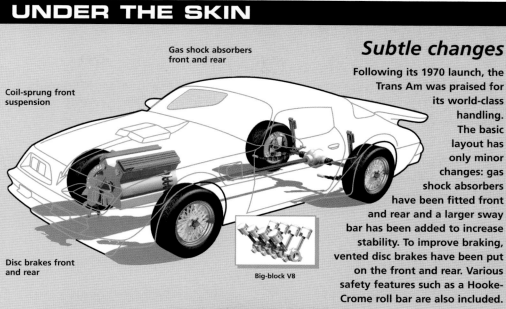

Gas shock absorbers front and rear

Coil-sprung front suspension

Disc brakes front and rear

Big-block V8

Subtle changes

Following its 1970 launch, the Trans Am was praised for its world-class handling. The basic layout has only minor changes: gas shock absorbers have been fitted front and rear and a larger sway bar has been added to increase stability. To improve braking, vented disc brakes have been put on the front and rear. Various safety features such as a Hooke-Crome roll bar are also included.

THE POWER PACK

"455" power

Powering this fiery Trans Am is a 455-cubic inch from a 1974 Pontiac. The V8 unit, with its cast-iron block and head, has undergone a variety of modifications. An Edelbrock Performer intake manifold has been added along with a 750-cfm Quadrajet injector, increasing intake flow. A Crane cam and variable lifters allow the engine to make more power than its stock configuration, a fact seen in the output figures, which see the maximum 350 bhp being produced at 4,800 rpm. Other additions include H.O. Enterprise TRI Y headers and dual Outlaw mufflers. The result is a really responsive motor.

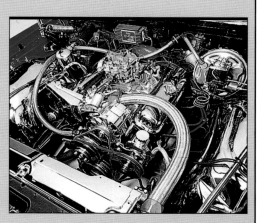

Super quick

In 1978, the most desirable of the Firebird/Trans Am range was the Grand Am Coupe. However, it could not compete with the 350-bhp car featured here. Its increased performance makes it one of the most competitive street racers out there.

From the outside, there are a few subtle clues to this Trans Am's performance.

Pontiac **TRANS AM**

The Trans Am name was perhaps even more important than Pontiac's throughout the 1970s, as it carried the mantle of the firm's only true performance car. It is still synonymous with power today.

Hood scoop

Despite the hood scoop this car has no Ram Air system. The scoop is decorative and is sealed, and has no effect on performance.

V8 engine

In 1974 the 455-c.i. engine was the largest in Pontiac's range. Modifications have enabled it to produce 350 bhp.

Safety features

To protect the driver in the event of an accident, Simpson race harnesses and a Hooke chrome roll bar have been fitted. To keep the driver firmly in position, there are also Recaro bucket seats.

Modified suspension

To enable the chassis to match the performance, the suspension has been uprated. Herb Adams chrome sway bars have been fitted front and rear, and H.O. Enterprises coil and leaf springs have replaced the stock items. In addition to this, KYB gas shocks are used instead of the previous telescopic variety.

Luxurious interior

Despite being built for speed, the owner of this Trans Am has added all the creature comforts including a CD deck.

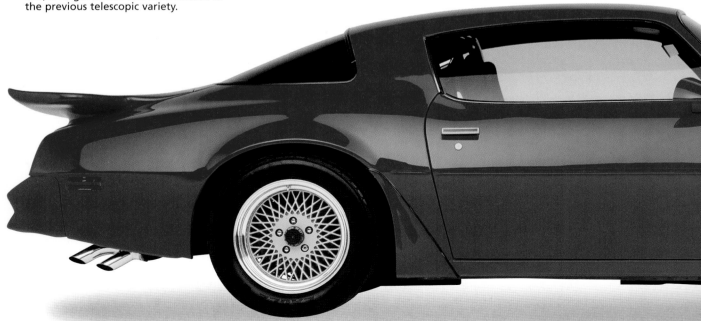

Non-stock mirrors

The door mirrors of this Trans Am come from a third-generation Firebird, which was immortalized as K.I.T.T. in the TV show *Knight Rider*.

Disc brakes

In contrast to its stock equivalent, this Trans Am has vented disc brakes at the rear, providing more consistent braking performance.

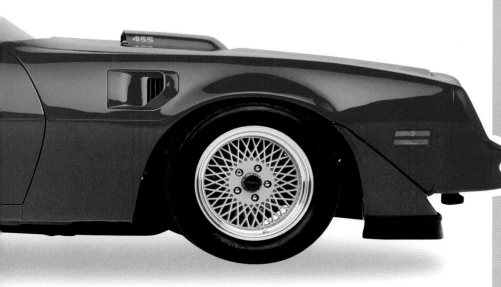

Specifications

1978 Pontiac Trans Am

ENGINE
Type: V8

Construction: Cast-iron block and heads

Valve gear: Two valves per cylinder operated by a single block-mounted camshaft with pushrods and rockers

Bore and stroke: 4.15 in. x 4.21 in

Displacement: 455 c.i.

Compression ratio: 8.0:1

Induction system: Four-barrel Rochester Quadrajet carburetor

Maximum power: 350 bhp at 4,800 rpm

Maximum torque: 360 lb-ft at 3,300 rpm

Top speed: 125 mph

0-60 mph: 5.1 sec.

TRANSMISSION
TH400 three-speed automatic

BODY/CHASSIS
Steel unitary chassis with steel body panels

SPECIAL FEATURES

The 455-c.i. engine was not available in the stock '78 Trans Am.

The aggressive look of the Trans Am has been augmented by a front spoiler.

RUNNING GEAR
Steering: Rack-and-pinion

Front suspension: Unequal-length A-arms with coil springs and gas shock absorbers

Rear suspension: Live axle with leaf springs and gas shock absorbers

Brakes: Vented discs (front and rear)

Wheels: 16 x 8 Enkei polished

Tires: Goodyear Eagle 255/50ZR16

DIMENSIONS
Length: 196.2 in. **Width:** 76.2 in.

Height: 47.6 in. **Wheelbase:** 108.0 in.

Track: 63.3 in. (front and rear)

Weight: 3,511 lbs.

Porsche **914/6**

The 914/4 is an inexpensive, Porsche/VW sports car, but the six-cylinder 914/6 is nearly all Porsche. It uses the 911's flat-six engine, and its mid-engined handling is superior to its more expensive 911 contemporaries.

"...the balance is perfect."

"With the roof off, the 914/6 feels wonderfully airy, and it's soon obvious why Porsche made it mid-engined. The balance is perfect and the direct steering requires little effort. What's more, in contrast to so many mid-engined cars, it's easy to catch the back end if you put too much power down and cause oversteer. Yes, the gear shifer could be better and outright performance isn't really stunning, but this car is still a joy to drive."

The linear layout of the 914/6's dashboard is still recognizable on today's 911s.

Milestones

1966 Ferry Porsche and
Volkswagen's Heinz Nordhoff agree that Porsche will design a new sports car, VW will market it as a VW/Porsche with a VW 411 engine and Porsche will sell it with a Porsche engine.

The 914/6 takes its flat-six from the legendary 911.

1970 The 914 goes on sale
after having made its debut at the previous year's Frankfurt Motor Show. Prices quickly rise before the cars go on sale in the U.S.

1971 By flaring the wheel
arches, welding on a steel roof and using the 190-bhp engine from the 911S, Porsche produces the very fast 916. Only around 20 are made before the project is discontinued.

The Boxster is the first mid-engined Porsche since the 914.

1972 Production of the 914/6
ends, although the cheaper 914/4 continues until the 1976 model year.

UNDER THE SKIN

Family likeness

Porsche sensibly used as much from the established 911 as possible in making the 914/6. That meant the same front suspension of struts operating longitudinal torsion bars and the same precise rack-and-pinion steering gear. The engine is mounted longitudinally with the five-speed transmission behind it—basically the 911's setup turned through 180 degrees.

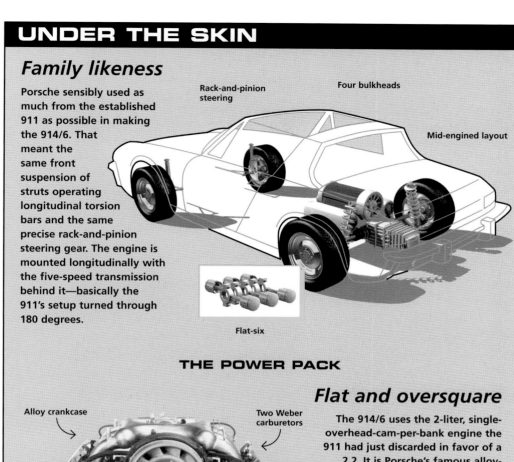

Rack-and-pinion steering

Four bulkheads

Mid-engined layout

Flat-six

THE POWER PACK

Flat and oversquare

The 914/6 uses the 2-liter, single-overhead-cam-per-bank engine the 911 had just discarded in favor of a 2.2. It is Porsche's famous alloy-crankcase flat-six. The pistons run in individual Biral barrels connected at the top by an alloy cam carrier and cylinder heads. There is a large belt-driven fan in a plastic housing on top of the engine to aid cooling. Designed to rev high, it is oversquare with a short stroke, while there are just two valves per cylinder and two triple-choke Weber carburetors.

Alloy crankcase

Two Weber carburetors

Two valves per cylinder

Belt-driven fan

Racing 916

The rarest and most desirable of the 914/6 family is the 916. Only a handful were made before the project was canceled because of costs. It has the 2.4-liter flat-six unit from the 911E (190 bhp), which gives 0-60 mph in less than seven seconds.

It's super-rare, but the 916—built for racing—is a phenomenal car.

Porsche 914/6

Porsche's first mid-engined production sports car was produced years before the current Boxster, but despite its great dynamic abilities, off-beat looks and a high price caused its downfall after only three years.

Pop-up lights

Gugelot, the 914/6's stylists, wanted an uncluttered and rectangular look, and dispensed with exposed headlights, opting instead for two round lights in pop-up pods.

Flat-six engine

Because the 914/6 was meant to be the affordable Porsche, it couldn't have the same power as the more expensive 911. So it uses the 125-bhp 2-liter.

Fiberglass roof

The 914/6 was designed as a targa top, and the lightweight fiberglass roof panel can be unclipped and lifted clear. It then stows under the rear compartment.

Magnesium wheels

All 914/6s have five-lug rather than four-lug wheels. Just a few cars have the desirable Mahle diecast magnesium wheels, although more were made with Fuchs five-spoke aluminum alloys. Either way, the wheels house excellent vented disc brakes.

Specifications

1970 Porsche 914/6

ENGINE

Type: Flat six-cylinder

Construction: Alloy crankcase with separate Biral (cast iron with alloy cooling fins) cylinder barrels and alloy cam carriers and cylinder heads

Valve gear: Two valves per cylinder operated by a single chain-driven overhead camshaft per bank of cylinders

Bore and stroke: 3.15 in. x 2.60 in.

Displacement: 1,991 cc

Compression ratio: 8.6:1

Induction system: Two Weber triple-choke downdraft carburetors

Maximum power: 125 bhp at 5,800 rpm

Maximum torque: 131 lb-ft at 4,200 rpm

Top speed: 123 mph

0-60 mph: 8.7 sec.

TRANSMISSION

Five-speed manual

BODY/CHASSIS

Unitary monocoque construction with steel targa top convertible two-seater body

SPECIAL FEATURES

Most 914/6s wore Fuchs five-spoke aluminum wheels.

Under-bumper driving lights supplement the pop-up headlights.

RUNNING GEAR

Steering: Rack-and-pinion

Front suspension: Struts with lower wishbones and longitudinal torsion bars

Rear suspension: Semi-trailing arms with coil springs and telescopic shock absorbers

Brakes: Vented discs (front), Solid discs rear

Wheels: 5.5 x 14 in.

Tires: 185 HR 14

DIMENSIONS

Length: 156.9 in.   **Width:** 65.0 in.

Height: 48.0 in.   **Wheelbase:** 96.4 in.

Track: 53.6 in. (front), 54.4 in. (rear)

Weight: 2,195 lbs.

Fixed passenger seat

With no room behind, there was no need for a movable passenger seat. Instead, there's a movable footrest in the footwell. Eventually, however, a movable seat was introduced for the 1972 model year.

Rear-mounted transmission

The only drawback to setting the transmission behind the mid-mounted engine is that this requires a long gear linkage—never as precise or good to use as the shorter one in the 911.

Porsche 911 TURBO

Porsche took the brave step of installing a turbocharger into its 911 road car. It may have been vastly expensive, but the thrill of driving a Porsche with such a massive rush of power was well worth it.

"...a raging animal."

"A superb driving position is one thing you can always count on in a 911. This instantly settles you into the car, which is a good thing because you need your wits about you. The turbo viciously builds boost at around 3,800 rpm, transforming this docile driver into a raging animal. This can be hair-raising on corners, especially with so much weight at the rear end. Lifting off in mid-corner produces truly dramatic oversteer that may cause the 911 to swap ends."

With its low and snug interior, the 911 offers a truly race-inspired driving position.

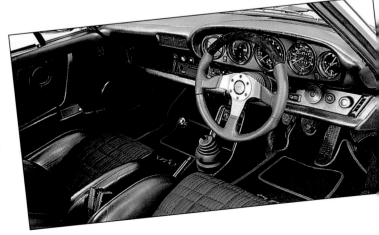

Milestones

1974 Porsche displays its outrageous new 911 Turbo at the Paris Motor Show.

Porsche's most ferocious 911 in 1974 was the European Carrera RS 3.0.

1975 Production begins at Porsche's Stuttgart Zuffenhausen factory.

The "Slant Nose" was Porsche's supercar of the early 1980s.

1976 The Turbo arrives in the U.S. as the 930 Turbo Carrera.

1978 The original 3.0-liter model is replaced by a new 3.3-liter version with an uprated chassis. This remains in production until 1989.

1991 With an all-new 3.6-liter engine the 911 Turbo is reborn using the basis of the 1989 Carrera 2.

UNDER THE SKIN

Serious chassis

A number of changes to the 911 were needed to control its ferocious level of power. Some of the modifications include a heavy-duty clutch, larger torsion bars from the Carreras and the suspension was tuned with anti-dive geometry used in the racing Carrera RSR. Turbo cars also boast different camber and caster settings and stronger anti-roll bars than standard 911s. Stopping the 911 Turbo are four-wheel vented discs.

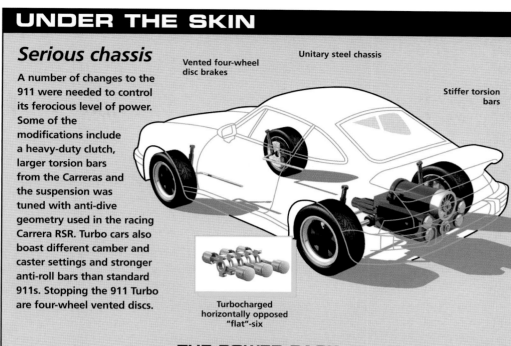

Vented four-wheel disc brakes

Unitary steel chassis

Stiffer torsion bars

Turbocharged horizontally opposed "flat"-six

THE POWER PACK

Turbo trailblazer

After BMW abandoned turbos in 1974, Porsche became just about the only manufacturer in the world to pick up the turbo gauntlet. It did so in spectacular style, thanks to its experience with the 917 racer. Porsche engineers took the flat-six air-cooled engine from the Carrera and gave it bigger pistons and cylinder bores. Then it modified the Bosch K-Jetronic fuel injection and installed a breakerless distributor. This was the first time any such ignition system was used on a production car. But the most important feature was the KKK Type 3 turbocharger. This increased power to 234 bhp in U.S. spec cars and 260 bhp in European versions.

Untamed

There is something magical about the very first 911 Turbo that subsequent versions never recaptured. Later 3.3-liter cars tamed the turbo lag, but the original model requires the absolute maximum driver effort to really exploit its full potential.

Fast and brutish, the 911 Turbo has now become an icon.

Porsche 911 TURBO

The addition of a turbocharger transformed the acclaimed 911 Carrera into a firecracker on wheels. The extra power was accompanied by a host of improvements derived from Porsche's racing program.

KKK turbocharger

In 1974, turbocharging had only really been tried by Chevrolet and BMW. Porsche knew that turbocharging had a strong appeal because of its successful turbocharged racing program. The roadgoing 911 Turbo uses a single KKK Type 3 turbocharger with a maximum 0.8 bar (about 12 PSI) of boost.

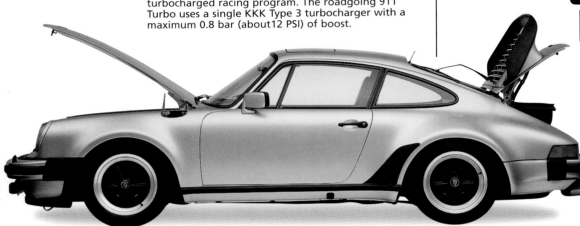

Wide wheels and tires

The wider cast-alloy wheels are a standard seven inches at the front and eight inches at the back. The standard tire specification was Pirelli Cinturato 205s up front and 215s at the rear, but wider, lower-profile 225/50 rear tires could be fitted as an option.

Stronger transmission

Although it still had only four speeds, the transmission was redesigned with longer ratios to take advantage of the higher possible speeds. The case casting was stronger and the synchromesh more resilient. Buyers were offered alternative final drivesets.

Luxury specification

The pricey Turbo was Porsche's top model. In the U.S., the Turbo came with standard air conditioning, leather upholstery, radio and power windows. A sliding sunroof was optional, but there was no targa roof option as with other 911 models.

Bulging arches

To cover the huge wheels and tires, the normally flush front arches have a notable flare in them. At the rear, the arches have gargantuan proportions.

'Whale tail' spoiler

Porsche's 'whale tail' rear spoiler was born on the 911 Turbo. It has two functions: The spoiler houses the turbo's intercooler and it also aids in high-speed downforce.

1976 Porsche 911 Turbo

ENGINE

Type: Horizontally opposed "flat" six-cylinder

Construction: Aluminum block and heads

Valve gear: Two valves per cylinder operated by a single chain-driven overhead camshaft per bank of cylinders

Bore and stroke: 3.74 in. x 2.77 in.

Displacement: 2,993 cc

Compression ratio: 6.5:1

Induction system: Bosch (K-jetronic) KKK turbo, intercooler fuel injection

Maximum power: 234 bhp at 5,500 rpm

Maximum torque: 245 lb-ft at 4,000 rpm

Top speed: 156 mph

0-60 mph: 4.9 sec.

TRANSMISSION

Four-speed manual

BODY/CHASSIS

Steel monocoque (unibody)

SPECIAL FEATURES

The deep-set front chin spoiler is unique to the 911 Turbo.

The 'whale tail' spoiler houses the Turbocharger's intercooler.

RUNNING GEAR

Steering: Rack-and-pinion

Front suspension: MacPherson struts, transverse lower A-arms, longitudinal torsion bars, anti-roll bar

Rear suspension: Semi-trailing arms with transverse torsion bars, shock absorbers and anti-roll bar

Brakes: Vented discs (front and rear)

Wheels: Alloy, 15-in. dia.

Tires: 215/60 VR15

DIMENSIONS

Length: 168.9 in.   **Width:** 69.9 in.

Height: 52.0 in.   **Wheelbase:** 89.4 in.

Track: 56.3 in. (front), 59.1 in. (rear)

Weight: 2,514 lbs.

Renault 16

We all take space-efficient front-wheel drive hatchbacks for granted these days, but in the early 1960s, there was no such thing. The ground-breaking Renault 16 changed all that.

"...durable and robust."

"The interior is typically French. The column shift is unusual for a European car but works very effectively, with a positive action and smooth shifts. The four-cylinder engine is lively enough, but it is the suspension that really impresses. The ride is very soft, yet the Renault has reassuringly good grip. While refinement may not be the first priority, practicality certainly is and all the materials in the cabin have a durable and robust feel."

Although family oriented, the turned aluminum-styled dash looks sporty.

Milestones

1964 In December, Renault reveals its revolutionary hatchback 16 with a standard 1,470-cc engine.

1968 The TS version is launched with a bigger 1,565-cc engine.

The swoopy 17 coupe uses Renault 16 engines.

1969 The 1565-cc engine is now available in automatic-transmission models.

1973 A range-topping TX version is launched with a bigger engine, five speeds and sports trim.

Underneath, the 16 owes a great deal to the Renault 4 of 1961.

1979 The 16 finally gives way to the new, larger Renault 20/30 series, which ironically does not prove to be as successful or long-lived as its predecessor.

UNDER THE SKIN

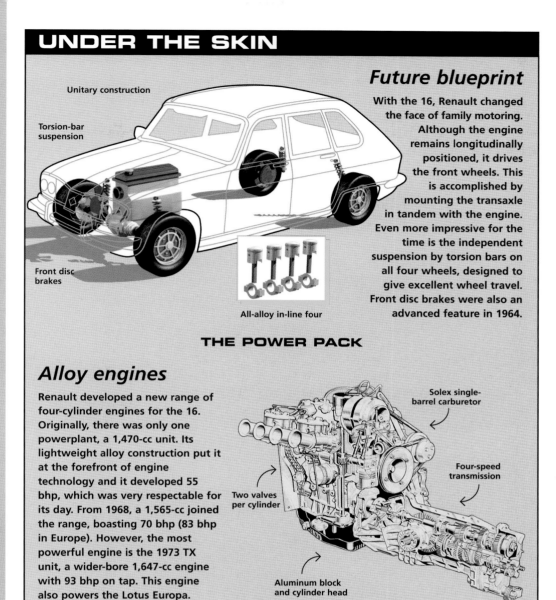

Unitary construction

Torsion-bar suspension

Front disc brakes

All-alloy in-line four

Future blueprint

With the 16, Renault changed the face of family motoring. Although the engine remains longitudinally positioned, it drives the front wheels. This is accomplished by mounting the transaxle in tandem with the engine. Even more impressive for the time is the independent suspension by torsion bars on all four wheels, designed to give excellent wheel travel. Front disc brakes were also an advanced feature in 1964.

THE POWER PACK

Alloy engines

Renault developed a new range of four-cylinder engines for the 16. Originally, there was only one powerplant, a 1,470-cc unit. Its lightweight alloy construction put it at the forefront of engine technology and it developed 55 bhp, which was very respectable for its day. From 1968, a 1,565-cc joined the range, boasting 70 bhp (83 bhp in Europe). However, the most powerful engine is the 1973 TX unit, a wider-bore 1,647-cc engine with 93 bhp on tap. This engine also powers the Lotus Europa.

Solex single-barrel carburetor

Four-speed transmission

Two valves per cylinder

Aluminum block and cylinder head

Bigger motor

The ultimate 16 is the TX, first seen in 1973. It has a larger engine (1,647 cc) producing 93 bhp, making it the most powerful in the range. It has a top speed of 106 mph and is fitted with a five-speed transmission, quad headlights and sports wheels.

Enthusiasts are drawn to the TX with its 93-bhp engine.

Renault 16

The Renault 16 remained in production for 15 years and won a big following for its innovative features and unrivaled practicality.

Front-wheel drive

In 1964, the benefits of front-wheel drive were just beginning to be appreciated. The Renault 16 led the way, showing its superior traction on bad surfaces and demonstrating its greater interior space.

Hatchback body

Back in 1964, most cars had a three-box shape (that is, with the trunk sticking out at the back), but Renault applied some logic and turned the trunk into a bigger area accessed by a large tailgate. Pundits at the time were not sure what to call it: was it a sedan or a station wagon? But the 16 launched a genre that we now know as the hatchback.

Adaptable cab

An attractive aspect the 16 was practic and extremely spacio interior. Front-wheel dri means that the floor flat and a colum gearshift provided great space to move around u front. Rear seat legroo was unrivaled at the tim The rear seats can als fold down for increase carrying capacit

Front disc brakes

Again, the 16 was ahead of its time in terms of braking. Few family cars could boast front disc brakes in 1964 and the 16 gained a reputation as a safe-braking and safe-handling car.

Specifications

1973 Renault 16 TS

ENGINE

Type: In-line four-cylinder

Construction: Aluminum block and head

Valve gear: Two valves per cylinder operated by a single camshaft via pushrods and rockers

Bore and stroke: 3.03 in. x 3.31 in.

Displacement: 1,565 cc

Compression ratio: 8.6:1

Induction system: Single Solex carburetor

Maximum power: 70 bhp at 5,200 rpm

Maximum torque: 86 lb-ft at 2,500 rpm

Top speed: 93 mph

0-60 mph: 16.2 sec.

TRANSMISSION

Four-speed manual or three-speed automatic

BODY/CHASSIS

Unitary construction with steel five-door hatchback body

SPECIAL FEATURES

To save yet more space, the spare tire is mounted in the engine bay.

A discreet tailgate spoiler is standard on the TX model.

RUNNING GEAR

Steering: Rack-and-pinion

Front suspension: Wishbones with torsion bars, anti-roll bar and shock absorbers

Rear suspension: Trailing arms with torsion bars, anti-roll bar and shock absorbers

Brakes: Discs (front), drums (rear)

Wheels: Steel, 14-in. dia.

Tires: 5 x 14 in.

DIMENSIONS

Length: 166.8 in.   **Width:** 65 in.

Height: 57 in.   **Wheelbase:** 106 in.

Track: 52.6 in. (front), 50.3 in. (rear)

Weight: 2,260 lbs.

Independent suspension

By 1960s standards, the Renault 16 was advanced in that it uses independent suspension all around. It has torsion bars front and rear, with wishbones up front and trailing arms at the rear. This system provides very generous suspension travel, allowing the springs to absorb potholes with ease.

Rolls-Royce **CAMARGUE**

The attractive Pininfarina-styled Rolls-Royce Camargue was the British company's flamboyant 1970s super-coupe—a car for Europe's ultra elite that was truly in a class of its own.

"...floating on air."

"As you would expect, the Camargue's cabin is ultra-luxurious, perfectly fitting its overall sense of occasion. The Camargue is in no way the best handling car around, but that's not its point. It's there for the effortless way it can travel long distances without being remotely tiring. The silence inside the cabin is uncanny, and the ride quality gives the impression of floating on air —which, with those hydraulics, is virtually what you're doing, anyway."

Rolls-Royce interiors are always luxurious, but the Camargue adds a little Italian style.

Milestones

1975 A flamboyant super-coupe slotting in at the top of the Rolls-Royce tree, the Camargue is launched to incredulous comments about its price tag.

1978 Production moves from Mulliner Park Ward in London to Rolls-Royce's own plant in Crewe.

The Rolls-Royce Corniche came just below the Camargue in the Rolls-Royce range.

1979 The suspension undergoes some improvements.

The Camargue is built on the Silver Shadow platform.

1986 As a final farewell, the last dozen fuel-injected Camargues are sold in the U.S. as a limited run 80th Anniversary edition, complete with white paint and twin red body stripes.

UNDER THE SKIN

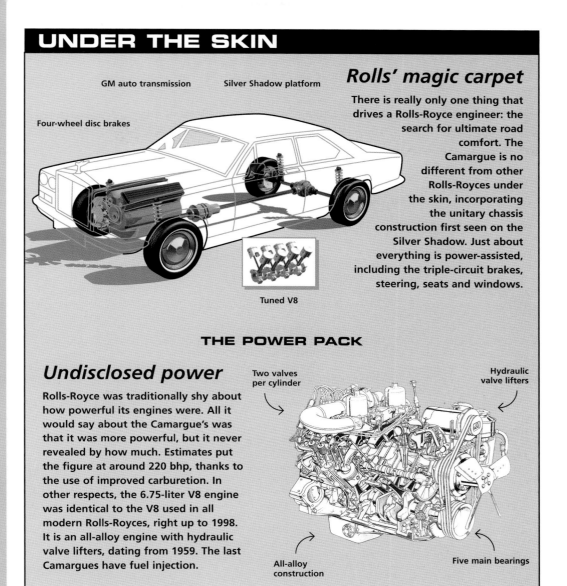

GM auto transmission   Silver Shadow platform

Four-wheel disc brakes

Tuned V8

Rolls' magic carpet

There is really only one thing that drives a Rolls-Royce engineer: the search for ultimate road comfort. The Camargue is no different from other Rolls-Royces under the skin, incorporating the unitary chassis construction first seen on the Silver Shadow. Just about everything is power-assisted, including the triple-circuit brakes, steering, seats and windows.

THE POWER PACK

Undisclosed power

Rolls-Royce was traditionally shy about how powerful its engines were. All it would say about the Camargue's was that it was more powerful, but it never revealed by how much. Estimates put the figure at around 220 bhp, thanks to the use of improved carburetion. In other respects, the 6.75-liter V8 engine was identical to the V8 used in all modern Rolls-Royces, right up to 1998. It is an all-alloy engine with hydraulic valve lifters, dating from 1959. The last Camargues have fuel injection.

Two valves per cylinder

Hydraulic valve lifters

All-alloy construction

Five main bearings

Italian style

The Camargue is unique among Rolls-Royces as an Italian-styled production coupe. It is assured of rising in value in coming years because, in its day, it represented the pinnacle of the Rolls-Royce stable—a two-door Rolls will always be collectible.

Styled by Pininfarina, the Camargue was initially built by Mulliner Park Ward.

Rolls-Royce **CAMARGUE**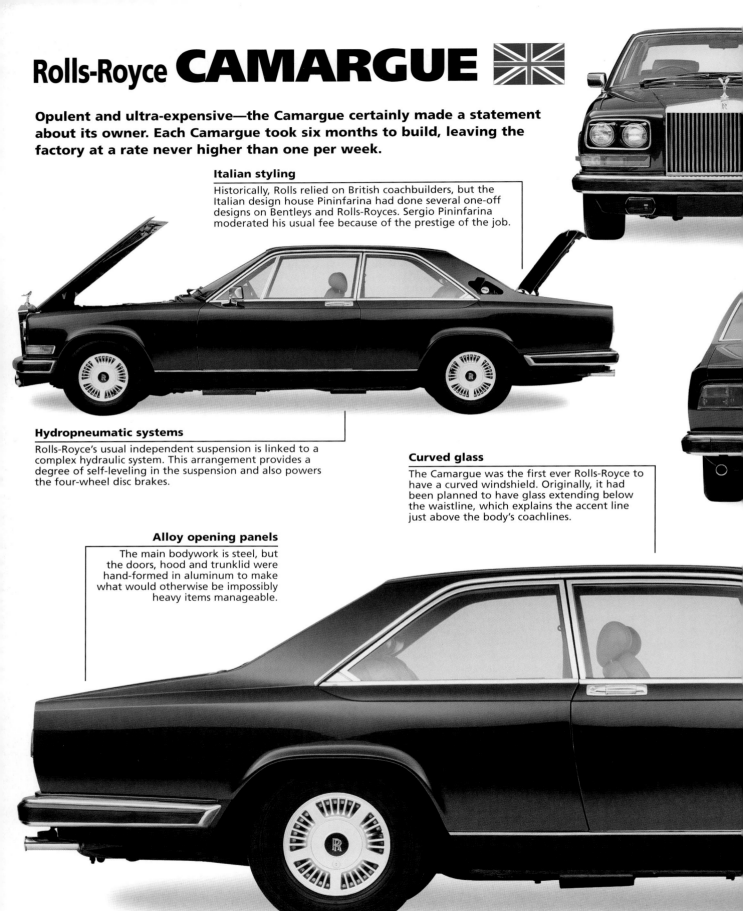

Opulent and ultra-expensive—the Camargue certainly made a statement about its owner. Each Camargue took six months to build, leaving the factory at a rate never higher than one per week.

Italian styling

Historically, Rolls relied on British coachbuilders, but the Italian design house Pininfarina had done several one-off designs on Bentleys and Rolls-Royces. Sergio Pininfarina moderated his usual fee because of the prestige of the job.

Hydropneumatic systems

Rolls-Royce's usual independent suspension is linked to a complex hydraulic system. This arrangement provides a degree of self-leveling in the suspension and also powers the four-wheel disc brakes.

Curved glass

The Camargue was the first ever Rolls-Royce to have a curved windshield. Originally, it had been planned to have glass extending below the waistline, which explains the accent line just above the body's coachlines.

Alloy opening panels

The main bodywork is steel, but the doors, hood and trunklid were hand-formed in aluminum to make what would otherwise be impossibly heavy items manageable.

Height of opulence

The luxurious interior has leather upholstery, split-level air conditioning, cigar lighters in the front and rear and folding trays.

Imposing grill

All Rolls-Royces have an impressive front grill, but the Camargue's is unusual in two respects. First, it is angled forward slightly at the top, and second, it is the widest grill ever to appear on a Rolls-Royce.

Split-level air conditioning

The star technical attraction of the Camargue was its amazing and effective split-level air conditioning system, which cost nearly 10 percent of the value of the car and had the cooling capacity of 30 domestic refrigerators.

Specifications

1980 Rolls-Royce Camargue

ENGINE

Type: V8

Construction: Aluminum block and heads

Valve gear: Two valves per cylinder operated by a single camshaft via pushrods and rockers

Bore and stroke: 4.10 in. x 3.90 in.

Displacement: 6,750 cc

Compression ratio: 7.3:1

Induction system: Twin SU sidedraft carburetors

Maximum power: 220 bhp at 4,000 rpm (est.)

Maximum torque: 330 lb-ft at 2,500 rpm (est.)

Top speed: 130 mph

0-60 mph: 9.7 sec.

TRANSMISSION

Three-speed automatic

BODY/CHASSIS

Unitary monocoque construction with subframes and steel two-door coupe body

SPECIAL FEATURES

The four headlights have their own individual wipers and washers.

On the Camargue, the traditional 'Flying Lady' mascot adorns the widest-ever Rolls-Royce grill.

RUNNING GEAR

Steering: Rack-and-pinion

Front suspension: Wishbones with coil springs, self-leveling, telescopic shock absorbers and anti-roll bar

Rear suspension: Semi-trailing arms with coil springs, self-leveling, telescopic shock absorbers and anti-roll bar

Brakes: Vented discs (front), solid discs (rear)

Wheels: Steel or alloy, 15-in. dia.

Tires: HR70 x 15

DIMENSIONS

Length: 203.5 in.   **Width:** 75.6 in.

Height: 57.9 in.   **Wheelbase:** 120.1 in.

Track: 60.0 in. (front), 59.6 in. (rear)

Weight: 5,175 lbs.

Saab 99 TURBO

With one stroke, Saab turned the rather unoriginal and boring 99 into the cult car of the early 1980s. All it took was the addition of a Garrett turbocharger and an extra 30 bhp and the 99 became a 120-mph rocket.

"...the handling is a surprise."

"You might expect the 99 Turbo to be heavy and clumsy, but it isn't. It's heavy all right, but that helps give an excellent ride while the handling is a real surprise. The Turbo turns sharply and, although the unassisted steering really requires effort at parking speeds, once you are on the move it is a delight. This is matched by impressive acceleration, especially once the turbo spools up. The 99 remains a solid, comfortable car."

Leather seats were a factory option in Europe's trend-setting turbo.

Milestones

1978 After 100 prototypes have covered over three million miles between them in a typically Saab thorough approach, the production Saab 99 Turbo makes its debut at the Frankfurt Motor Show.

Saab's 99 remained in production for 20 years.

1979 Saab quickly puts the 99 Turbo into action in the World Rally Championship as a replacement for the existing normally-aspirated 2.0-liter EMS. When Stig Blomqvist wins the Swedish Rally (for the fifth time), it is the first ever win for a turbocharged rally car.

Saab still carries on the tradition of turbocharging its cars, including the larger 9000.

1980 Even with turbo power the 99 is becoming outdated in world rallying, where it's up against purpose-built rally cars. With the launch of the 900 Turbo, the 99 is discontinued in early 1981.

UNDER THE SKIN

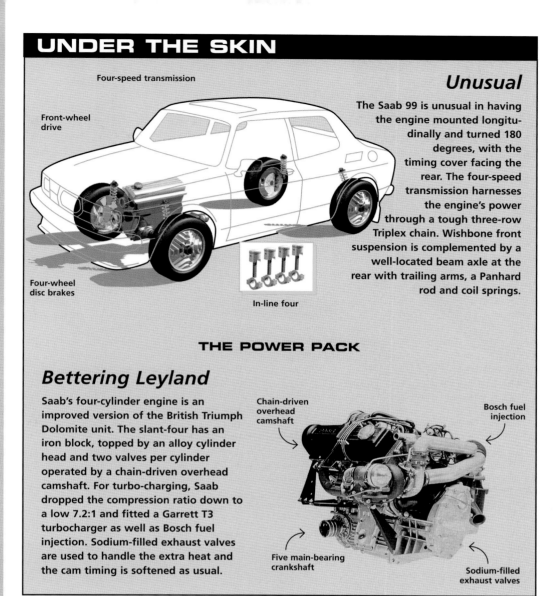

Four-speed transmission

Front-wheel drive

Four-wheel disc brakes

In-line four

Unusual

The Saab 99 is unusual in having the engine mounted longitudinally and turned 180 degrees, with the timing cover facing the rear. The four-speed transmission harnesses the engine's power through a tough three-row Triplex chain. Wishbone front suspension is complemented by a well-located beam axle at the rear with trailing arms, a Panhard rod and coil springs.

THE POWER PACK

Bettering Leyland

Saab's four-cylinder engine is an improved version of the British Triumph Dolomite unit. The slant-four has an iron block, topped by an alloy cylinder head and two valves per cylinder operated by a chain-driven overhead camshaft. For turbo-charging, Saab dropped the compression ratio down to a low 7.2:1 and fitted a Garrett T3 turbocharger as well as Bosch fuel injection. Sodium-filled exhaust valves are used to handle the extra heat and the cam timing is softened as usual.

Chain-driven overhead camshaft

Bosch fuel injection

Five main-bearing crankshaft

Sodium-filled exhaust valves

Two doors

Although the three-door hatchback version is the most common, the two-door sedan models are more desirable because of their rarity (only 1,000 were made) and because they are lighter and therefore faster. All were either red or black.

Because of their rarity, enthusiasts prefer the two-door 99 Turbo sedan.

Saab 99 TURBO

Although the 99 first appeared in 1968, Saab managed to make the 99 Turbo look impressive by adding special wheels and making the cars exclusively red or black.

Four-cylinder engine
Saab worked wonders on the British-designed slant-four engine and made it tough and reliable. These models have different pistons and a lower compression ratio because of the use of the turbocharger.

Front spoiler
The ordinary 99 had excellent ground clearance—useful in Swedish winters. Although the Turbo wasn't lowered for its performance role, it was given a deep front spoiler to prevent excess air from getting under the car at speed.

No rocker panels
Part of the strength of a conventional modern monocoque design is in the door sills. The Saab did without and still proved to be extremely strong. The doors come right down to the bottom of the car and there are no sills to step over as you get in.

Special wheels
One way the Turbo was made to stand out from the lesser 99s was by fitting special 'Inca' alloy wheels. Rally versions used eight-spoke Minilite alloy wheels.

Rack-and-pinion steering

All the 99s use rack-and-pinion steering. Surprisingly for such a heavy front-wheel drive car there is no power assistance. The steering wheel is therefore unusually large to give enough leverage.

Front-hinging hood

Extending all the way to the cowl, the hood can be slid forwards and then hinged forward at the front for access to the engine.

Specifications
1978 Saab 99 Turbo

ENGINE

Type: In-line four-cylinder

Construction: Cast-iron block and alloy head

Valve gear: Two valves per cylinder operated by a single chain-driven overhead camshaft

Bore and stroke: 3.54 in. x 3.07 in.

Displacement: 1,985 cc

Compression ratio: 7.2:1

Induction system: Bosch fuel injection with Garrett T3 turbocharger

Maximum power: 145 bhp at 5,000 rpm

Maximum torque: 174 lb-ft at 3,000 rpm

Top speed: 120 mph

0-60 mph: 9.1 sec.

TRANSMISSION

Four-speed manual

BODY/CHASSIS

Unitary construction steel monocoque two-door sedan or three-door hatchback body

SPECIAL FEATURES

Vents on the rear quarter panels are a feature of all 99s.

Big black bumpers are fitted to all later 99s; early cars use chrome bumpers.

RUNNING GEAR

Steering: Rack-and-pinion

Front suspension: Double wishbones with coil springs, telescopic shock absorbers and anti-roll bar

Rear suspension: Beam axle with coil springs, Panhard rod, trailing arms and telescopic shock absorbers

Brakes: Discs (front and rear)

Wheels: Alloy, 5.5 x 15 in.

Tires: Pirelli P6, 175/70 HR15

DIMENSIONS

Length: 178.3 in.   **Width:** 66.5 in.

Height: 56.7 in.   **Wheelbase:** 97.5 in.

Track: 55.1 in. (front), 55.9 in. (rear)

Weight: 2,715 lbs.

Talbot SUNBEAM-LOTUS

Out of an unpromising car—the Talbot Sunbeam—a championship-winning rally car was created. Lotus supplied an engine that made this car the fastest of the hot hatches that appeared around this time.

"...generous power."

"Unlike front-wheel drive cars such as the Volkswagen Rabbit, the rear-wheel drive Sunbeam is easier to control finely between understeer and oversteer with the throttle. The generous power of the twin-cam engine means that there's plenty of wheelspin and oversteer available. The engine is the star of this car, with its willing, free-revving nature and wonderful exhaust note. Throttle response is immediate and there's plenty of torque."

A chunky-rimmed steering wheel and a tachometer hint at the car's performance.

Milestones

1977 Chrysler launches the Sunbeam range of hatchbacks for Europe. The new car is based on the previous Plymouth Cricket sedan floorpan, but shortened by 3 inches and topped by a neat three-door hatchback body.

1979 After a European takeover by Peugeot, the name changes to Talbot. To celebrate, the Sunbeam-Lotus is launched.

The next hottest Sunbeam was the 1600 Ti.

1980 Six world championship events are entered; Henri Toivonen wins the Lombard-RAC rally.

The Lotus Elite, launched in 1974, shares its twin-cam engine with the Sunbeam-Lotus.

1981 As Talbot wins the World Rally Championship or makes against the might of the Audi Quattro, the plug is pulled on the whole Sunbeam range, including the Lotus.

UNDER THE SKIN

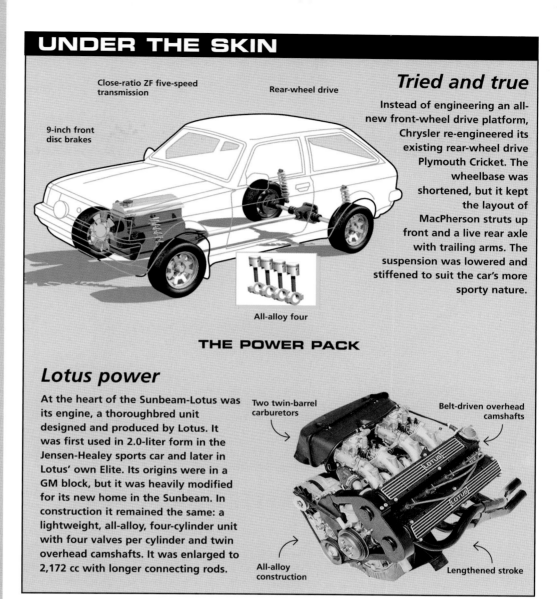

Close-ratio ZF five-speed transmission

Rear-wheel drive

9-inch front disc brakes

All-alloy four

THE POWER PACK

Tried and true

Instead of engineering an all-new front-wheel drive platform, Chrysler re-engineered its existing rear-wheel drive Plymouth Cricket. The wheelbase was shortened, but it kept the layout of MacPherson struts up front and a live rear axle with trailing arms. The suspension was lowered and stiffened to suit the car's more sporty nature.

Lotus power

At the heart of the Sunbeam-Lotus was its engine, a thoroughbred unit designed and produced by Lotus. It was first used in 2.0-liter form in the Jensen-Healey sports car and later in Lotus' own Elite. Its origins were in a GM block, but it was heavily modified for its new home in the Sunbeam. In construction it remained the same: a lightweight, all-alloy, four-cylinder unit with four valves per cylinder and twin overhead camshafts. It was enlarged to 2,172 cc with longer connecting rods.

Two twin-barrel carburetors

Belt-driven overhead camshafts

All-alloy construction

Lengthened stroke

Lotus hatch

The Sunbeam was an extremely drab little hatchback, hastily conceived to fill a gap in the market for parent company Chrysler. The Sunbeam-Lotus was the opposite: a rally-winning homologation special with the magic Lotus badge.

With just over 2,000 units built, the Sunbeam-Lotus is highly collectable.

Talbot **SUNBEAM-LOTUS**

A Lotus engine, modified suspension, racing transmission and unique cosmetic appeal, as well as a distinguished competition pedigree, a Lotus badge and considerable rarity, make the Sunbeam-Lotus a classic.

Lotus engine

The very heart of the Sunbeam-Lotus was its engine. The 2.2-liter unit was a modified version of that used in the Lotus Elite—it boasted probably the most advanced specification of any roadgoing four-cylinder engine then being produced.

Five-speed transmission

Unlike all other members of the Sunbeam family, which had a four-speed transmission, the Lotus has a close-ratio ZF five-speed. The transmission and a higher axle ratio allowed much higher cruising speeds.

Unique color scheme

The Sunbeam-Lotus had a distinctive paint finish. Early cars have a black main body color with a wide silver stripe at waist level. Later cars like this one had a light metallic main body color with a black stripe.

Lowered suspension

Although the suspension is lowered and the spring and shock rates are stiffer, the suspension is basically shared with the unmodified Sunbeams. That means a live rear axle located by four links, and front struts and coils with an anti-roll bar.

Standard interior

The Sunbeam-Lotus was based on the top-of-the-range GLS model. This means it is well equipped, but it also means that it doesn't feel as special as the rest of the car: for instance, there is no Lotus badging on the interior. Equipment includes special rally-style front seats with headrests, tinted glass, brushed nylon trim and a split/fold rear seat.

Lotus badging

Talbot liberally applied Lotus badges to the body, notably on the front fenders and grill. The connection was more than just show, though, because Lotus gave one of its coveted Type numbers to the project—Type 81.

Specifications
Talbot Sunbeam-Lotus

ENGINE
Type: In-line four-cylinder

Construction: Aluminum cylinder block and head

Valve gear: Four valves per cylinder operated by belt-driven double overhead camshafts

Bore and stroke: 3.75 in. x 3.0 in.

Displacement: 2,174 cc

Compression ratio: 9.44:1

Induction system: Two twin-barrel carburetors

Maximum power: 150 bhp at 5,750 rpm

Maximum torque: 150 lb-ft at 4,500 rpm

Top speed: 121 mph

0-60 mph: 7.4 sec.

TRANSMISSION
ZF five-speed manual

BODY/CHASSIS
Unitary monocoque construction with three-door steel hatchback body

SPECIAL FEATURES

The Sunbeam-Lotus was unique in the range in having special Lotus-designed double four-spoke alloy wheels.

The engine is based on a GM block and was designed by Lotus.

RUNNING GEAR
Steering: Rack-and-pinion

Front suspension: MacPherson struts with coil springs, shock absorbers and anti-roll bar

Rear suspension: Live axle with trailing arms, coil springs and shock absorbers

Brakes: Discs (front), drums (rear)

Wheels: Alloy, 6 x 13 in.

Tires: 185/70 HR13

DIMENSIONS
Length: 151.2 in. **Width:** 63.1 in.

Height: 55.3 in. **Wheelbase:** 95.0 in.

Track: 51.75 in. (front), 51.25 in. (rear)

Weight: 2,116 lbs.

Toyota CELICA

Before the Celica, most Japanese mass-market coupes were simply two-door versions of mundane sedans. The Celica changed all that. It was genuinely stylish, extremely reliable and loaded with extras.

"...a fine-sounding engine."

"Faced with the mass of gauges and controls, your expectations are high. Start the engine and you're not disappointed. This is a fine-sounding engine that's not especially powerful but is fun to use. The controls—clutch, steering and gearshift—are light, and ride comfort is soft and forgiving. What's more, the performance is quiet and refined. Handling is hardly super taut, but although the Celica is no top-grade sports car, it's a capable coupe."

A racy steering wheel complements the deep-set gauges and body-hugging seats.

Milestones

1970 Toyota launches its all-new Celica brand—a smart coupe based on the Carina sedan—which is available in liftback coupe and notchback coupe styles.

A liftback version was also offered and has even sportier styling than the hardtop.

1971 U.S. imports begin with a 2.0-liter engined model.

1975 In the U.S., engine displacement grows to 2.2 liters to cope with emissions regulations.

Celicas are still being built but they are now front drive.

1977 The original Celica is replaced by an all-new second-generation series with more angular styling.

UNDER THE SKIN

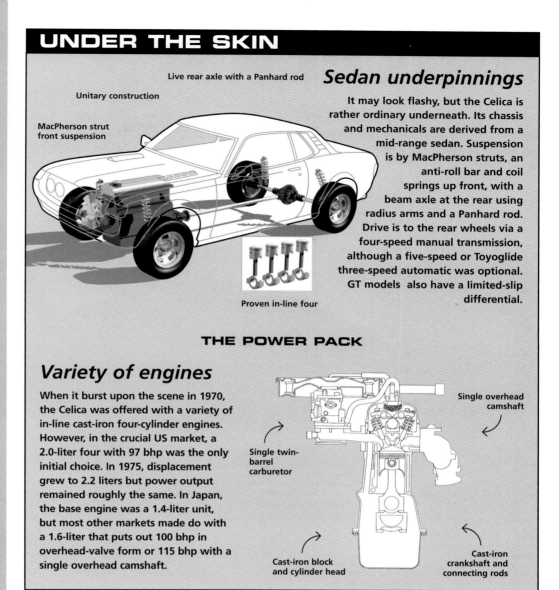

Unitary construction

MacPherson strut front suspension

Live rear axle with a Panhard rod

Sedan underpinnings

It may look flashy, but the Celica is rather ordinary underneath. Its chassis and mechanicals are derived from a mid-range sedan. Suspension is by MacPherson struts, an anti-roll bar and coil springs up front, with a beam axle at the rear using radius arms and a Panhard rod. Drive is to the rear wheels via a four-speed manual transmission, although a five-speed or Toyoglide three-speed automatic was optional. GT models also have a limited-slip differential.

Proven in-line four

THE POWER PACK

Variety of engines

When it burst upon the scene in 1970, the Celica was offered with a variety of in-line cast-iron four-cylinder engines. However, in the crucial US market, a 2.0-liter four with 97 bhp was the only initial choice. In 1975, displacement grew to 2.2 liters but power output remained roughly the same. In Japan, the base engine was a 1.4-liter unit, but most other markets made do with a 1.6-liter that puts out 100 bhp in overhead-valve form or 115 bhp with a single overhead camshaft.

Single twin-barrel carburetor

Single overhead camshaft

Cast-iron block and cylinder head

Cast-iron crankshaft and connecting rods

Sporty Celica

If there is a model to choose, the sporty GT tops the list. It boasts a twin-cam engine, improved handling and standard factory alloy wheels. Today, these early Celicas are still underrated as classics, and good examples are reasonably priced.

GTs are the most interesting of the first-generation Celicas.

Toyota **CELICA**

If you wanted a good value, a sharply styled coupe with compact dimensions, good gas mileage and total reliability, the Celica was hard to beat in the early 1970s. Not surprisingly, it became extremely popular.

Overhead valve or overhead cam
Four different engine sizes were offered in the Celica worldwide: 1.4, 1.6, 2.0 and 2.2 liters. Smaller engines were overhead-valve units, although GTs had a 97-bhp, 2.0-liter unit with a single overhead camshaft.

Live rear axle
Like most Japanese cars of this era, the Celica is conservatively engineered. It retains a live rear axle, but it uses coil springs and is located by radius arms and a Panhard rod.

Choice of transmission
A four-speed manual was standard, but a five-speed could be ordered. Synchromesh was fitted to all gears, resulting in smooth and refined shifts.

Two body styles
Early Celicas came as either two-door hardtops or three-door fastbacks with lift-up tailgates. Styling was heavily influenced by U.S. cars of the era, a factor that proved instrumental in its sales success.

Double headlights

The quad headlights mounted in a recessed grill bear a strong resemblance to those found on 1970-1971 Ford Torino Cobras. Early models have distinctive chrome bumpers that lasted until 1973 on U.S. cars.

Spacious interior

Unusual for a compact coupe, the Celica has ample room for four and can accommodate a fifth person in a pinch.

Specifications
1971 Toyota Celica GT

ENGINE
Type: In-line four-cylinder
Construction: Cast-iron block and head
Valve gear: Two valves per cylinder operated by a single overhead camshaft
Bore and stroke: 3.37 in. x 3.15 in.
Displacement: 1,968 cc
Compression ratio: 8.5:1
Induction system: Single twin-barrel carburetor
Maximum power: 97 bhp at 5,500 rpm
Maximum torque: 106 lb-ft at 3,600 rpm
Top speed: 104 mph
0-60 mph: 13.3 sec.

TRANSMISSION
Five-speed manual

BODY/CHASSIS
Unitary monocoque construction with steel two-door coupe body

SPECIAL FEATURES

Large turn signals are housed in the end of the front fenders.

Vents in the hood are an American design feature copied by Toyota.

RUNNING GEAR
Steering: Recirculating ball
Front suspension: MacPherson struts with trailing links, coil springs, telescopic shock absorbers and anti-roll bar
Rear suspension: Live axle with radius arms, Panhard rod, coil springs and telescopic shock absorbers
Brakes: Discs (front), drums (rear)
Wheels: Steel, 13-in. dia.
Tires: 6.45 x 13 in.

DIMENSIONS
Length: 169.2 in.   **Width:** 63.0 in.
Height: 51.6 in.   **Wheelbase:** 95.5 in.
Track: 51.2 in. (front), 51.4 in. (rear)
Weight: 2,430 lbs

Triumph **TR6**

To the enthusiast, the TR6 was the final Triumph TR. It was the last to have a separate chassis and more power than grip; a car that needed a real driver to get all the performance out of its old-fashioned design.

"...performance is excellent."

"It helps if you know what you're doing with a TR6. Some cars look after you, but not the TR6. It's easy to get the front-heavy Triumph into corners too fast, but it is well mannered enough for the tail not to come around. The steering is heavy, low geared, and the wheel is at the driver's chest. The ride is harsh and firm and yet the TR6 rises above all that. Straight-line power is excellent, and once you realize the chassis' limitations, it really is great fun."

The simple wooden dashboard is typically British. The steering wheel is right in your lap and gauges clear and easy to read.

Milestones

1953 Triumph TR line starts with the four-cylinder TR2 and progresses through TR3 in 1955, TR3A in 1958, TR4 in 1961, and TR4A in 1961, by which time engine size has grown to 2.2 liters and independent rear suspension has appeared.

TR2 started the famous TR line.

1967 Fitting the 2.5-liter straight-six to the TR produces the TR5. It has Italian styling, like the TR4 and 4A.

1969 Karmann of Germany restyles the front and rear to give the TR6 its characteristic chopped tail and full-width front grill. It has wider wheels than the TR5 and a front anti-roll bar. American spec cars uses two Stromberg carburetors rather than fuel injection for emissions reasons.

1973 The engine characteristics are changed, and power reduced with a different camshaft.

1976 Production ends.

The TR5 uses a straight-six engine.

UNDER THE SKIN

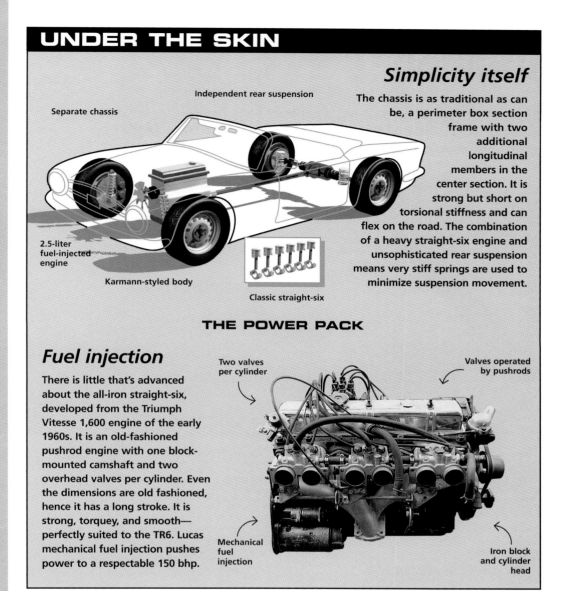

Independent rear suspension

Separate chassis

2.5-liter fuel-injected engine

Karmann-styled body

Classic straight-six

Simplicity itself

The chassis is as traditional as can be, a perimeter box section frame with two additional longitudinal members in the center section. It is strong but short on torsional stiffness and can flex on the road. The combination of a heavy straight-six engine and unsophisticated rear suspension means very stiff springs are used to minimize suspension movement.

THE POWER PACK

Fuel injection

There is little that's advanced about the all-iron straight-six, developed from the Triumph Vitesse 1,600 engine of the early 1960s. It is an old-fashioned pushrod engine with one block-mounted camshaft and two overhead valves per cylinder. Even the dimensions are old fashioned, hence it has a long stroke. It is strong, torquey, and smooth—perfectly suited to the TR6. Lucas mechanical fuel injection pushes power to a respectable 150 bhp.

Two valves per cylinder

Valves operated by pushrods

Mechanical fuel injection

Iron block and cylinder head

Euro-Brit

Most TR6s were sold in the U.S. where emission laws ruined engine output, dropping it to 106 bhp with twin carburetors. That means the pre-1974 European spec 150-bhp car is the one to go for, despite the sometimes troublesome mechanical fuel injection.

Pre-1974 TR6s have a 150-bhp fuel-injected engine and the best performance.

Triumph **TR6** 🇬🇧

Rugged and uncompromising, crude and old fashioned, the TR6 was one of the last of its breed and it had enough performance, style, and character to make up for all its shortcomings.

Rack-and-pinion steering

British manufacturers were the first to be convinced of the advantages of rack-and-pinion steering and the TR6 is so equipped.

Straight-six engine

The TR5 and TR6 were the only TRs to have a six-cylinder engine. The earlier cars had four-cylinders, as did the TR7. TR8s had V8s.

Foldaway top

The top is easy to put up and down. When stowed, it fits neatly away behind the seats and fits flush with the bodywork so it won't spoil the lines of the car.

Wishbone front suspension

In Britain, a sports car's front suspension was traditionally double wishbone. The TR6 is no exception.

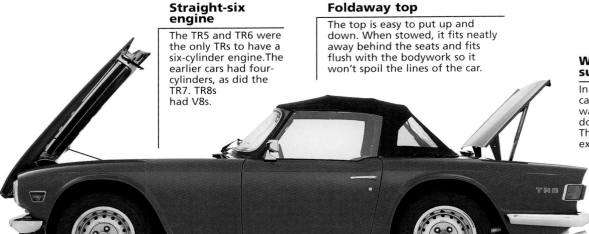

Front disc brakes

The TR6 uses 10.9-inch Girling disc brakes in the front, while the rear brakes still use drums.

Semi-trailing arm suspension

The semi-trailing arm independent rear suspension was better than the old TR's live axle but it was not perfect, so Triumph gave it wide (for the time) rear tires along with stiff springs to limit its movement.

Overdrive transmission

Although the TR6 has a four-speed transmission, it's equipped with overdrive, operating on the top three ratios to effectively give seven gears.

Karmann styling

Karmann skillfully transformed the look of the TR with minimal changes. It added wraparound and squared tail lghts and redesigned the front end.

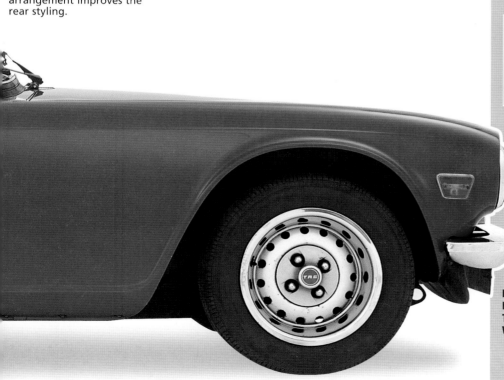

Dual exhaust

With a straight-six engine there was no need for twin exhaust tail pipes but this arrangement improves the rear styling.

Specifications
1970 Triumph TR6

ENGINE
Type: Straight-six
Construction: Cast-iron block and head
Valve gear: Two valves per cylinder operated by single block-mounted camshaft, pushrods and rockers
Bore and stroke: 2.95 in. x 3.74 in.
Displacement: 2,498 cc
Compression ratio: 9.5:1
Induction system: Lucas mechanical fuel injection
Maximum power: 150 bhp at 5,500 rpm
Maximum torque: 164 lb-ft at 3,500 rpm
Top speed: 119 mph
0-60 mph: 8.4 sec.

TRANSMISSION
Four-speed manual transmission with overdrive on top three ratios

BODY/CHASSIS
Box section perimeter chassis with steel two-door convertible body

SPECIAL FEATURES

Lucas mechanical fuel injection was intended to increase power, but it proved to be temperamental and unreliable at low speeds.

Karmann's restyle of the front and rear gave the TR6 a muscular look.

RUNNING GEAR
Steering: Rack-and-pinion
Front suspension: Double wishbones with coil springs, telescopic shocks and anti-roll bar
Rear suspension: Semi-trailing arms with coil springs and telescopic shocks
Brakes: Discs 10.9 in. dia. (front), drums (rear)
Wheels: Steel disc, 5.5 in. x 15 in.

DIMENSIONS
Length: 159 in.   **Width:** 58 in.
Height: 50 in.   **Wheelbase:** 88 in.
Track: 49.3 in. (front), 48.8 in. (rear)
Weight: 2,473 lbs.

Triumph GT6

The Spitfire was a huge success for Triumph, so the company built on this by expanding the range with a hard-top GT version. A straight-six engine improved performance and the roof added refinement.

"...endowed with power."

"The GT6 was built to be a step above the Spitfire, and it shows. The interior has more luxurious embellishments. The driving position is comfortable, with an abundance of leg room and well located pedals. The smooth straight six is endowed with ample power that really gives the GT6 a very decent rate of speed. On early swing-axle cars, uncontrollable at-the-limit situations can occur, but the ensuing models are much more manageable."

A polished wooden dashboard makes the GT6 much more luxurious than the Spitfire.

Milestones

1962 Triumph launches its Spitfire, a new small, separate-chassis sports car with a four-cylinder engine.

The Spitfire was launched four years before the GT6.

1966 A new Spitfire variant is introduced. The GT6 uses the straight-six engine from the Triumph Vitesse and has a fastback grafted onto the Spitfire shell. It produces 95 bhp.

The 2-liter straight-six engine was also fitted to the Vitesse.

1968 Following criticism of the wayward rear end, the rear suspension is modified. The new model is known as the GT6 Mk II, or GT6+ in the U.S.

1970 The styling is modified like the Spitfire Mk IV's to produce the GT6 Mk III. It lasts until 1973. More than 40,000 have been built.

UNDER THE SKIN

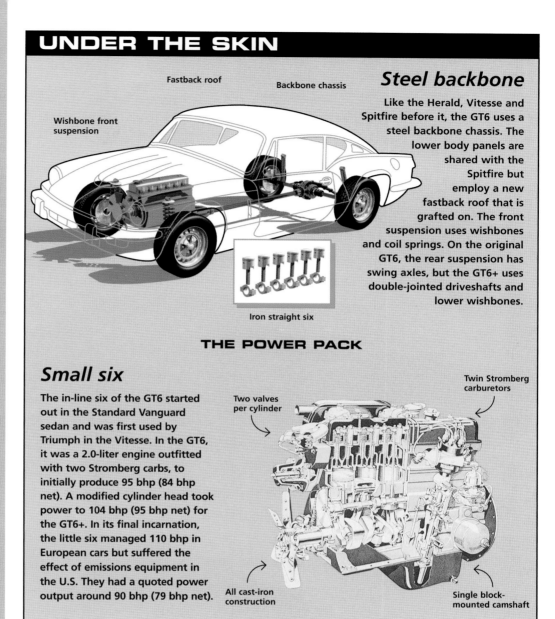

Fastback roof

Backbone chassis

Wishbone front suspension

Iron straight six

Steel backbone

Like the Herald, Vitesse and Spitfire before it, the GT6 uses a steel backbone chassis. The lower body panels are shared with the Spitfire but employ a new fastback roof that is grafted on. The front suspension uses wishbones and coil springs. On the original GT6, the rear suspension has swing axles, but the GT6+ uses double-jointed driveshafts and lower wishbones.

THE POWER PACK

Small six

The in-line six of the GT6 started out in the Standard Vanguard sedan and was first used by Triumph in the Vitesse. In the GT6, it was a 2.0-liter engine outfitted with two Stromberg carbs, to initially produce 95 bhp (84 bhp net). A modified cylinder head took power to 104 bhp (95 bhp net) for the GT6+. In its final incarnation, the little six managed 110 bhp in European cars but suffered the effect of emissions equipment in the U.S. They had a quoted power output around 90 bhp (79 bhp net).

Two valves per cylinder

Twin Stromberg carburetors

All cast-iron construction

Single block-mounted camshaft

Last and best

The final Mk III iteration of the GT6 is regarded by many as the finest. Its sharper styling is much more crisp than the earlier cars and, at least in European form, it offers the most power. The very last cars have a brake booster and tinted glass.

Cleaner styling makes the last GT6 the most popular.

Triumph **GT6**

It may look like a fastback version of the Spitfire, but the GT6 is much more than that. A smooth six-cylinder engine and luxurious interior turn it into a kind of mini E-Type.

Tight turning circle

Like other small Triumphs, the GT6 has an incredibly tight turning circumference of only 25 feet. It almost rotates around its rear wheels. In fact, it turns so tightly that there is severe wheel scrape on full lock.

Six-cylinder engine

Instead of the Spitfire's frail four-cylinder engine, the GT6 uses the six-cylinder unit from the Triumph Vitesse. It offers a more substantial amount of power and torque than the Spitfire's unit and is more refined.

Fastback roof

The racy fastback roof is grafted onto the same lower body panels as used by the Spitfire. The styling is similar to that of Spitfire Le Mans racers.

Backbone chassis

Although its main competitor, the MGB GT, used unitary construction, the GT6 stuck with a separate chassis. It is a steel-backbone design with a fork at either end to hold the engine, final drive and suspension.

Specifications

1971 Triumph GT6 Mk III

ENGINE

Type: In-line six-cylinder

Construction: Cast-iron block and head

Valve gear: Two valves per cylinder operated by a single camshaft via pushrods and rockers

Bore and stroke: 2.94 in. x 2.99 in.

Displacement: 1,998 cc

Compression ratio: 8.0:1

Induction system: Twin Stromberg carburetors

Maximum power: 79 bhp at 4,900 rpm

Maximum torque: 97 lb-ft at 2,700 rpm

Top speed: 107 mph

0-60 mph: 12.3 sec.

TRANSMISSION

Four-speed manual with overdrive

BODY/CHASSIS

Steel chassis and two-door coupe body

SPECIAL FEATURES

Louvered vents on the C-pillar improve cabin ventilation.

The fold-forward, clamshell hood allows excellent access to the engine.

RUNNING GEAR

Steering: Rack-and-pinion

Front suspension: Double wishbones with coil springs and telescopic shock absorbers

Rear suspension: Swing axles with a transverse semi-elliptic leaf spring and telescopic shock absorbers

Brakes: Discs (front), drums (rear)

Wheels: Steel, 4.5 x 13 in.

Tires: Dunlop, 15SR-13

DIMENSIONS

Length: 149.0 in.   **Width:** 58.5 in.

Height: 47.5 in.   **Wheelbase:** 83.0 in.

Track: 49.0 in. (front), 51.0 in. (rear)

Weight: 2,013 lbs.

Revised rear suspension

The handling of the GT6 Mk I was much criticized, and so later cars gained a modified rear suspension with lower wishbones and double-jointed driveshafts.

Hood bulge

In order to clear the taller, longer engine, the Spitfire's hood had to be remodeled with a bulge. It was not only functional, but very agreeable with the car's performance image.

Triumph STAG

Launched in 1970, the Stag was intended to move Triumph into the sporty grand touring segment. Gutsy, handsome, fast and practical, it became an automotive icon through the 1970s.

"...refined and comfortable."

"Because it was an entirely unique car in 1970, it was difficult at the time to appreciate the Stag's attributes. The V8 engine is smooth, with a refined rumble resonating from the exhaust. Acceleration is average at best. The Stag is more at home high-speed cruising than standing-start drag racing. The coil-sprung suspension results in a comfortable ride and, although it rolls through turns, the car is easy to control."

As befitting a grand tourer, the Stag has leather upholstery and a wood dash.

Milestones

1970 Triumph boldly launches its Michelotti-styled V8-powered Stag. It is the first Triumph sports car to embody unitary construction and the first to be powered by a V8 engine.

1971 Triumph begins to export the Stag to the U.S.

Also styled by Michelotti, the gutsy TR6 was far removed from the refined Stag.

1973 A Mark II version is finally introduced. It has a more refined V8 engine, better steering, improved seating and a different soft top.

Dolomite Sprints use a slant four which is essentially half of the Stag's 3.0-liter V8.

1977 The final Stags are produced after a relatively small production run.

UNDER THE SKIN

Unitary construction

Independent rear suspension

Power front disc brakes

Refined V8

Sedan-based

Italian design house Michelotti asked for a Triumph 2000 sedan to use as the basis for a styling exercise in 1965. This eventually evolved into the Stag. The floorpan is a shortened 2000 unit, resulting in unitary construction—a first for Triumph sports cars. The front suspension consists of MacPherson struts and an anti-roll bar, while the independent rear end benefits from coil springs and semi-trailing arms.

THE POWER PACK

Home-grown

Triumph remained fiercely independent even after its merger with Leyland. Thus, when it came to fitting an engine into the Stag, Triumph decided to use its own V8, a single overhead-cam, 3.0-liter unit with alloy cylinder heads. In 1973 the unit received reshaped combustion chambers and higher compression pistons with domed tops making it both smoother and quieter. However, early engines suffered from cooling and reliability problems which severely tarnished the Stag's image.

Single overhead camshaft

Twin SU carburetors

Cast-iron block with alloy heads

Seven main-bearing crankshaft

Mk II Stag

Post-1973 Stags, with a reworked V8 engine, improved seating and attractive five-spoke wheels, are preferred by collectors. The best investment is an all-original, low-mileage Mk II. If well maintained, Stags can be very reliable.

The best buy is the later, post-1973 Stag Mk II.

Triumph STAG

The Stag may have gained a reputation as being a fragile sports car—and an unreliable one at that—but its mix of good road manners, Italian styling, rarity and practicality make it an attractive classic today.

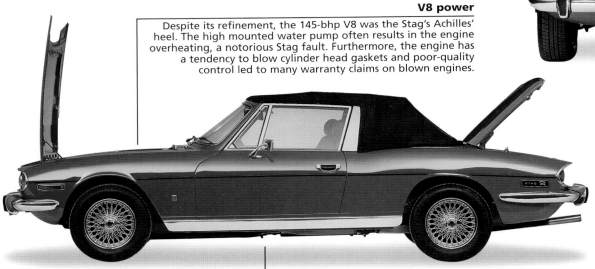

V8 power

Despite its refinement, the 145-bhp V8 was the Stag's Achilles' heel. The high mounted water pump often results in the engine overheating, a notorious Stag fault. Furthermore, the engine has a tendency to blow cylinder head gaskets and poor-quality control led to many warranty claims on blown engines.

BMW-like suspension

The Stag's suspension—MacPherson struts and lower wishbones up front and semi-trailing arms at the rear—is strongly reminiscent of contemporary BMW's.

Italian styling

The attractive final shape was a combination of Michelotti and Triumph ideas. Prototypes were shuttled between the Triumph factory and the Italian design house in Turin for modifications. The padded roll-over bar was a unique feature, as were the generously-sized rear seats.

Choice of tops

Customers could specify whether they wanted soft or hard tops (or both). The soft top worked very effectively with the T-bar, and the hard top. While it looked very attractive the top was often criticized for being heavy and cumbersome to fit.

Four-seater layout

The notion of a full four-seater convertible was very unusual in Europe. The Stag embodied a belief at the time that Leyland should be setting trends, not following them. It was thought that the Stag was the type of car that would sell well in the U.S., but this did not prove to be the case.

Unitary construction

Because the Stag used a much-modified version of the 2000 Sedan floorpan, it became the first Triumph sports car to use integral unitary construction. This improved handling and reduced chassis flex.

Specifications
1977 Triumph Stag

ENGINE

Type: V8

Construction: Cast-iron block and aluminum heads

Valve gear: Two valves per cylinder operated by a single overhead camshaft

Bore and stroke: 3.38 in. x 2.54 in.

Displacement: 2,997 cc

Compression ratio: 8.8:1

Induction system: Two Stromberg carburetors

Maximum power: 145 bhp at 5,500 rpm

Maximum torque: 170 lb-ft at 3,500 rpm

Top speed: 118 mph

0-60 mph: 9.3 sec.

TRANSMISSION

Four-speed manual plus overdrive or three-speed automatic

BODY/CHASSIS

Integral chassis with two-door steel convertible body

SPECIAL FEATURES

The four-speed overdrive transmission came from the 2000 sedan.

Stags are not true convertibles because they have a fixed B-pillar.

RUNNING GEAR

Steering: Rack-and-pinion

Front suspension: MacPherson struts with lower wishbones, coil springs, shock absorbers and anti-roll bar

Rear suspension: Semi-trailing arms with coil springs and shock absorbers

Brakes: Discs (front), drums (rear)

Wheels: Steel wire, 14-in. dia.

Tires: 185 x 14

DIMENSIONS

Length: 174.0 in. **Width:** 63.5 in.

Height: 49.5 in. **Wheelbase:** 100 in.

Track: 52.6 in.(front), 53.0 in. (rear)

Weight: 2,795 lbs.

Triumph DOLOMITE SPRINT

This car's award-winning 16-valve engine turned a competent but essentially dowdy four-door family runabout into a championship-winning racer. In Sprint form, the Dolomite was turned into a luxury performance sedan able to perform as good as Alfa Romeos and BMWs.

"...16-valve unit loves to rev."

"The cosy, comfortable interior with its wooden dashboard is just so English and old fashioned, although the performance is anything but. The 16-valve engine loves to rev and will gallop enthusiastically to 6,500 rpm, but the old chassis struggles just a bit to keep up. The steering is excellent, but the ride tends to deteriorate once you get away from smooth roads. The brakes could do with more power, too, but the Sprint still has charm."

Wood-faced dashboards are a typical feature of 1960s and 1970s Triumphs.

Milestones

1970 Triumph's owner
British Leyland introduces the new Toledo. The car is basically the previous Triumph 1300 re-engineered from front-wheel drive to rear-wheel drive, mildly restyled and given a larger engine.

The Dolomite enjoyed a long production run.

1973 The fastest of all the
Dolomites appears. The Sprint has its engine stretched to 1,998 cc, a new 16-valve head and 127 bhp.

The cheaper Triumph Toledo has shorter trunk.

1974 Andy Rouse
wins the manufacturers' title in the British Saloon Car Championship.

1980 British Leyland ends the Dolomite
Sprint production run after 22,936 cars have been made.

UNDER THE SKIN

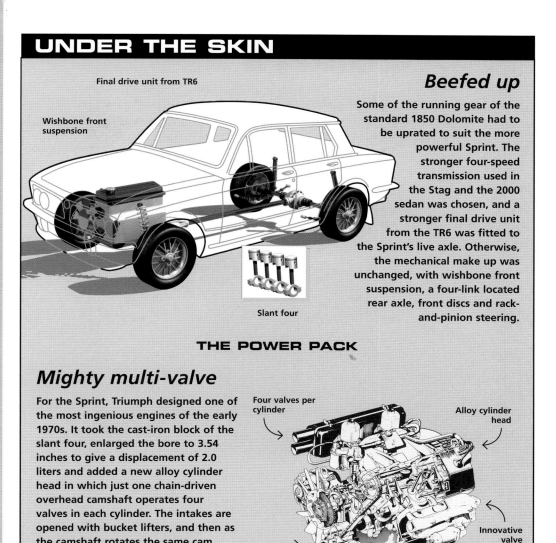

Final drive unit from TR6

Wishbone front suspension

Slant four

Beefed up

Some of the running gear of the standard 1850 Dolomite had to be uprated to suit the more powerful Sprint. The stronger four-speed transmission used in the Stag and the 2000 sedan was chosen, and a stronger final drive unit from the TR6 was fitted to the Sprint's live axle. Otherwise, the mechanical make up was unchanged, with wishbone front suspension, a four-link located rear axle, front discs and rack-and-pinion steering.

THE POWER PACK

Mighty multi-valve

For the Sprint, Triumph designed one of the most ingenious engines of the early 1970s. It took the cast-iron block of the slant four, enlarged the bore to 3.54 inches to give a displacement of 2.0 liters and added a new alloy cylinder head in which just one chain-driven overhead camshaft operates four valves in each cylinder. The intakes are opened with bucket lifters, and then as the camshaft rotates the same cam lobes operate long rockers across the head to open the exhaust valves.

Four valves per cylinder

Alloy cylinder head

Innovative valve operation

Cast-iron block

Peak performer

The Sprint represents the peak of the Dolomite's evolution, which started with the Triumph 1300 and spawned the TC and Toledo models. Toward the end of the production run an exclusive 'Rio' Panther-bodied version was built but prices were sky high.

The Sprint's racing heritage makes it a very collectible Triumph.

Triumph **DOLOMITE SPRINT**

A trademark black vinyl roof masked just how tall and upright the old Dolomite bodyshell was. However, in Sprint form the Dolomite had one of the most powerful 2.0-liter engines in production—with performance to match.

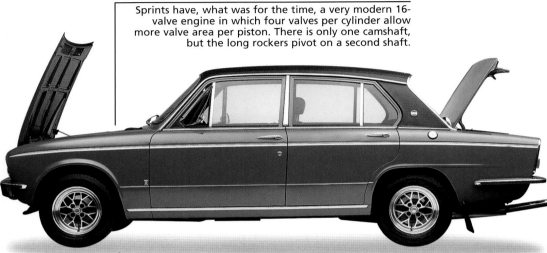

16-valve engine

Sprints have, what was for the time, a very modern 16-valve engine in which four valves per cylinder allow more valve area per piston. There is only one camshaft, but the long rockers pivot on a second shaft.

Uprated radiator

The extra power generated by the 16-valve engine required an uprated radiator. This uses a viscous-coupled cooling fan, which is driven off the engine.

TR6 rear brakes

Although Triumph did not go as far as fitting discs on the rear brakes, it did uprate them by fitting the larger drums from the TR6. On the Sprint they incorporate a brake balance unit.

Unique alloy wheels

One feature unique to the Sprint is the painted black and silver alloy wheels. Until the launch of the Sprint, no British manufacturer had fitted alloy wheels as a standard feature on a mass-production model.

Vinyl roof

With so few changes to the bodywork, Triumph wanted some way of distinguishing the Sprint from the ordinary Dolomite. It chose what was then a popular feature—a black vinyl roof.

Overdrive transmission

The earliest Sprints were only available with a four-speed manual transmission, although a three-speed automatic was added a few months after launch. From 1975, however, a Laycock overdrive became standard, operating on third and fourth gears, effectively giving a six-speed transmission.

Wishbone suspension

As usual with Triumphs, the front suspension is a double wishbone arrangement, but with a concentric coil spring shock unit working on the top wishbone. This is a legacy of the previous front-drive design which could not accommodate a bottom-mounted spring.

Specifications
1975 Triumph Dolomite Sprint

ENGINE

Type: In-line slant four

Construction: Cast-iron block and alloy head

Valve gear: Four valves per cylinder operated by a single chain-driven overhead camshaft

Bore and stroke: 3.54 in. x 3.07 in.

Displacement: 1,998 cc

Compression ratio: 9.5:1

Induction system: Two SU carburetors

Maximum power: 127 bhp at 5,700 rpm

Maximum torque: 122 lb-ft at 4,500 rpm

Top speed: 115 mph

0-60 mph: 8.8 sec.

TRANSMISSION

Four-speed manual with overdrive on third and fourth gears

BODY/CHASSIS

Unitary construction steel monocoque with four-door sedan body

SPECIAL FEATURES

Though late compared to other global auto builders, the Sprint was the first Triumph production car to feature alloy wheels.

The Sprint is distinguished from basic Dolomites by its distinctive rear badge.

RUNNING GEAR

Steering: Rack-and-pinion

Front suspension: Double wishbones with coil springs, telescopic shock absorbers and anti-roll bar

Rear suspension: Live axle with four trailing links, coil springs and telescopic shock absorbers

Brakes: Discs (front), drums (rear)

Wheels: Alloy, 5.5 x 13.0 in.

Tires: 175/70 HR13

DIMENSIONS

Length: 162.2 in.   **Width:** 62.5 in.

Height: 54.0 in.   **Wheelbase:** 96.5 in.

Track: 53.4 in. (front), 50.4 in. (rear)

Weight: 2,300 lbs.

TVR **3000S**

TVR's first convertible came 20 years after the company began building cars. Using a Ford V6 engine, some are even turbocharged to give a higher level of performance, with better acceleration than a Ferrari 308.

"...plenty of muscle to flex."

"Drive a 3000S and it is easy to see how TVR could effectively reintroduce it in the 1980s without it feeling incredibly old fashioned. 'Traditional' is a better word, with plenty of muscle to flex from the pushrod Ford 3.0-liter. The transmission is super slick and the steering is very direct. Handling is neutral, thanks to good weight distribution. By today's standards, the tires are narrow so outright grip isn't veery stable making four-wheel drifts inevitable at speed."

The 3000S cockpit is a little cramped and crude but it has all the right equipment.

1978 TVR introduces its first open car. The 3000S convertible shares its running gear and 3.0-liter Ford V6 with the Taimar coupe.

The S2 uses a 2.9-liter Ford 'Cologne' V6.

1979 Turbo specialist Broadspeed is employed to modify the 3000S, boosting power to 265 bhp. 3000S production comes to an end after 258 have been made.

The ultimate S in performance terms is the 4.0-liter V8 of 1991.

1986 Popular Demand sees the launch of the S—a modern version of the 3000S with a similar but wider body and Ford's 2.8-liter V6 engine. The S2 of 1988 has a 2.9-liter V6, and the S3 of 1990 has longer doors and a restyled front end. 1991 sees the launch of the V8S. Production comes to an end in 1993.

UNDER THE SKIN

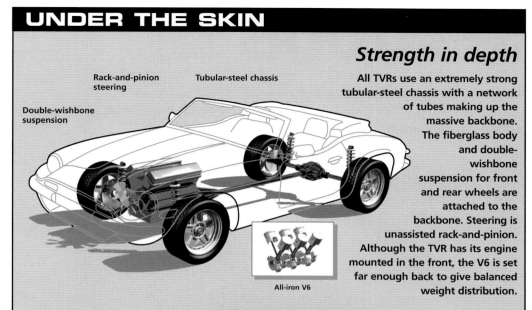

Rack-and-pinion steering

Tubular-steel chassis

Double-wishbone suspension

All-iron V6

Strength in depth

All TVRs use an extremely strong tubular-steel chassis with a network of tubes making up the massive backbone. The fiberglass body and double-wishbone suspension for front and rear wheels are attached to the backbone. Steering is unassisted rack-and-pinion. Although the TVR has its engine mounted in the front, the V6 is set far enough back to give balanced weight distribution.

THE POWER PACK

Ford V6s

TVR used the British Ford 3.0-liter Essex engine for the 3000S because it was strong (as its huge turbocharged output proved), powerful enough in standard form (142 bhp), and relatively affordable. It is a simple design and uses a cast-iron block and cylinder heads. For the S, which was launched in 1986, TVR changed to the German Ford 'Cologne' V6, which displaces 2.8 liters. It, too, follows a simple design structure but is a much more modern powerplant. The more muscular 1990 S3 was introduced with a much larger, 2.9-liter version of the 'Cologne' engine which could easily top 140 mph.

Affordable fun

With current convertible TVRs so expensive, the least expensive way to buy an open-top TVR is to find a 3000S, S1, S2 or S3. They offer fantastic performance (the S3 will hit 60 mph in under seven seconds) and also boast rewarding and unforgettable handling.

The V6 TVR convertible should not be ignored as a bargain sports car buy.

TVR **3000S**

When many sports car manufacturers were giving up on open-roofed sports cars, TVR took a gamble and chopped the roof off the Taimar coupe to produce the outstanding 3000S.

Fiberglass body

Every TVR has been built with fiberglass bodywork. It is perfectly suited to small-volume production and means that styling changes can be made relatively easily and without vast expense.

Front-hinged hood

Engine access is at a premium because the car's nose tips forward and the engine is mounted well back.

Ford V6

TVR brought in the overhead-valve V6 engine that Ford used in its high-performance Capri in England. There was no competition as the cars covered different markets.

Cutaway doors

The lines of the 3000S are enhanced by a dip in the doors, an echo of narrow pre-war sports cars.

Separate chassis

In its early days, TVR decided that the main strength of its cars should come from a large, central backbone of tubular steel. The company has kept with that concept ever since.

Convertible roof

In the first version of the 3000S, the roof was a conventional fold-away type. From 1986, TVR used roof panels with a separate rear-window section.

Wishbone suspension

TVR gave the 3000S a double-wishbone suspension at the front, as usual, and it also uses double wishbones at the rear, with the bottom arms extremely wide-spaced to give the best possible wheel location.

Perfect weight distribution

TVR mounted the Ford V6 far back in the chassis, giving the car a near-perfect front-to-rear weight distribution.

Specifications
1978 TVR 3000S

ENGINE
Type: Ford V6

Construction: Cast-iron block and heads

Valve gear: Two valves per cylinder operated by a single centrally mounted camshaft with pushrods and rockers

Bore and stroke: 3.70 in. x 2.85 in.

Displacement: 2,994 cc

Compression ratio: 8.9:1

Induction system: Single downdraft carburetor

Maximum power: 142 bhp at 5,000 rpm

Maximum torque: 172 lb-ft at 3,000 rpm

Top speed: 124 mph

0-60 mph: 7.8 sec

TRANSMISSION
Four-speed manual

BODY/CHASSIS
Separate tubular-steel backbone chassis with fiberglass two-seat convertible body

SPECIAL FEATURES

A front-tilting hood gives good access to the Ford V6 engine.

Neat, five-spoke alloys give the 'S' its required sporty feel without looking too ostentatious.

RUNNING GEAR
Steering: Rack-and-pinion

Front suspension: Double unequal-length wishbones with coil springs and telescopic shock absorbers

Rear suspension: Double unequal-length wishbones with coil springs and telescopic shock absorbers

Brakes: Discs (front), drums (rear)

Wheels: Alloy, 14-in. dia.

Tires: Radial, 185/70 VR14

DIMENSIONS
Length: 155.0 in. **Width:** 64.0 in.

Height: 47.0 in.   **Wheelbase:** 90.0 in.

Track: 53.8 in. (front and rear)

Weight: 2,340 lbs.

Volvo **P1800ES**

The uniquely styled Volvo P1800 coupe was looking a little dated by the start of the 1970s, so Volvo decided to spruce it up by adding a station wagon rear end. This improved its luggage capacity.

"...supportive seats."

"The elderly design of the P1800ES's engine means that you really need to work the shifter—which is slick, with well-spaced ratios—in order to overcome the lack of torque. Because the steering is heavier than suits most people's tastes, it is only on the freeway that the Volvo shines, with its overdrive transmission working very well. Prominent body roll makes forceful driving a hair-raising experience. At least you sit comfortably on very supportive seats."

An overdrive transmission makes the Volvo a fine cruiser.

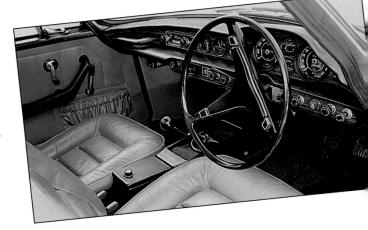

1963 Volvo moves into the sports car market with the P1800 coupe.

The sporty 123GT uses the same 1.8-liter engine as the ES.

1969 As the renamed 1800E, the coupe gains fuel injection, disc brakes and alloy wheels.

The P1800 sports coupe was originally made by Jensen.

1971 The 1800ES sports station wagon is launched. Despite its good looks, in Europe it gains the nickname 'Snow White's hearse.'

1972 Automatic transmission becomes available as an option.

1973 A year after the coupe is withdrawn, 1800ES production ends. Some 8078 examples were built. Most were exported to the U.S.

UNDER THE SKIN

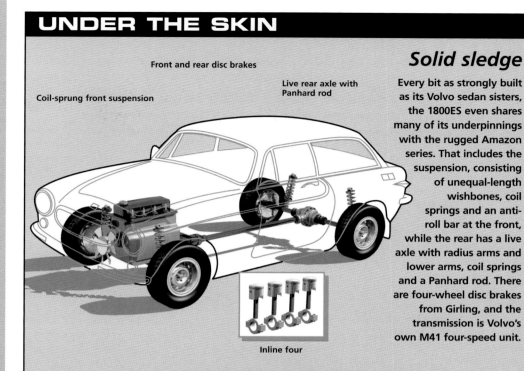

Coil-sprung front suspension

Front and rear disc brakes

Live rear axle with Panhard rod

Inline four

Solid sledge

Every bit as strongly built as its Volvo sedan sisters, the 1800ES even shares many of its underpinnings with the rugged Amazon series. That includes the suspension, consisting of unequal-length wishbones, coil springs and an anti-roll bar at the front, while the rear has a live axle with radius arms and lower arms, coil springs and a Panhard rod. There are four-wheel disc brakes from Girling, and the transmission is Volvo's own M41 four-speed unit.

THE POWER PACK

Rugged design

Volvo engines have a reputation for rugged reliability and longevity. Certainly the overhead-valve four-cylinder unit in the 1800ES lasted a long time in production, as it is derived from the PV444 engine of the 1940s. It even shares its 80-mm stroke, although by the 1970s it had expanded to 2.0 liters. From 1969, the sporting Volvos had Bosch electronically controlled fuel injection, in which form the engine puts out 130 bhp, or just 112 bhp in the U.S.

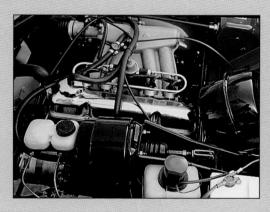

Characterful

While the early P1800 coupe may get collectors more excited than the later 1800E, the ES sports station wagon is unique among Volvos and is highly regarded. It is more practical, just as satisfying and reliable to own and has an individual character.

The P1800ES combines style, safety and performance.

Volvo **P1800ES**

Volvo's 1800ES was part sports car, part station wagon and a real image breaker for the Swedish firm. The specification was hardly state-of-the-art, but it was in many ways a lively, charismatic car.

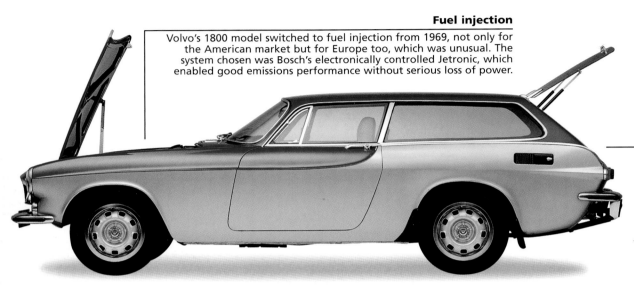

Fuel injection

Volvo's 1800 model switched to fuel injection from 1969, not only for the American market but for Europe too, which was unusual. The system chosen was Bosch's electronically controlled Jetronic, which enabled good emissions performance without serious loss of power.

Rear fins

Despite its rear-end makeover, the 1800ES retained the prominent rear fins of the 1800 coupe. This is one styling quirk that was well out of fashion by the 1970s.

Glass tailgate

A deep, glass rear hatch lifts up to access a neatly carpeted luggage area, usefully boosted in capacity over the regular coupe's. The station-wagon-style rear end also provides more headroom for rear-seat passengers and offers much better visibility.

Four-wheel disc brakes

As part of Volvo's safety-first policy, it adopted all-around disc braking from 1969. That meant the 1971–1973 1800ES model always came with powered discs on each wheel.

Overdrive or auto

After experimenting with ZF transmission, Volvo fitted the 1800ES with its own four-speed, all-synchromesh manual unit with Laycock de Normanville overdrive. From 1972, there was also the option of a Borg-Warner three-speed automatic.

Specifications

1972 Volvo P1800ES

ENGINE

Type: Inline four

Construction: Cast-iron cylinder block and head

Valve gear: Two valves per cylinder operated by a single camshaft with pushrods and rockers

Bore and stroke: 3.55 in. x 3.2 in.

Displacement: 1,986 cc

Compression ratio: 8.7:1

Induction system: Bosch fuel injection

Maximum power: 112 bhp at 6,000 rpm

Maximum torque: 115 lb-ft at 3,500 rpm

Top speed: 116 mph

0-60 mph: 11.3 sec.

TRANSMISSION

Four-speed manual with overdrive

BODY/CHASSIS

Unitary monocoque construction with steel two-door station wagon body

SPECIAL FEATURES

Unlike earlier P1800 models, the ES has a black plastic grill.

Bosch fuel injection allowed the ES to meet strict U.S. emission tests.

RUNNING GEAR

Steering: Worm-and-roller

Front suspension: Wishbones with coil springs, shock absorbers and anti-roll bar

Rear suspension: Live axle with trailing arms, radius arms, Panhard rod, coil springs and shock absorbers

Brakes: Discs (front and rear)

Wheels: Steel or alloy, 15-in. dia.

Tires: 185/70 HR15

DIMENSIONS

Length: 172.6 in. **Width:** 66.9 in.

Height: 50.6 in. **Wheelbase:** 96.5 in.

Track: 51.6 in. (front and rear)

Weight: 2,570 lbs.

Index